A Powerhouse of the Spirit

A Powerhouse of the Spirit

The Life and Art of Sister Margaret Watson of Grahamstown

William Barham

Published in South Africa on behalf of the author
by NISC (Pty) Ltd, PO Box 377, Makhanda, 6140, South Africa
www.nisc.co.za

First edition, first impression 2024
© The author 2024

All rights reserved. No part of this publication may be reproduced or transmitted in any form or by any means, electronic or mechanical, including photocopying, recording, or any information storage or retrieval system, without prior permission in writing from the publisher.

ISBN: 978-1-991458-07-0 (softcover)
ISBN: 978-1-991458-08-7 (pdf)

Project manager: Liz Gowans
Copy editor: Russell Martin
Indexer: Sanet le Roux
Cover designers: Advance Design Group

The authors and the publisher have made every effort to obtain permission for and acknowledge the use of copyright material. Should an inadvertent infringement of copyright have occurred, please contact the publisher and we will rectify omissions or errors in any subsequent reprint or edition.

Contents

Foreword		vii
Acknowledgements		ix
Introduction		xi
Chapter 1	A Clergyman's Daughter	1
Chapter 2	City of Saints	21
Chapter 3	Preparation for Good Things	40
Chapter 4	Bestowal of the Habit	68
Chapter 5	St Monica's Home	79
Chapter 6	St Mary and All the Angels	95
Chapter 7	A Life of Prayer without Ceasing	116
Chapter 8	Christ the King	143
Chapter 9	The Beauty of Holiness	160
Chapter 10	Fulfilment of the Work	189
Chapter 11	Before the Throne	208
Illustration credits		229
Bibliography		231
Index		240

'Grace be unto you and peace from Jesus Christ', a devotional card by Sister Margaret CR, Easter 1942

Foreword

When I joined the community as a postulant on Ash Wednesday in 1962 and went into the chapel, I remember Sister Margaret's little form all in black except for the white collar everyone wore in those days. She would be walking up to the altar to refresh the six vases of flowers on the reredos, looking quite frail but busy.

We did not ever speak as newcomers, and juniors did not fraternise with the rest of the Sisters – we lived separately and only passed each other in passageways etc. However, we all knew about her work as an artist and greatly respected her. She still had her studio at the top of the noviciate but had largely given up painting by then, although she was probably still making exquisite holy cards for Sisters' birthdays.

I was working in East London as a novice when Sister Margaret died on St Peter's Day in June 1964. When I came to make my final profession a few weeks later, I wanted to be given her silver cross because she had been an artist. So I prayed hard to be given hers and was so glad when it was given to me on that day. I felt God was encouraging me and that, like Sister Margaret, I would be doing art as time went on and contributing in a similar way.

I am pleased that Sister Margaret's story has been told in full after all these years.

Sister Carol CR
Superior, 1998–2005

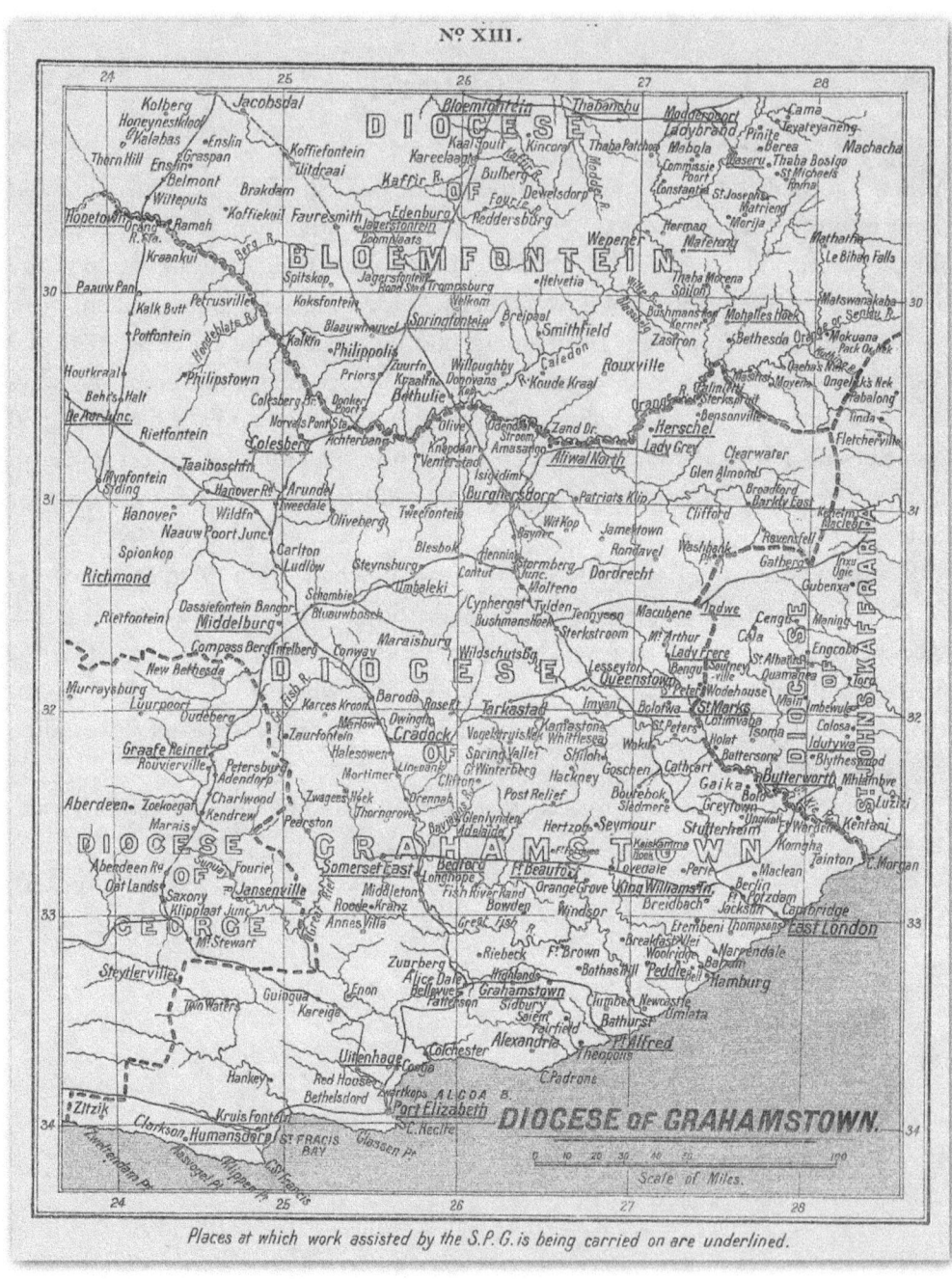

From *The Churchman's Missionary Atlas*, published by the Society for the Propagation of the Gospel in Foreign Parts, Westminster, 4th edition, 1922

Acknowledgements

As was the custom for Sisters in the Grahamstown Community of the Resurrection of Our Lord (CR), Sister Margaret left no diary or personal records. Indeed, she noted shortly before her death that she had destroyed what she had. Yet she did leave a trail of artworks, memories, publications and letters. With these and family records, together with some records left in the community's archive by other English women of her time, it has been possible to piece together the events and achievements of her life. The fullness of her story has often come from oblique sources, including logbooks and journals, and contemporary accounts by other Sisters at St Peter's.

Although the story is about her, it has also been written as a tribute to the dozens of English women who made similar commitments to a religious life in South Africa, whose names and contributions lie hidden in the community's archive. Therefore, as well as Sister Margaret, this work has been written in tribute to the 329 Sisters of the Community of the Resurrection and many others who contributed to their work as aspirants, helpers and friends.

At the start of the second millennium, Random House in Johannesburg published Guy Butler's magnificent tribute to Sister Margaret's art, *The Prophetic Nun*. My purpose has been to complement Professor Butler's work by helping to document the fullness of her secular and religious life. Towards this, I have received much kindness and help, from her family and goddaughters, the Reverend Mother, Sisters, oblates, priests and friends of the community, especially Jean Kelly. I am most grateful for all their assistance.

I would like to thank the Cory Library for Humanities Research at Rhodes University, custodians of the Sister Margaret Collection and some of the community's archives. I also extend my gratitude to archivists at the Amazwi South African Museum of Literature, the William Cullen Library at the University of the Witwatersrand, the Community of St Mary the Virgin in Wantage, St John's College in Cambridge, St Stephen's House and Pusey House in Oxford, Lambeth Palace Library, the Community of the Resurrection in Mirfield, the Africana City Library in Port Elizabeth, and the Anglican Diocese of Johannesburg. I am particularly grateful to Russell Martin for editing the final version of this work.

William Barham
June 2024

Sister Margaret CR, undated but possibly taken on the occasion of her profession in the Sisters' Chapel of the Resurrection at St Peter's Home, Grahamstown, on 22 January 1914, when aged thirty-five

Introduction

This work tells how Margaret Watson eschewed her comfortable but unfulfilled Cambridge existence, sailed to the Cape Colony and, then, after reconciling her doubts, made her commitment to putting aside temporal concerns and entering the religious life. The work also examines another aspect of her life, for which Sister Margaret is better known, as an artist and fresco painter, and how this aspect fused with her religious commitment through unexpected circumstances.

For a young woman of Margaret's intellect and standing, her transition to Sister of Mercy would seem almost unimaginable today. She was, however, a child of the Victorian era in which service to Great Britain and the Empire, to the Queen and the Church, was enshrined in the values of her class and, for her, driven home by the example of her parents. Yet, despite all that she had to offer, opportunities at the start of the twentieth century for respectable young English women of her standing were heavily constrained by a paternalistic social tradition. Accordingly, unless she sought to carve a new furrow like other social reformers of her day and live independently or take on a position in one of the few areas where respectable women could excel to a certain degree, she was more likely to remain an ornament at home, caring for siblings and parents, and confined to the drawing rooms until she married.

In contrast, the philanthropic works that Margaret's father introduced her to provided an acceptable, respectable and admired means of circumventing social constraints and enriching her life. However, for Margaret, even that was not enough. Instead, she freed herself from social constraints and chose a simple, consecrated existence as a bride of Christ.

Margaret Watson in 1905, aged twenty-six

Chapter One

A Clergyman's Daughter

✱✱✱

SISTER MARGARET'S STORY starts in the small Norfolk village of Starston, where her father was the parish priest, in 1879. Britain was at the height of its imperial age, and Queen Victoria had been on the throne for almost forty-two years. Among respectable upper-middle-class families like hers, a duty to the Crown and pride in the Empire rested alongside commitments to undertaking good works through the Church. These values shaped Margaret Watson and her family's way of life.

Margaret was the first of ten children of the Reverend Frederick and Margaret Lockhart Watson, who had married the year before she was born. Her father came from a prosperous Evangelical merchant family in York, where he was sent to York Minster's St Peter's College. Frederick was to break his family's provincial and Evangelical associations by winning an exhibition at St John's College at the University of Cambridge, where he matriculated in 1864. Cambridge proved to be transformational. Not only did he find the prevailing Anglo-Catholic orthodoxy in his college 'most congenial to his temper', but, having gained a degree in mathematics in 1869, he stayed on at St John's, rather than return to his father's world of banking and finance, to study Hebrew and theology in preparation for the Anglican ministry.

Although Tractarianism had commenced nearly forty years earlier, the Oxford Movement, the Camden Society and the English Ritualists continued to exert significant influence in the Church of England, which Margaret's

Margaret's father, the Reverend Frederick Watson, from a photograph in the vestry at St Margaret's Church, Starston

father was to serve. They sought to elevate all aspects of worship and reconnect the Church with its medieval, catholic and apostolic values. Accordingly, the 1860s and 1870s were times of great tension between the Evangelical and High Church wings in the Anglican Church, placing Frederick in a dilemma of allegiance between his family's values and the new Anglo-Catholicism which he began to embrace. Among these contrasting parties within the Church, their approaches to mission and growth of the Church overseas were particularly marked. They became of importance too for Frederick's daughter Margaret, as the High Church practice stood for a structured approach and the planting of an established Church to serve settlers as well as indigenous populations, and to impart British values as a responsibility of Empire.

The completeness of Frederick's transformation, and therefore his later influence on Margaret, is revealed by his appointment in 1875 to a curacy at St Giles, Cambridge, which was firmly in the hands of the Tractarians. The church had reopened in June of that year, having been greatly extended and rebuilt in the fashionable Gothic Revival style to provide room for the enormous congregations attracted to its Anglo-Catholic style of worship.[1] Under Father Slater, the rector of St Giles, Frederick was not only opened to the solemnity and richness of Anglo-Catholicism but 'led quietly towards the calm and cautious churchmanship' which he came to embody in his future life and ministry. Into these values, Margaret was born.

Frederick met his wife-to-be, Margaret Lockhart Adam, through parish work at St Giles. She was the eldest daughter of the Reverend George Read Adam, another Anglo-Catholic advocate, who had spent considerable efforts and private funds building the new church of St Mary with All Souls in Kilburn, North London. Following its consecration in 1862, George served as parish

---

[1] *Saint Giles' Church: A History and Guide.*

priest and was to have eight children, five of whom survived at the time of his untimely death in July 1867 at the age of thirty-eight.

Owing to his ambitious church building, George was to leave his wife, Margaret Euphemia, with debts and great uncertainty. However, her plight came to the attention of the Edward Storey Foundation, which had been established in Cambridge two centuries earlier to provide for clergy widows. As the Foundation agreed to support her, Margaret Euphemia and her children moved into one of their almshouses in Cambridge, in the parish of St Giles, just a stone's throw from the church. Through his work as curate

Margaret's mother, Margaret Lockhart Adam

at St Giles, Frederick supported the Adam family, especially after Margaret Euphemia died, leaving the younger children to be taken in by an aunt. Margaret Lockhart, Sister Margaret's mother, was aged twenty at the time of her own mother's death. Two years later, on 13 August 1878, Margaret Lockhart was married to Frederick by Father Slater at St Giles's Church.

Earlier in 1878, Frederick acquired his first incumbency when he accepted the living at Starston, near Diss in Norfolk. The couple moved there after their marriage. Margaret was born on 31 May 1879 and baptised by her father on 6 July. She was followed, while the Watsons lived at Starston, by Frederick in May 1800, Henry in November 1881, Arthur in June 1883, and Christopher in October 1885, before Ethel Mary, Margaret's first sister, was born in May 1886.

Margaret's father took on a part-time lectureship at St John's College while at Starston, which involved a lot of inconvenient travel. But the chance arose of being closer to the university when in 1886 the Bishop of Ely offered Frederick the parish of St Mary the Virgin, Stow-cum-Quy, just north of the city. However, before the family could move, Frederick needed to oversee the building of a new vicarage, as there had not been a resident parish priest since the 1650s.

Margaret's family were warmly received on their arrival in Quy in January 1887. Accounts reveal that St Mary's Church was 'packed' for her father's installation, which must have provided a lasting memory for Margaret, who

Postcard image of Starston Church

Starston rectory 1878 to 1886

reached the age of seven that May. As their new vicarage would not be ready for another eighteen months, the family was obliged to live in a temporary home on Chesterton Road in Cambridge, where Dorothy, Margaret's second younger sister, was born in March 1888. The new three-storey vicarage was finally ready

Chapter 1 | A Clergyman's Daughter

Church of St Mary the Virgin, Stow-cum-Quy

for the Watsons in June 1888 and would remain Margaret's home for five years.

Parish records reveal that from the outset, both parents worked to support the parish. From their first Christmas at Quy, Margaret's mother arranged a festival for village children, which became an annual event. She also established a branch of the Mothers' Union, which met at the vicarage each week. Through its network of local branches, such as at Quy, the Mothers' Union had grown to help spread Christian values of motherhood and education and contribute to social and moral reform.[2]

Henry, Frederick and Margaret (right) aged three, on 18 August 1883

Margaret's parents also set up a branch of the Society for the Propagation of the Gospel, the SPG, which similarly met at the vicarage with an agenda to help advance the Empire through

---

2 Maughan, *Mighty England Do Good*, p. 357.

Margaret's second and temporary family home from 1887, at 157 Chesterton Road, Cambridge (the taller house, right of centre)

High Church missionary values, encouraging men and women to support and commit to service in the Empire, by drawing on feelings of cultural superiority and commensurate responsibility towards less advantaged populations. The SPG's works ultimately depended on the money raised and support obtained from small branches, such as the Watsons set up, towards which a public meeting was arranged at Quy School when missionaries came to share their experiences abroad. Such philanthropy and church work were common across upper-middle-class society in this era of High Empire when Great Britain had never looked so secure nor had so confidently regarded itself as a force for good. Many women of Mrs Watson's standing took it upon themselves to do what they could to help, and many improving societies, such as the Mothers' Union and the SPG, relied on the organising power and commitment of women such as her. These values and commitments became enshrined in the lives of Margaret's generation.

Margaret reached the age of ten in May 1889. Although imperceptible at the time, her experience of these meetings, the influences provided in her vicarage home, and all the other good works that her parents took on as priest and vicar's wife must have been formative. Perhaps because of this, her mind opened to the possibility that she might one day commit to philanthropy, undertake church work and serve in the mission field.

Dorothy, Margaret's second younger sister, recalled that the 'vicarage was large to accommodate so big a family, and we had maids and nurses and a receiving

CHAPTER 1 | A CLERGYMAN'S DAUGHTER

The Vicarage, Stow-cum-Quy, after completion in 1888

nursery governess, a big garden and two cows, and other things, no doubt'. Dorothy also described her brothers' noisy adventures in the garden and their blowing up wasp nests after discovering that their father kept gunpowder in his desk drawer. The boys went to the village school until they became too much of a handful, and then were packed off to boarding school. However, as was customary for respectable families such as the Watsons, the girls were kept at home and taught in the nursery upstairs by a governess. Two further children were born at Quy: Basil Lockhart in August 1889 and Grace Hilda in February 1891. According to that year's census, fifteen people lived at the vicarage: the Reverend Frederick and Mrs Margaret Lockhart Watson, nine children ranging from two months to eleven years, and a governess, cook and maids.

In March 1891, Margaret's father arranged his first confirmation service at Quy. Her confirmation probably came a couple of years later, when she was twelve or thirteen. She later recalled what a treasured day it had been, when writing to one of her goddaughters. 'I know how I felt, it seemed to me that something wonderful had happened, and that the Holy Spirit had come to dwell with me.'[3] 'I had hoped it was going to be that best of all gifts – the gift of the Holy Spirit (the "strengthening gift" as the Church calls it) bringing his sevenfold treasure.'[4]

---

3 Sister Margaret, letter to Merle Metcalf, 6 August 1956.
4 Sister Margaret, letter to Merle Metcalf, 15 October 1956.

Margaret (central back) with parents and grandmother Susannah Watson and eight siblings at Stow-cum-Quy vicarage in 1892. Back: Christopher, Margaret and Arthur. Middle: Grace on her mother's knee, Henry, Frederick and Basil on his father's knee. Front: Dorothy and Ethel.

Around this age, Margaret began taking charge of Sunday School classes in the vicarage under her parents' supervision. As a reward each summer, all the Sunday School children were invited for a large tea party at the vicarage. In this way young Margaret was drawn further into her father's work.

Since being reappointed to St John's College as a Divinity lecturer in 1882, Frederick had keenly participated in the university's initiative to establish missionary parishes to serve the fast-growing population in south-east London. In 1883, St John's College took responsibility for the parish of Walworth in the Diocese of Southwark. Frederick was appointed the college's secretary, and, under his supervision, funds were raised to build a substantial red-brick church with a missionary centre and parsonage. The Lady Margaret parish, named after the college's foundress, Lady Margaret Beaufort, became a passion for Frederick, which Margaret and her mother also came to share. Both contributed to the work of the Ladies' Committee in Cambridge, so as to raise funds for the parish.[5]

From all these accounts of the good works and responsibilities that Margaret's parents carried out, we can gain an impression of how her early years were influenced by their example of public duty and parish service, doing what

---

5 Minute book of the Ladies' Committee for St John's Missionary Parish of Lady Margaret, Walworth, Archive of St John's College, Cambridge.

they could to support less fortunate parishioners and with a missionary interest in work at home and abroad. From their parents' example of devotion and hard work and from the stability that their loving, traditional and religiously principled household provided, all the children would go on to prosper in their adult lives. Their father believed that no one should be satisfied with the world in its current state. He therefore encouraged his children to strive for improvement rather than accept what they saw around them. He believed, and preached, that if this could be done and everyone assumed this challenge rather than tolerate the inadequacies around them, then a 'golden age lay ahead in the not-too-distant future'.[6]

The Reverend Canon Frederick Watson, MA, DD, c.1893

In September 1893, after six years at Stow-cum-Quy, Margaret's father wrote in the parish magazine that 'God has called me to work in another plot in his Vineyard'. He had been appointed priest at the eleventh-century church of St Edward King and Martyr in the centre of Cambridge.[7] Although it covered only a small area tucked between Market Square and King's College, his new pastoral and preaching roles were considerable. At St Teddy's, as the church had become affectionately known, Frederick was popular with students; the parish included King's College within its bounds. His appointment brought another change for Margaret, as the family moved from their large country vicarage to a more restricted terraced house at 10 Harvey Road, which was to be her home for the next three years. University families lived in many of the houses around them. Dorothy recalled that she 'could mention at least half a dozen names of the children we played with, who afterwards became famous. Maynard Keynes was one. He was about my eldest brother's age and despised our childish activities.'[8]

Margaret was fifteen at the time of the move from Quy in 1894. Perhaps

---

6 Watson, *Sacramental Grace*, pp. 1–3.
7 *Crockford's Clerical Directory* 1898, p. 1427.
8 Dorothy Watson's childhood reflections.

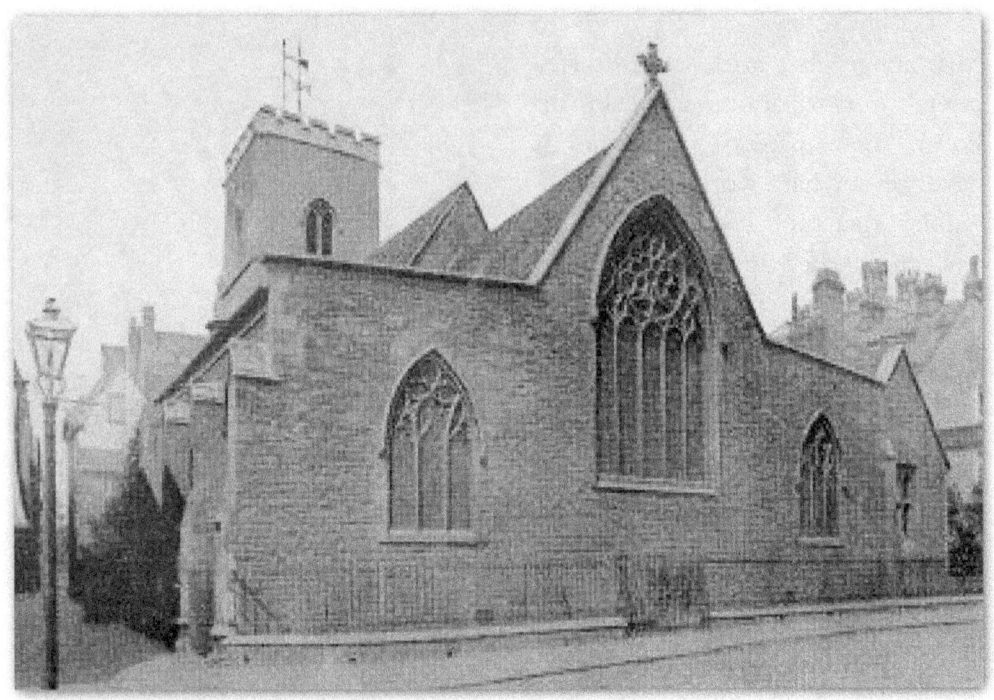
Church of St Edward King and Martyr, Peas Hill, Cambridge

View of Frederick Watson's new parish including King's College beyond Trinity College, from the tower of St John's College

Chapter 1 | A Clergyman's Daughter

Hills Road in Cambridge, c.1890, from which Harvey Road led off (middle view to the right), with the Hills Road Wesleyan Chapel (foreground left), distant tower of the Anglican Church of St John the Baptist, and the spire of the Roman Catholic Church of Our Lady and the English Martyrs

during this year, she was sent off to boarding school, most likely a family-run 'dame' school for just a few girls.[9] Of the girls, she alone was sent away, as her younger sisters attended the Perse School in Cambridge, to which they walked each day. In contrast, her brothers went to well-known public schools: Frederick to the King's School in Canterbury, Christopher to St Edward's School ('for gentlemen's sons') in Oxford.[10] Later, the much younger John was to be sent to Sedbergh School.

With Margaret and her brothers away during term time, the whole family could only meet up during school holidays. Each summer, their father took a locum for a few weeks to provide a family break together, usually at a large seaside parish. In 1893, they went to stay at Hunstanton on the Norfolk coast and returned there for several summers. On one occasion, when they arrived, the station porter assumed that they must be a school party as there were so many children and was astonished to learn that they were all from the same family.[11] Photographs reveal the children's adventures on the beach, usually with an aunt in attendance to keep a sharp lookout. One summer, a tragedy nearly occurred when eleven-year-old Arthur was swept out to sea after he lost the paddle of

---

9   Dorothy Watson's childhood reflections.
10 Venn and Venn, *Alumni Cantabrigienses*, vol. VI, p. 369; & The National Census, April 1901.
11 Dorothy Watson's childhood reflections.

Hunstanton on the northern Norfolk coast, a favoured summer holiday location for the Reverend Frederick Watson and his family

Margaret (standing second from left) with her family, complete with infant John, at Hunstanton in 1899

the canoe he had made. The family thought he would surely drown. After much distress, he was spotted and rescued. Afterwards, when their father was missing from the picnic lunch, the children were told: 'Leave him alone. Father is saying thank you to God for saving Arthur's life.'[12]

The Watsons soon outgrew their house in Harvey Road, particularly as the garden was inadequate for the brothers' boisterous games. In 1896, they moved to a more substantial, newly built house on a secluded driveway just off Cambridge's busy Station Road. At 6 Salisbury Villas, the children could enjoy a 'well-designed garden with covered way running half-way down, with a tennis court, croquet lawn, large greenhouse and plentiful supply of fruit trees'.[13] Dorothy recalled their new home as being 'full to brimming' when her brothers held tennis parties for their friends who came to stay.[14]

Margaret on the beach at Hunstanton with Grace in 1898

The year 1898 was an important one for Margaret, as following the birth of John Douglas, the family's tenth and final child, she was to become godmother at his baptism on 17 April. That summer, when she left school and reached the age of nineteen, she travelled to North Yorkshire to stay with her aunt Susan, her father's sister, who was married to George Pierson. He was the land agent at Baldersby Park, a sizeable Palladian country house near Ripon. The Piersons lived on the estate with three children, including a two- and a ten-year-old, whom Margaret was most likely taken on to help. Her stay coincided with the patronal festival of the parish church of St James the Great at Baldersby on 24 July. This striking Gothic Revival building by the prominent Victorian architect William Butterfield was consecrated in 1857, embodying every conceivable aspect of rich and beautiful high-Victorian Anglo-Catholic worship. Her visit was never to be forgotten, partly as the church had become a place of sanctuary and pilgrimage for those 'seeking to reflect on the goodness of God and a deeper realisation of

---

12 Dorothy Watson's childhood reflections.
13 Dorothy Watson's childhood reflections.
14 Dorothy Watson's childhood reflections.

The Watson family home at 6 Salisbury Villas, Station Road, Cambridge

Jesus Christ as Lord and Saviour'.[15] What also made her visit memorable was that she received an inspirational gift: a copy of *The Cloud of Witness*.

This book, containing daily sequences of religious thoughts from many minds, was often given as a coming-of-age present. Its prayers and passages sought to

---

15 *The Parish Church of St James the Great, Baldersby St James.*

Chapter 1 | A Clergyman's Daughter

Church of St James the Great, Baldersby, as completed in 1856

serve as a guide for the Christian year and provide inspiration for life's trials. Margaret's copy, inscribed 'M.W., St James's Day, Baldersby 1898', was to be of great relevance in her life partly because of its content and partly as it had been compiled by the tireless social reformer and Christian activist, the Honourable Mrs Littleton Gell. Not only was she a strong supporter of traditional Victorian family values and a prominent advocate of the Mothers' Union, which Margaret's parents keenly supported in their parishes, but Mrs Gell was also a member of the British Women's Emigration Society. In 1901, she became chairwoman of the South African Emigration Expansion Committee, set up to encourage gentlewomen like Margaret to settle in and help anglicise the southern colonies. Margaret's copy was one of the few possessions she took with her and kept during her journey of faith that she was to embark on. Later she gave it away as a coming-of-age present in 1945.

Amongst her father's friends who called at 6 Salisbury Villas was the philosopher, clergyman and Greek scholar, the Reverend Dr Alfred Caldecott. He had arrived at St John's College in 1876; his time there overlapped with Margaret's father. Dr Caldecott wrote *English Colonialism and the Empire* as a textbook to justify British imperial expansion. He also strongly advocated women's rights and later petitioned the Prime Minister over women's voting rights at the time of the suffragette movement. Perhaps Dr Caldecott's visits and conversations

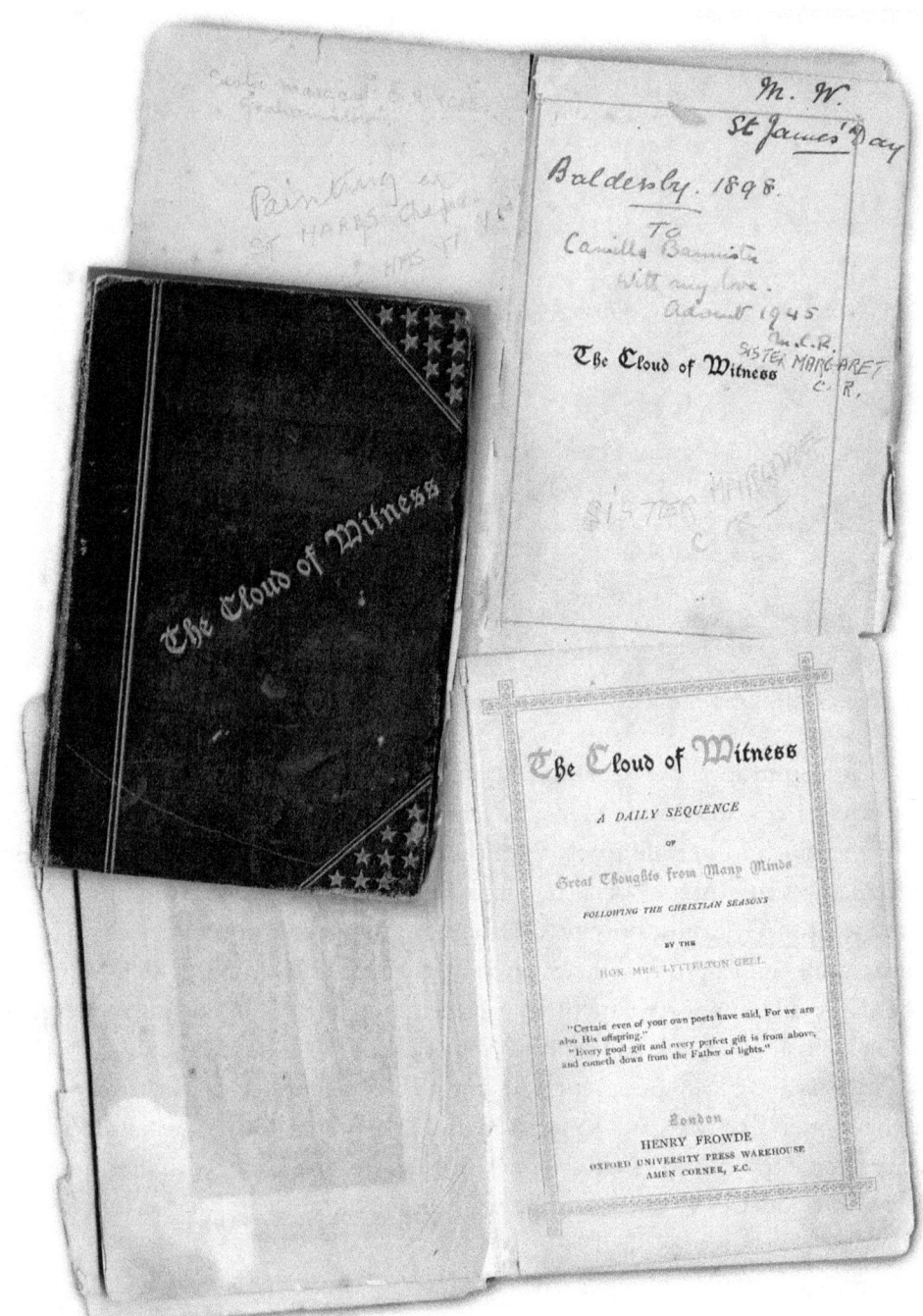

Margaret's copy of *The Cloud of Witness*, inscribed 'M.W. St James's Day Baldersby, 1898'

encouraged the germinating thoughts in Margaret's mind that she might eschew a conventional life and seek even greater fulfilment elsewhere.

In March 1901, Margaret was living at home with her parents in Cambridge.[16] That year, Henry, the first of her brothers to venture off, left for southern Africa to serve in the Imperial Yeomanry during the Anglo-Boer War (1899–1902). However, it is uncertain where Margaret went after then, as she was unusually absent from photographs in her sister Ethel's family album until reappearing in 1904. She later once wrote that she 'went to France and trained as an artist mixing with many who became famous', so it may have been at this stage that she joined the colony of bright young English artists training in Paris.[17]

Margaret in 1904, aged twenty-five

Over the years, Margaret's father had taken on a heavy workload. He had become the principal lecturer in Hebrew and Theology at St John's College and director of Theological Studies.[18] He also taught mathematics and continued to oversee the missionary parish in Walworth. These responsibilities must have placed a considerable burden on him, especially given his own parish commitments, which included four services each Sunday at St Edward's; this required him to present three separate sermons, as well as conduct Sunday School. Each sermon was 'prepared with scrupulous attention and delivered with emphasis and must have drawn considerably on his mental forces'.[19] Beyond Cambridge, Frederick had been appointed examining chaplain for the Bishop of St Albans and an honorary canon of Ely Cathedral. He also had his large family and household to manage.

On her twenty-sixth birthday on 31 May 1905, Margaret entered the final year of her family's halcyon existence in Cambridge. That autumn Ethel recorded in her diary that their father had been unwell for several months. On doctor's orders, he took two weeks off over Christmas to rest. Although there had been

---

16 The National Census, 31 March 1901.
17 *Sunday Express*, 12 November 1939.
18 Obituary Rev. Canon Frederick Watson, *The Eagle*, vol. XXVII, 1906, p. 215.
19 Caldecott, *English Colonization and Empire*, p. vi.

Glimpses of Cambridge life with her brother John and sisters Grace and Dorothy on the River Cam, c.1904, in a photograph taken by Ethel (above) and with Arthur and his future fiancée Olive, and a punnet of strawberries in 1905 (below)

concern, it must have come as a terrible shock when their father had a seizure after several recurrences of exhaustion and heart trouble. After breakfast on 1 January 1906, Frederick lay 'on his study-couch and closed his earthly life'.[20] He was sixty-six. Dorothy wrote about the family's great shock and distress; they believed that he had worked himself to death.[21]

As he was one of the university's most prominent members, news of Margaret's

---

20 Obituary Rev. Canon Frederick Watson, *The Eagle*, vol. XXVII, 1906, p. 215.
21 Dorothy Watson's childhood reflections.

CHAPTER 1 | A CLERGYMAN'S DAUGHTER

Margaret at 'King's Messengers' in Norfolk during the summer of 1906

father's death travelled quickly. Obituary notices appeared in the national newspapers the following morning and were repeated across the country in the following days. Then, on 4 January, just three days later, his funeral took place at his church, St Edward King and Martyr, before burial in the parish plot on Mill Road. With fortitude, the family held together, but their father's death made a great deal of difference, as it suddenly left them very badly off.[22] Parishioners and godparents rallied to pay the boys' school fees, but there was no other money to support the girls. Margaret and her sisters would have to make their own way in life.

Before his death, Frederick had written two manuscripts to add to the five that had already been published. The family turned to his old friend Dr Caldecott to prepare them, and, with Margaret's help, *Inspiration* and *The Seven Words from the Cross* were ready for publication by year's end. On 16 February 1907, just over a year after her father's death, with his final manuscripts published and his affairs tidied up, Margaret could move on and set out on her own. Her father had

---

22 Dorothy Watson's childhood reflections.

provided an example of commitment to public duty. It seemed that for Margaret, English society did not appeal, and as a result of her childhood experiences, she may never have sought a conventional life.

Instead, she decided to escape from the comfortable drawing rooms and break from the polite society she knew, in which she was profoundly limited by her gender, her lack of money and her family's need to maintain their respectability. She followed her father's vocation and picked up his challenge to help confront what was wrong and put it to rights. She decided to go overseas and set off for Grahamstown (today known as Makhanda) in the Colony of the Cape of Good Hope.

Chapter Two

City of Saints

✸✸✸

LYING BETWEEN RUGGED escarpments in the hills about seventy miles north-east of Port Elizabeth and five hundred miles east of Cape Town, the small cathedral city of Grahamstown was founded as a military outpost in 1812. Although by the time of Margaret's arrival it had become a significant cultural, legal and market town, the main railway lines had bypassed Grahamstown and it had never gained commercial prominence.[1]

Grahamstown had become known as the City of Saints, not only as the seat of an Anglican diocese but also because it had more towers, spires and parish churches than almost any other town of its size in the Colony. Since 1855, several boarding schools had been founded along the lines of Britain's famous public schools, and the city's prestige as a seat of learning rose even further with the establishment of St Paul's Theological College in 1902 and Rhodes University College in 1904. That year, the town's settler population reached fourteen thousand, with many more in the surrounding district.

On the eve of Margaret's arrival in 1907, London's *Morning Post* newspaper described the tranquil scene:

> Unique amongst South African centres, Grahamstown is devoted wholly to the interests of education. Descending into the picturesque, wooded hollow, the traveller finds a trim little city characterised by church spires and large

---

1 Thomson, *A Short History of Grahamstown*, p. 34.

scholastic buildings. Soon, he is inhaling once more the long-forgotten atmosphere of Cambridge, England or Cambridge, Mass. Cap and gown pervade the way. Spectacled ladies toil to and fro on bicycles, a satchel of notebooks swinging from the handlebar. Mellow walled academies hide behind the oaks, while others flaunt the new-born nakedness of red brick and galvanised iron upon the dusty streets.[2]

The Cathedral Church of St Michael and St George had not always been a prominent landmark. Originally built as a parish church, it was considered inadequate for the bishop's seat after the diocese was created in 1853. Sir George Gilbert Scott, the renowned Gothic Revival architect, agreed to draw up plans for a significantly larger and worthier building with the tallest spire in southern Africa. Construction had been delayed by shortages of money and ecclesiastical conflicts, which meant that only the new chancel, tower and spire were complete by the time of Margaret's arrival in 1907. Work on the new nave had commenced and would last until 1912. However, the totality of Sir Gilbert Scott's plan for this enormously imposing and important cathedral was not fully realised for another forty years, until the completion in 1952 of the Lady Chapel, to which Margaret would make a contribution.

Margaret would have known that all the English familiarity and neatness belied Grahamstown's turbulent past in this frontier land between white settlers and Africans. She would also have known that twenty years earlier, the cathedral had been the centre of a bitter schism between bishop and dean, which had led to the bishop being excluded from his cathedral seat. The matter was not resolved until after Dean Williams's death in 1885, by when the fourth Bishop of Grahamstown, the Right Reverend Allan Becher Webb, DD, had been translated to the diocese.

In his previous diocese of Bloemfontein, Bishop Webb had recognised that for the Church to best meet the need to educate the local residents, it should involve women. To this end Webb founded the first Anglican sisterhood in southern Africa, the Community of St Michael and All Angels, in 1874. Following his translation to Grahamstown in 1883, Webb sought to draw in women who would make a sustained difference, building on his experience in Bloemfontein. Again, he sought to tap into English women's sense of concern and their willingness to volunteer to improve the lives of families whose circumstances fell short of Victorian ideals. However, Webb was cautious about inviting individual women to travel to the Cape, as he felt sure that they would drift off or 'be absorbed by marriage'.[3] Instead, he preferred that they come as members of a religious

---

2 *Morning Post*, London, 26 October 1906.
3 Webb, *Women's Work for Foreign Missions*, pp. 3–5.

CHAPTER 2 | CITY OF SAINTS

Postcards from Grahamstown in the early 1900s, as Margaret would have first seen the city when she arrived in 1907

community or make some other kind of pledge to stay. Either way, Webb envisaged women working as part of the Church, secured into the diocesan structure and under local control rather than as a branch house of an established English religious order.[4]

---

4 Webb, *Women's Work for Foreign Missions*, pp. 3–5.

Cathedral Church of St Michael and St George, Grahamstown, as Margaret would have first seen it in 1907

The proposal that English women serve in large numbers in a missionary capacity was untested, but the notion that they should form their own religious communities was not. One of the outcomes of the mid-nineteenth-century Oxford Movement was the re-establishment of religious communities, with the first ones being founded in the late 1840s. These included the great convents of St Mary the Virgin in Wantage from 1848 and St John Baptist in Clewer from 1851. Both had been founded in the Anglo-Catholic tradition and were to influence the fledgling community in Grahamstown that Bishop Webb had in mind. By 1900, more than ninety Anglican religious orders for women existed across the British Isles, involving an estimated ten thousand women, who stayed for anything from a few months to a lifetime.[5]

These communities provided middle- and upper-class women with opportunities to break away from Victorian social constraints and contribute as church workers much more than was ever likely if they remained at home. Sisterhoods offered a demanding and consecrated life, fulfilled through prayer, community living, and worthwhile work for those confident that this was their calling. Although some English communities sent Sisters to work in branch houses abroad, the numbers who could be released were usually small, given the commitments at home. For women who sought to serve overseas, the attraction of Bishop Webb's proposal was not only the certainty that they would do so but the security offered, as they would travel out to a community anchored within the Anglican Church and enfolded within its diocesan structure.[6]

Bishop Webb had been reluctant to leave his Bloemfontein diocese and part from the sisterhood he had founded in 1874, the Community of St Michael and All Angels. Nonetheless, he was persuaded to accept the See of Grahamstown, which had become vacant owing to the death of his predecessor, Bishop

---

5 Mumm, *Stolen Daughters*, p. 277.
6 Webb, *Women's Work for Foreign Missions*, p. 13.

CHAPTER 2 | CITY OF SAINTS

Interior of the Cathedral Church of St Michael and St George, following completion of the replacement nave in 1912

Nathaniel Merriman, following a carriage accident the year before. Having received approval from the diocese and the Metropolitan Bishop in Cape Town, Webb's translation to Grahamstown occurred during a prolonged stay in London in 1883.[7] Being confident that he would need more English women to assist in his new diocese, he took the opportunity to renew his call for women to commit to helping before sailing to the Cape.

The bishop was a frequent preacher at St Peter's, Eaton Square, an important society church serving the upper-class area of Belgravia, where his friend and fellow Anglo-Catholic, the Reverend George Howard Wilkinson, had developed a strongly supportive ethos for High Church overseas missions. Thus, one Sunday in July 1883, the new Bishop of Grahamstown climbed up to the pulpit and used the text 'Whereupon, O King Agrippa, I was not disobedient to the heavenly vision' to call for women to sail with him and assist in the Church's work in the Cape Colony.[8] Among those listening to the sermon was twenty-year-old Annie Cecile Ramsbottom Isherwood, an orphan who had committed herself to church work at St Peter's and had already decided on missionary work abroad. 'The words of the text went home to her heart.'[9] Webb gladly accepted the offer from such a vibrant and committed young woman. Four other women volunteered,

---

7   Gould, *Grahamstown Cathedral*, p. 34.
8   Acts of the Apostles 26:19.
9   A Sister of the Community, *Mother Cecile in South Africa*, p. 1.

Mother Cecile CR, c.1905

along with a priest from St Peter's and one other. After sailing to Cape Town, they reached Grahamstown in November 1893.

One of Cecile's first achievements was to set up an orphan school, initially with just one girl. From this modest start, she began her work of education and care. Out of the initial group, some returned to England not liking the work, while others found better opportunities and drifted away. In response, Bishop Webb determined it was right to invite Cecile to help establish a new religious community, building on his experience at Bloemfontein. Impressed with her vitality and leadership, he asked Cecile to become the foundress of the Community of the Resurrection of Our Lord in Grahamstown. He clothed her as a novice on St Mark's Day, 25 April 1884, when she was only twenty-one years old. On making her profession three and a half years later, she became the community's first Superior, taking the name in religion of Mother Cecile.[10]

Half a century later, when Margaret Watson, by then Sister Margaret CR, wrote *The Mind of Our Founders*, she explained that Bishop Webb's decision to establish the community was partly an act of atonement for the controversies caused by Bishop Colenso of Natal.[11] His trial for heresy in 1863, due to his apparent abandonment of fundamental religious tenets, had rocked the Anglican Church. After much controversy, the matter was finally resolved upon Bishop Colenso's death in 1883, the year of Webb's translation to Grahamstown. Margaret also wrote that Bishop Webb's decision to name the community after the Resurrection was an attempt to dispel the trouble that the schism between Dean Williams and his preceding bishop had caused. This had led Grahamstown to become another 'byword for disunity and bitterness in the Anglican Church', which he sought to lay to rest.[12]

---

10 CR Profession Register, entry 1.
11 Sister Margaret, *The Mind of Our Founders*, p. 7.
12 Sister Margaret, *The Mind of Our Founders*, p. 5.

> The Bishop had come to a terrible state of affairs in the Cathedral City, and it was his wide Vision that saw the need for a Religious Community, whose members might offer reparation by their lives for the wrong done; thus striking a very solemn note in our first beginnings. As self-will and disobedience had been at the root of the present scandal, so the Sisters could rejoice in being given the opportunity of offering their Vows and themselves at the Foot of the Cross.[13]

> It seemed most fitting that her [Mother Cecile's] Community should become that of the Resurrection and that its ideal should be life springing from complete self-sacrifice.[14]

Within months, an attractive property at Eden Grove, on the city's western side, had been purchased and rebuilt to become a permanent home. It was named St Peter's, maintaining the link with Eaton Square. In 1886, the Chapel of the Resurrection was built to serve the Sisters, a place that would become very dear to Margaret later. Other works commenced to provide accommodation for destitute children, a school for girls within the community's grounds, and the Good Shepherd School for 'coloured' (mixed race) children nearby. As the number of Sisters and available helpers increased, missionary work began among the Chinese community in Port Elizabeth in 1886, as, from its beginning, the community sought to serve people across the spectrum of Cape society.

By 1887, just four years after its establishment, when the community numbered only five professed Sisters, it was decided to enlarge St Peter's Home. More space was needed as, with the community approaching its tenth anniversary, there were five novices and nine professed Sisters, with several additional helpers. As their number grew, the Sisters opened new missions, including educational institutions in the eastern districts of the Colony: in King William's Town, Herschel, Keiskamma Hoek and East London. In 1894, the community started another great endeavour by offering teacher training to the older girls in their St Peter's School so as to help provide staff for their elementary schools.

The community depended as much on the flow of money as on the supply of helpers from England to enable it to grow. As a result, much work took place in the mother country to build a network of supporters who would run appeals, hold public meetings, help with recruitment and generally promote the Sisters' work. As the community's standing in the Cape Colony grew, the Sisters were asked to do more work. Mother Cecile's enthusiasm could not let the community stand still, nor did she want to miss any opportunities provided she

---

13 Sister Margaret, *The Mind of Our Founders*, p. 7.
14 Sister Margaret, *The Mind of Our Founders*, p. 5.

had available Sisters. Arguing 'that we must go forward as the need increases', she returned to England several times to seek funds and more helpers.[15] Her charismatic meetings generated great interest as she toured the country, and senior Anglican clergy, including the Archbishop of Canterbury, were keen to lend their support.[16]

While funds were forthcoming, there could never be enough. Nor could there ever be enough women prepared to travel out to the Cape to meet the community's needs. The Sisters recognised this and recorded in their letter to English supporters in April 1905 that 'it would tax the energies of twice the number of Sisters and workers to keep pace with the growth'.[17] They needed more. Through the English Helpers Union, a supporting network of helpers across England, including Cambridge, an appeal was made:

Workers Wanted for St Peter's Home

This is an old cry, but it comes with redoubled force just now. The work has grown so vastly that help of all kinds is more and more needed, not only the more technical teaching work, but, from what I gather from Mother Cecile's Letters, workers of 'all sorts and conditions of women' for the Home itself, the Schools, Colleges. St Peter's provides a wonderfully varied field of work, and surely there might be some among our readers and friends who would answer to this call, and give their best. As Mother Cecile reminded us in a letter a year or two ago, 'great gifts are not necessary, but a desire to give self up honestly and self-forgettingly for Christ's work'.[18]

By removing any presumption that showing an interest in helping might also involve entering the sisterhood, it was hoped that more women would be willing to come, even for short stays. The community would welcome all kinds of skills.

In November 1906, *The Queen: The Lady's Newspaper* carried a favourable report of the community's achievements and, by doing so, played its part in urging young women to go out.[19] A further piece in the community's quarterly letter to English supporters in April 1907 addressed misconceptions about St Peter's Home.

---

15 CR, *Church Education in South Africa* (c.1907), p. 28.
16 A Sister of the Community, *Mother Cecile in South Africa*, p. 119.
17 CR Quarterly Letter, April 1905, p. 2.
18 CR Annual Report 1903–1904, p. 10.
19 *The Queen: The Lady's Newspaper*, 17 November 1906, p. 892.

Appeal for Volunteers

Perhaps many are stirred by all the missionary ardour that is in the air these days, making itself felt in increased interest taken in Missionary books and prayers, but are kept back by thinking that they could never 'be a Missionary' or preach to the heathen. 'Oh no, that is not in my line at all,' one may say; or another, 'I could not live in a hot climate, nor could I bear the loneliness we read of'; or again, 'I never could speak decent French even, so how could I hope to master the language of these heathen?' Would it not be well, first of all to settle the point as to what a Missionary is? Is it not one who obediently keeps God's commandments? When He says 'Go' they go (or let go – help go).

Where for such work could a better field be than at S. Peter's Grahamstown? There the doors (those kindly doors) are open to all earnest seekers after work with God. The climate is most healthy; English is spoken; work abounds to suit all aspirations from the lowliest to the most ambitious. There, a start on the shores of Africa may be made, which may end in the darkest hinterland – in the almost unpenetrated Soudan. In these days of cheap fares and quick steamers a personal visit to S. Peter's would be the best way of judging whether it is a good mission field.[20]

All these efforts had some effect, as by October 1906, in addition to those seeking a religious life, 129 women had come out to help for longer or shorter stays. Sixteen had arrived in 1906.[21] Somehow, and unsurprisingly, given her upbringing, news of the community reached Margaret. Although she had already sailed when the 'Appeal for Volunteers' was published in April 1907, it may have offered some comfort and explanation to her family.

On Saturday, 16 February 1907, six weeks after the first anniversary of her father's death, Margaret, aged

Margaret Watson at Hunstanton, Norfolk, on holiday with her family, early in the 1900s

---

20 CR Quarterly Letter, April 1907, pp. 8–9.
21 CR Quarterly Letter, October 1906, The Warden's Report, p. 3.

RMS *Saxon* of the Union-Castle Mail Steamship Company (left) alongside the company's wharf at the Princess Dock, Southampton, in early 1907, receiving attention to her paintwork prior to her next voyage to the Cape of Good Hope

twenty-seven, made her way to Southampton's Princess Dock. Since Cecile Isherwood first made the same journey to Cape Town in 1883, passenger liners on the Cape run had grown four times in size. Margaret sailed on one of the newest ships of the Union-Castle Mail Steamship Company, RMS *Saxon*, which was also the largest and most powerful vessel in the company's fleet when delivered in 1900. She could carry 310 first-, 203 second- and 132 third-class passengers and assorted cargo. At a speed of 17½ knots, the voyage to Cape Town usually took two weeks, including a brief call at Madeira.

Margaret travelled third class in a portion of the ship set aside for migrants at the stern, well away from the comfortable saloons and fine food. The third-class fare was £10 10d, for which she would have been allocated a berth in a spartan cabin for four, without bedding, and received basic meals from the third-class galley.

Margaret's journey was likely to have been very similar to a report included in the community's quarterly letter to English supporters four months earlier.

Scattered Impressions of Voyage to S. Africa and of S. Peter's Home

THE VOYAGE – What a wearisome voyage that is to some of us, yet how its details stand out in our memories! The arrival at the boat at Southampton, the inspection of our cabin, the waiting on deck while we wonder as we look round which among the crowd are to be our fellow passengers; then the last half-hour before starting – our friends standing on the pier just beyond speaking distance and so many last words left unsaid, while to the left of us comes the reiterated call 'Away, there!' as the mails are being put on board. Now the boat is off, and most of us prefer to go to our cabins and unpack, even though it necessitates the last look at English shores.

MADEIRA – After four days, during which not many of the passengers are to be seen, Madeira is reached. How refreshing to wake up and know that we shall see land! Most of us hurry on shore about 7 a.m. to wander about the town, which has an interesting old part and a picturesque market. Then there is the attraction of a meal on terra firma; for the rest, there was distraction enough in the sale of baskets and other wares, which were hurriedly brought out to the boat directly we cast anchor, whilst small boys from various boats shrilly invite the passengers to throw them coppers for which to dive.

Margaret Watson watching a dance performance on the promenade deck of RMS *Saxon* during her voyage to Algoa Bay in 1907

CAPE TOWN – Three hours' respite, and then the voyage is resumed; this time ten days without a break is before us, during four of which the heat is intense, and every effort to think or read profitably is quite futile. Then, as the Wednesday approaches on which we are due to reach Cape Town, our excitement visibly grown, we can think and talk of nothing else, and on the morning itself many of us are on deck by 5.30 a.m. to welcome the first sight of land. And what a glorious morning it was! Robben Island lay to our left, and behind it rose a long row of mountains, while the sky was already tinged with the deep red glow of a cloudless sunrise. On our right a full moon was setting in all her glory, throwing up in deep blackness the great mass of Table Mountain. Can you conceive the beauty of colour! Still the moonshine on the water and the deep blues of night to the west, yet the glory of the future day to the east – such was our welcome to the new country. And how we did enjoy the day on shore! In the morning we went up to All Saints' Home, where the All Saints Sisters have a large orphanage for boys and girls, and schools; then to lunch at the GFS [Girls Friendly Society] Home, where we were most hospitably received – and then in the afternoon we trammed and

RMS *Saxon* of the Union-Castle Mail Steamship Company

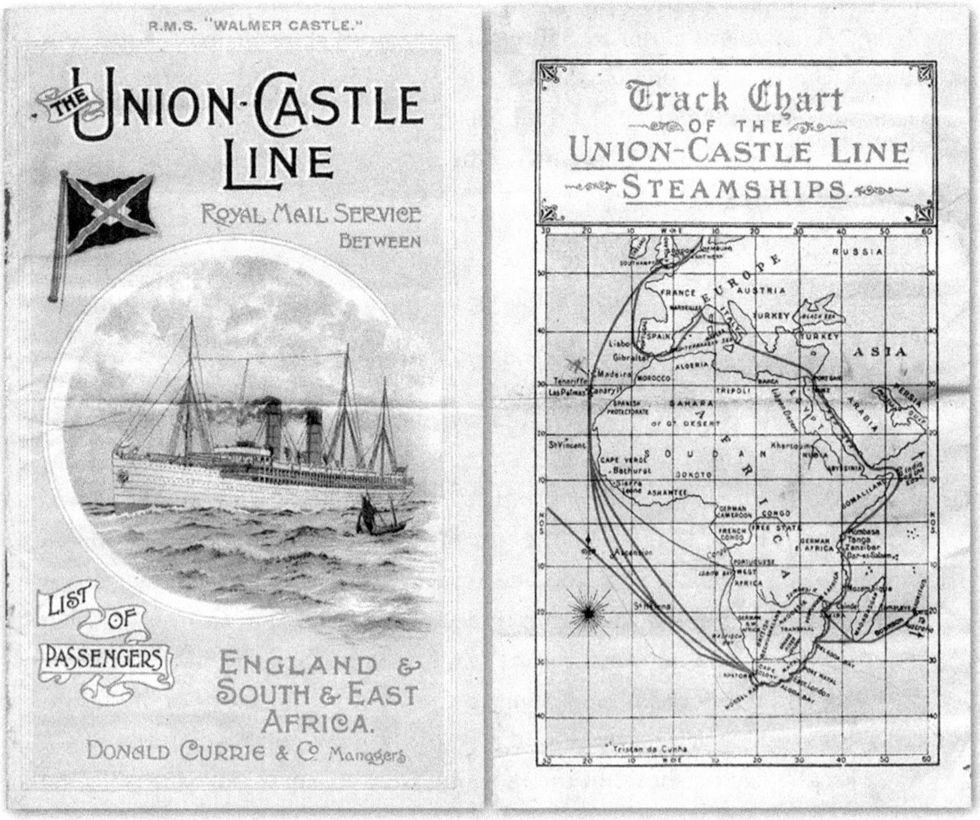

Union-Castle Line passenger information leaflet, 1911

RMS *Saxon*, or sister ship, in Cape Town docks, postcard image from 1910

walked out to Bishop's Court, where the Archbishop lives, and where we had a kindly welcome, bringing as we did messages from mutual friends in England.

Port Elizabeth – But Cape Town was not our destination. We left it during the beautiful sunset, and we felt we had indeed seen the famous Cape in its glory. On the Friday morning we anchored early at Port Elizabeth, where after breakfast, a tug came out to fetch us ashore. As we drew near to the landing stage we caught sight of a habit already dear to many of us, and a Sister of St Peter's Home gave us a loving welcome. Somehow, with that warm greeting all feeling of being in a strange land passed away, we felt among our own people. Having seen our luggage we went by tram up to the Mission House in the North End. Here a delicious cup of tea refreshed us much after the so-called ship's tea, and each of the four Sisters now stationed there had a welcome greeting to give us, as she came in from her morning's work. I only had time for a short visit to the school and laundry, which is about six minutes' walk from the Mission House, but it was nice to see a little of the work done there.

The Night Journey to Grahamstown – 9 p.m. saw us at the station with a night journey before us up to Grahamstown – a very short one – as the train waits at the station for two hours, besides many other shorter stoppages. I was lucky in getting a carriage to myself till about 4 a.m., when three people tumbled in and settled themselves to sleep as best they could. At about 7 a.m.,

Algoa Bay anchorage off Port Elizabeth, 1911

Basket used to transfer passengers over the side onto tugs riding alongside, as used at Algoa Bay and other ports without deepwater berths

half an hour before we were due in Grahamstown, dawn began to break, and we saw more of our surroundings. We were winding up the sides of what seemed to be great gorges, and we had a glimpse of Grahamstown, only to lose it again as we circled round the city; but it all looked very beautiful in the early morning light.

As we steamed into the station once again, as at Port Elizabeth, we caught sight of a loving face greeting us, and almost before the train stopped, a warm welcome was given us, and the long-anticipated moment of arrival at Grahamstown was accomplished.

CHAPTER 2 | CITY OF SAINTS

Lighters being towed away from a Union-Castle steamer, c.1910

Postcard showing passengers landing at the North Jetty, Port Elizabeth, from a mailship anchored in Algoa Bay

Grahamstown railway station, c.1910

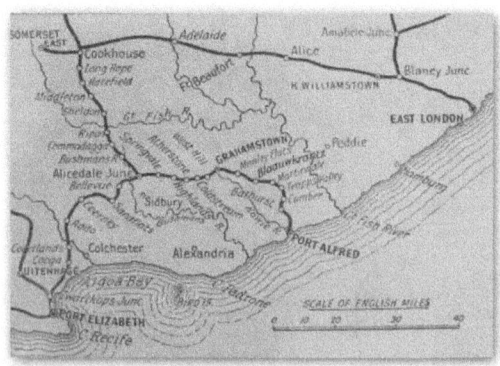

Cape Colony railway connections to Grahamstown, from *The Railways of Cape Colony*, by J.W. Courtenay (1907)

ST PETER'S — Then came the walk up from the station, past the Cathedral, and on to a gateway, just at a dip in a road, close by which a small stream runs. As we came through the gateway I noticed St Peter's School on the left, then the rose garden, the last bit of gardening Mother Cecile herself superintended with such keenness, and which, typical perhaps of the other parts of her work, promised to flourish despite of being planted out at what some thought an unseasonable time. Behind the rose garden lie the College Tennis Courts, backed by the 'Junior House', where the First Year Students and Boarders have their meals and recreation. By the time this is passed we are close up to the Home itself. A long building two stories high. The western end is chiefly given up to the College dormitories and a schoolroom; the centre has a good entrance hall, with Workers' and Sisters' refectories on each side, and the kitchen behind.

CHAPTER 2 | CITY OF SAINTS

Hill Street, Grahamstown, towards the Cathedral, from the railway station in 1906

To the eastern end of the central block is the Chapel, and as we approached it, we recognised at once the steps leading up to it where Mother Cecile was photographed by Miss Amy Bonsor. The craving to see her there once more seemed overwhelming at that moment, but I need not dwell on that – in every part of the House she so loved, one longs to see her and to hear her steps.

When I arrived I was led beyond the Chapel to the entrance of the wing, where Mother Cecile had her own little room, and about which she had spoken to me; a tiny room, yet I felt somehow that it was a room she would have loved, and did love.

It was by this time about 8.30, and having had some breakfast, I was sent to rest most of the day, but at 4 p.m. I was taken up to see Woodville, another house belonging to the Sisters, where the Home children live. Of these I can say little, only that they look very nice in their blue frocks and white hats, as my work is not to be with them …

THE CHAPEL – But in all this while I have not mentioned the Chapel; the truth is, it was not till I had been there two or three times that I began to know what my impression was. It is small – too small, as some of you probably know – from our present large numbers, and the little Oratory above the Chapel – where one can hear but not see – is in constant use. I can only speak of it as it struck me; but seldom have I been into a Church which so quickly conveyed

Shopping emporia in the High Street, Grahamstown, as in 1907

a sense of quiet restfulness; everything is so absolutely simple, nothing ornate, no mural decorations, nothing to distract the eye from the Altar, which one feels to be at the centre of its life – yet everything is strong and good, and at times the eye is caught by the light on the polished pillars of the screen. Reminding us of the Psalmist's words – especially the early Celebrations – bear the same stamp of the quiet restfulness of strength.

One little touch always attracts me, and that is the soft singing of a hymn with pauses between each verse during the actual Communicating on Sundays. On Trinity Sunday especially, Hymn 160 was beautifully rendered this way.[22]

THE WALKS – I need not speak further of the Chapel, as all would guess it as such a centre of our life out here that we could spend any length of time dilating on it. It somehow seems natural to speak next of another source of rest here – namely, the quiet time out on the rough ground which rises almost immediately behind the Home, and where, under the pines, one can always get a feeling of being alone and apart. Here is also, within ten minutes' walk of the Home, a charming view of Grahamstown, with its encircling hills, looking so quiet and peaceful. Here it is pleasant to walk with a congenial friend and dream of those in England – in fact, in the month of June, the

---

22 Most likely 'Holy! Holy! Holy!', Hymn 160 in *Hymns Ancient and Modern*, traditionally sung on Trinity Sunday.

climate is so like that of the Mother Country that this might be England itself, and Grahamstown an English country town, except for the [African] faces to be seen everywhere. Then to go back strengthened for the work by the knowledge that those at home are thinking and praying for us constantly; yet we are not without an occasional great longing to see those dear faces again, but withal, fully under the spell of the fascination of St Peter's – a fascination which seizes with a firm grip most of those who come within the charm of its circle.[23]

---

23 CR Quarterly Letter, October 1906, pp. 9–12.

Chapter Three

Preparation for Good Things

✽✽✽

BY THE TIME Margaret arrived in Grahamstown in March 1907, Mother Cecile and Bishop Webb had both departed, and the community they founded was now under its second Superior, Mother Florence.

Having served as Bishop of Grahamstown since 1883, Allan Webb preached his farewell sermon and bid farewell to the Sisters at Evensong before sailing to England on 7 May 1898, a decision taken for the sake of his wife's frail health.[1] Convinced that she and the heart of the community should follow Bishop Webb to Scotland so that he could continue with his oversight and help with its recruitment, Mother Cecile had also left Grahamstown in 1898. After finding a suitable house in Forres, several other Sisters joined her there.[2] However, the move was short-lived, as, after being recalled to Grahamstown in July 1899, Mother Cecile found that she could not return to Scotland owing to the outbreak of the Anglo-Boer War. Perpetually driven by the need to do more, Mother Cecile undertook several return visits to England after the war to raise funds and promote the community's work. Weak and exhausted by illness and overwork, she was sent back to London for the final time in August 1905 and died after emergency surgery for cancer on 20 February 1906 at the

---

1 *Inverness Cathedral Magazine*, July 1898, 'Bishop Webb's Farewell to his Diocese'. He was to serve as Provost of the Cathedral Church of St Andrew in Inverness until being appointed Dean of Salisbury Cathedral in 1901, where he died in June 1907.
2 A Sister of the Community, *Mother Cecile in South Africa*, p. 65.

St Peter's Home, Grahamstown at the time of Margaret's arrival, after first enlargement and construction of the Sisters' wing (to the left) in 1892

age of forty-three.³ Mother Cecile had been a woman of extraordinary energy and progressive views, and was held in such high regard that the Archbishop of Canterbury officiated at her funeral.

Arriving at St Peter's Home just over a year after her death, Margaret Watson was struck that the community still seemed 'full' of Mother Cecile and was still mourning for her.⁴ She wrote that the foundress's 'gay, gracious personality seemed to be everywhere. Everything was referred to as "what dear Mother

---

3 A Sister of the Community, *Mother Cecile in South Africa*, p. 153.
4 Sister Margaret, *The Mind of Our Founders*, p. 3.

would like". It seemed as if her love was still watching over the place, as we are sure her prayers still do.'[5] As a new 'helper', Margaret would almost certainly have been drawn into the thick of activities on the campus at St Peter's with its teacher training college and large girls' school, and in the nearby streets where some of the community's other schools and orphanages were housed.

Bishop Webb had been clear about the practical and moral qualities he sought in women coming to help and had written that, above all, 'can do is easily carried about'.[6] An account of life within the 'hive' at St Peter's conveys the busy environment that Margaret joined.

The Life of a Worker at St Peter's Home

It is a very difficult task to describe the life of a worker at St Peter's Home, because of the varied work carried on there, and the individual capacity and talent of each worker; so perhaps the best way of giving a faint idea of what is going on in this busy 'hive' is to tell a little bit about the many branches of work as they present themselves to a newcomer, and to sketch a rough outline of the routine of an ordinary day. Of course the part that absorbs into its activities the majority of the workers is the big Training School for Pupil Teachers, which is now so large that, unless you are accustomed to the rush and bustle of school life, is almost bewildering, until you begin to grasp the details of its machinery; then you begin to realise the importance of the work, and to see that to have the slightest influence for good in the lives of these girls, either in school as their teacher or out of school in the many opportunities which continually arise, is a great privilege and missionary work in a very true sense. At the present time most of the big building is given up to dormitories and class rooms for the Pupil Teachers, but one end is still reserved for the Sisters and Workers, where each one has a small cubicle to herself, simply furnished with a bed, washing stand, a nice capacious cupboard, a few pegs for clothes, etc., and it is surprising how soon one learns to do without things that at home seemed indispensable. Everybody rises early out here, for it is no hardship in this land of sunshine, and when the great bell rings at 6 a.m., you are quite ready to get up and, after a refreshing cold tub, set to work at seven!

The girls prepare their day's work before breakfast, so there is plenty to do for the workers in terms of taking charge. At 8 a.m. we all have breakfast with the older girls, but at a separate table with the Sister-in-Charge. After this, bed-making and dusting our rooms, and then begins the regular work of the day; those who are teachers going off to different schools, for the Sisters

---

5 Sister Margaret, *The Mind of Our Founders*, p. 3.
6 Webb, *Women's Work for Foreign Missions*, p. 11.

are responsible for at least four; and this year, besides these, a new branch of kindergarten has begun, for which some of the girls are being trained.

Many too, who have already passed their Pupil-Teacher Examinations have now come back as Matriculation Students, with the view of continuing their studies for the Certificate for Secondary School Teachers; and to help with these classes, teachers who have gone in for Higher Education at home of course are needed for domestic service; whilst at the same time all the cooking and washing for this immense household are done by them under the supervision of skilled workers. And in these departments a few native girls are also engaged, who have come from far distant Mission Stations specially to be trained in the technical work; and to get into touch with them outside their fixed occupations, to take them for walks, preside over their meals, read prayers for them, and other offices of that kind, fall to the lot of some of the appointed workers, who cannot fail to be interested in this special branch, and to feel that the time these girls spend down here in such surroundings must have lasting results when they return to their own homes. The workers dine together at 1 o'clock, after which they have a quiet restful time until the girls and teachers come out of school at 2 p.m. After this, there is much to be done with the students out of school, going for walks, playing tennis, taking a general interest in their occupations, drawing them out as much as possible, and getting to know their individual characters – and these differ so much from those of English girls.

There is a Debating Society, for which all workers are eligible as members, and much interest and keenness is shown about the various topics which are brought up for discussion at the monthly meeting, for the Colonial girls dearly love a good argument!

At 6 o'clock comes our evening meal, after which we all go to Vespers, and, though other duties fall to the lot of some before bedtime, this practically ends the worker's day.

But no sketch of this busy life would be in any way complete without reference to the Chapel and its helpful Services, which seem as it were the keynote of this life of service, bringing into harmony the varied occupations, so that we can all realise, whatever our task may be, that the object of our work is one. The Chapel itself is beautifully cared for, and the Altar always adorned with the loveliest flowers; it is open all day for private prayer, and the peace and quiet within its walls are real rest and refreshment in the daily round.

Besides this, four times a week we are able to begin our day with a Celebration of the Holy Eucharist, and of the Offices we attend Prime or Terse and Vespers daily. On Fridays there is a Special Evensong at 5.30 for the Sisters and Workers, with an Address always helpful and instructive, and very often we enjoy the special privilege of hearing the Bishop himself. On Sundays we all go to the Cathedral for Matins, and to Evensong in our own Chapel, when it is full to overflowing, because at this time the whole big family is present, from the Sisters down to the small home children, including also the Native girls. It is very difficult in a few words to give any real idea of the life, because it is so different from anything at home, and comprises a very wide sphere of work; but, in spite of sacrifices which must be met and difficulties which must be overcome, there is some charm about it which grows stronger the longer you are here, and the only advice one who is out here can give to one at home, is 'come and try!'[7]

Margaret would have had much to contribute with all that she had done at home in Cambridge to help look after her younger brothers and sisters, her artistic training, and her principled judgement derived from her upbringing as a clergyman's daughter. 'Come and try' had been the call. So, she did. Although there is no record of where Margaret helped during her first months in Grahamstown, others have recounted that they initially worked in the community's elementary schools and orphanages, with St Peter's Woodville orphanage for white girls being likely.

Setting up a home for destitute children had been one of Mother Cecile's first works after she arrived in Grahamstown to help Bishop Webb. She had been appalled to discover that in the absence of any children's homes, the only place for waifs and strays was prison, where they were housed with adults 'under deplorable conditions'.[8] 'Some of the little ones came through district visiting.'[9] Others were sent to the orphanage by the magistrates. Three years before Margaret's arrival, Woodville, a property close to St Peter's Home, had been purchased to accommodate 132 children up to the age of thirteen, with room for its elementary school.[10] For the older girls, training was provided in housekeeping, laundry, cookery and needlework on a 'thoroughly Christian basis' to prepare them for work and adult life.[11]

In testimony to Mother Cecile's determination to improve the provision of education across the Colony by extending its schools, the community had,

---

7   CR Quarterly Letter, July 1903, pp. 3–5.
8   CR, *Woodville Orphanage and Industrial School* (c.1917).
9   CR, *Woodville Orphanage and Industrial School*.
10 CR, *Woodville Orphanage and Industrial School*; & *Church Education in South Africa* (c.1907).
11 CR Annual Report, July 1904 to July 1905, September 1905, p. 16.

CHAPTER 3 | PREPARATION FOR GOOD THINGS

St Peter's School situated below St Peter's Home, 1907

Laundry at the Industrial School for European Girls in 1907

Grahamstown Training College buildings in 1907

St. Peter's Home, Grahamstown.

Rules for Workers and Visitors.

It is hoped that Ladies offering for a time as Workers at St. Peter's Home, will regard it for the time as their home, observing the same loyalty and consideration as they would in their own family circle. In this spirit of thoughtful care for the general well being of all, they are asked to observe the following Rules:—

1. — To keep silence.
   (a) From 10 p.m. until after breakfast. In the Common Room quiet talking is allowed from after Compline until 10 p.m.
   (b) At all times in passages and on the stairs.
2. — To be present at two Offices daily unless permission is given to the contrary.
3. — To make their own beds, to keep their rooms tidy and to be punctual at all times.
4. — Not to give presents to the Home Girls without permission.
5. — Not to visit each other in times of sickness without permission, or to go into each others' rooms from the Compline Bell until after breakfast and from 2.0 p.m. till 4.0 p.m.
6. — To put their lights out by 10.30 p.m. unless permission is given to the contrary.
7. — Not to go into the Infirmaries, Kitchen or Pantry without permission.
8. — Not to smoke in the House, but Workers and visitors are free to smoke in specified places within the grounds.
   N.B.—The Garden Nook is for Workers and Visitors.
9. — To notify the Guest Mistress when they will be out after 10 p.m. or when absent from meals, and not to go out for country walks alone, because it is not safe to do so in this country.

In conclusion, Workers are lovingly asked to remember at all times that they are Workers in St. Peter's Home, that the Chapel altar is the true centre of their life and work, and that they are in close contact with impressionable young life. Therefore there is need of the highest standard of attendance at Public Worship, as well as the ordering of the personal life, both within and without the precincts of the Home.

Rules for Workers and Visitors at St Peter's Home, c.1906

as we have seen, commenced teacher training in 1894, involving the upper form of their St Peter's School. Two years later, in 1896, this provision was significantly increased when St Peter's School moved to a new building at Eden Grove, allowing for the establishment of a separate teacher training school in the now disused classrooms at St Peter's Home. From these small beginnings, the Grahamstown Training College was founded in 1904 and, under the Sisters' leadership, grew into an important and prestigious institution, which that year moved into purpose-built accommodation at Eden Grove, just below St Peter's Home. Gradually, the college campus expanded across a range of adjoining buildings, bringing much activity to the Sisters' lives. Their community had never intended to be contemplative but to engage with the world. With the presence of dozens of teacher trainees and tens of scores of girls at St Peter's School, the Sisters' home and grounds were anything but quiet.

Disaster struck in late August 1907 when a new boarding house for college girls, Canterbury House, caught fire just before it was to be handed over by the builders. Helpers had spent the day carrying in furniture to get it ready for the start of term a week later. The cause was a gas leak, and the building was substantially damaged. This disaster aside, 'I cannot express to you how thoroughly happy I am here,' wrote a recently arrived worker in a message published in the community's quarterly letter for English supporters. 'The very atmosphere seems full of love and joy and homeliness.'[12] These words could have been Margaret's, and possibly were, as the anonymous helper also wrote that she 'hoped to go up to a farm for a week, as it is difficult to rest here, there are so many odds and ends to do in a huge place like this'.[13]

Margaret indeed went up to Highlands Farm, a sheep farm in the hills to the west about ten miles from Grahamstown. Highlands was easy to reach as it was a railway halt on the Alicedale line. The farm had been home to the pioneering botanist Mary Elizabeth Barber, daughter of one of the early English settlers from 1820, who had taken advantage of the Colonial Government's offer of a hundred acres of land for every man over eighteen prepared to settle and farm. Mary Barber had become an accomplished poet and painter before she died in 1899, making Highlands a place of curiosity for Margaret no doubt.[14]

Margaret took the opportunity to escape from the summer heat in the early weeks of 1908 to paint. She produced a landscape, dimly lit by the midsummer night, entitled 'Night at Highlands', which captured a view from atop the Milner Dam, which was completed to create a reservoir for the city in 1898.

---

12 CR Quarterly Letter, April 1910, pp. 3–5.
13 CR Quarterly Letter, April 1910, pp. 3–5.
14 Mary Elizabeth Barber, Wikipedia.

The Botanical Gardens above St Peter's Home, which can be seen below to the left, leading to the Sisters' gardens, in April 1906

'Night at Highlands', a watercolour by Margaret Watson, 1908

Shortly after her return from Highlands, Margaret's life changed. On Saturday, 7 March 1908, on the eve of Lent, she made her first step into the religious life. On this day, she was accepted as a postulant into the Community of the Resurrection of Our Lord. So began a 'preliminary course of discipline and training to prepare her for admission to the Noviciate and eventual reception of the Habit'.[15]

Margaret's acceptance would have been achieved through an interview with the novice mistress, who would have already decided on her suitability by observing her at St Peter's since her arrival. Her father's standing in Cambridge undoubtedly had already marked her out. At some stage, references from England would have been sought to confirm her depth of faith, leadership potential, natural demeanour, and how she might cope under stress.[16]

Experienced Sisters knew that a steady stream of postulants was essential for the community's health to ensure its continuity by replacing less active members as they grew old and thus enabling it to expand. They also knew it was desirable to have a good number of aspirants to select from, to avoid the necessity of accepting any applicant through lack of choice. Therefore, drawing in postulants was of the greatest importance to secure the community's longevity. With a good supply of postulants and novices, the community could look ahead with strength and certainty. However, the Sisters also knew they had to ensure that newcomers would fit in and not disrupt their ordered existence.

Margaret Watson was the hundred-and-tenth woman to take this initial step.[17] The community she joined numbered seventy-one women in 1908, including two other postulants who entered in the months just before and after her. Out of that year, there were fourteen novices, fifty-three active Sisters and one aged over seventy.[18] Advice to those who had reached this stage was to be cautious and to be sure they were ready to enter the religious life. While not doubting that they had been led to this point by God through his calling, and therefore not challenging their sincerity, the community urged a pause before they took each step, to make sure, as the final profession would be irrevocable.

In a letter to an unknown candidate the Warden at the time that Margaret became a postulant commented on the merits of entering the community at St Peter's Home:

As you know different Communities have different methods and standards,

---

15 Advisory Council on Religious Communities, *Guide to the Religious Communities of the Anglican Communion*, p. 13.
16 CR Reference Form for Aspirants.
17 CR Register of Novices [from] 1908, entry 110.
18 CR Profession Register and Register of Novices [from 1908].

> and while some seem to aim at crushing individuality in more or less degree, in order to develop disciplinary and regulated method of life, your Community seems to aim at greater freedom of work, while at the same time developing the spiritual and devotional side as the mainspring and safeguard. I feel very strongly that the St Peter's method is the one which will be most likely to suit your character, and to develop what is best and strongest in you. You will have the necessary discipline which Community Life gives. The working under Rule and Order. And you will also have the freedom which will enable you to avoid the feeling of being cramped which might take the spring and life out of your work. I also think the warmth of a community like St Peter's will give you what you value, and what will much help you, and so I am very glad you are being drawn to it.[19]

Since 1 May 1906, the community had been under the superiorship of Mother Florence. She had been unanimously elected after the foundress's death in March of that year, having already served as Assistant Superior from 1904.[20] Among her many qualities, Mother Florence was strict and businesslike. She was aware of the need to place the community on a sound footing after the somewhat idealistic approach of the founder.

> A greater contrast to the late mother could hardly be imagined. Mother Cecile was the novice-foundress at twenty-one and died at forty-three, a pioneer until the end. What she wanted was to consolidate and carry on the work. Sister Florence was in middle life. She had entered the community three years after its start and had been sent for a period of novice training to the Community of St John the Baptist, Clewer. After that she became the mother's right hand, employed in many capacities.

> Without the personal charm and prestige of the Foundress, she worked her way with sound and sterling qualities. She was short of stature, but every inch counted. Her blue eyes were practical, not dreamy. In interviews, they sparkled with silver specks, which seemed to search your every being. The Mother was called 'the little lion' by her contemporaries in training and 'the mighty atom' by members of the men's CR [the Community of the Resurrection based at Mirfield, Yorkshire], who came to take retreats.[21] She was, in the earlier years, hard on herself and others, but with the cares of office, she softened greatly.[22]

Having first arrived in Grahamstown as a worker in 1887 and entered the

---

19 Phelps, *Some Letters and Counsels of Francis Robinson Phelps*, pp. 28–29.
20 A Sister of the Community, *The Story of a Vocation*, p. 105.
21 Fathers of the Community of the Resurrection, Mirfield, Yorkshire.
22 Naylor, *South Africa: My Venture*, ch. IV.

noviciate in 1888 as only the sixth sister,[23] Mother Florence was one of the cornerstones of the community. As part of her training, she had been sent back to England in 1890 to learn from 'one of the oldest and most numerous active communities [for women] in England'.[24] Her stay was with the Community of St John Baptist, which had been founded at Clewer, near Windsor, in 1852 to undertake rescue work with 'fallen' women and girls.[25] Under the vision of their founder, Canon T.T. Carter, the rector of Clewer, the Clewer Sisters had pioneered this work within the Anglican Church. They also defined their version of the religious life, firmly bound by Anglo-Catholic values. With forty years of experience since being founded, the Clewer sisterhood had a great deal to offer the fledgling community in Grahamstown. Links stretched back to Bishop Webb's friendship with Canon Carter, the founder of Clewer, and Mother Cecile had been a regular visitor during her stays in England after 1885.[26]

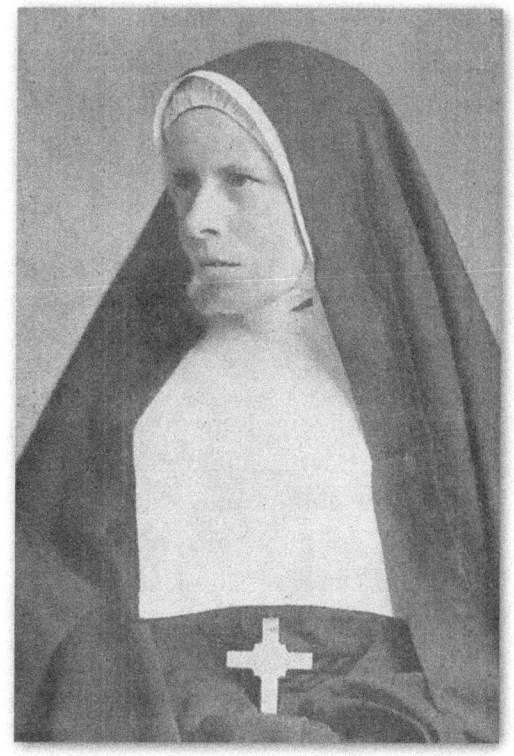
Mother Florence CR, c.1906

Sister Florence sought to learn as much as possible during her two-month stay in the noviciate at Clewer between June and August 1890.[27] As Superior, Mother Florence was able to draw on this to benefit the Grahamstown sisterhood. She had been elected at a time of significant expansion, with the number of Sisters and aspirants doubling from forty to eighty between 1900 and 1910. Under her superiorship, several new projects commenced. With so much going on, she needed to be astute. Mother Florence held high expectations for herself and accepted no less from others. At times, she needed to be tough; according to

---

23 CR Profession Register, entry 6.
24 Anson, *Call of the Cloister*, p. 304.
25 Anson, *Call of the Cloister*, pp. 305–306.
26 Annuals of the Community of Saint John Baptist, 1885–1906, Berkshire Records Office.
27 Annuals of the Community of Saint John Baptist, 1885–1906; & A Sister in the Community, *Mother Cecile in South Africa*, p. 232.

reports, she certainly could be.[28] Nonetheless, Mother Florence carried great dignity, was much respected within and beyond the convent's walls, and, as one novice observed, she had 'the light of vision in her eyes'.[29]

Under the Constitution, the Superior's appointment was for seven years. She pledged to govern constitutionally rather than autocratically or capriciously. It was 'her part to supply a mother's love, and to act in all matters of grave concern'.[30] Neither the obedience shown to the Superior by all other members of the community nor adherence to the community's rules was to be seen as 'servile or mechanical, but trustful and generous'. Mother Florence was honoured 'for the office's sake', which required that she always be addressed with respect.[31]

Aside from the Superior, regulating the community fell to the Warden, who was always an ordained priest. As well as acting as chaplain at St Peter's Home and administering the Holy Sacraments daily, it was his duty to 'direct the entire spiritual concern of the Sisterhood'.[32] At Margaret's arrival, the Reverend Douglas Ellison held this post, but he retired to England in 1908 because of ill health.

Not knowing any likely priest in the Colony who could fill the gap, Mother Florence returned to England in March 1908 to seek a replacement. The appointment of a new Warden to help ensure stability in the community after the foundress's death was of great importance. Through the assistance of friends, the Reverend Francis Robinson Phelps, rector of Thorpe Episcopi in the Diocese of Norwich, was identified as a possible candidate.[33] Mother Florence's prayers were answered after she contacted this 'saintly priest', who had been born in Newfoundland and educated at Oxford, for he agreed to the appointment. She wrote to the Archbishop of Canterbury, Randall Davidson, to express her confidence that he would be a great help and blessing to the community and to say that his wife was entirely in support of his decision.[34] Phelps travelled to Grahamstown with his wife and daughter and took up his new position on 25 March 1909, becoming the community's beloved Warden for the next six years until being raised to the episcopate of Grahamstown.[35]

Overseeing the community was the Visitor, an appointment that defaulted to the Bishop of Grahamstown. His role was to act as superior authority for the

---

28 A Sister in the Community, *The Story of a Vocation*, pp. vii–viii.
29 A Sister in the Community, *The Story of a Vocation*, pp. vii.
30 CR, *The Constitution and Rule, Book II: The Rule* (1914), pp. 17–19.
31 CR, *The Constitution and Rule, Book II: The Rule* (1914), pp. 17–19.
32 CR, *The Constitution and Rule, Book II: The Rule* (1914), pp. 5–8.
33 A Sister of the Community, *The Story of a Vocation*, p. 37.
34 Mother Florence CR, letter to the Most Reverend Randall Davidson, 8 October 1908, Lambeth Palace Library.
35 A Sister of the Community, *The Story of a Vocation*, pp. 38–39.

Chapter 3 | Preparation for Good Things

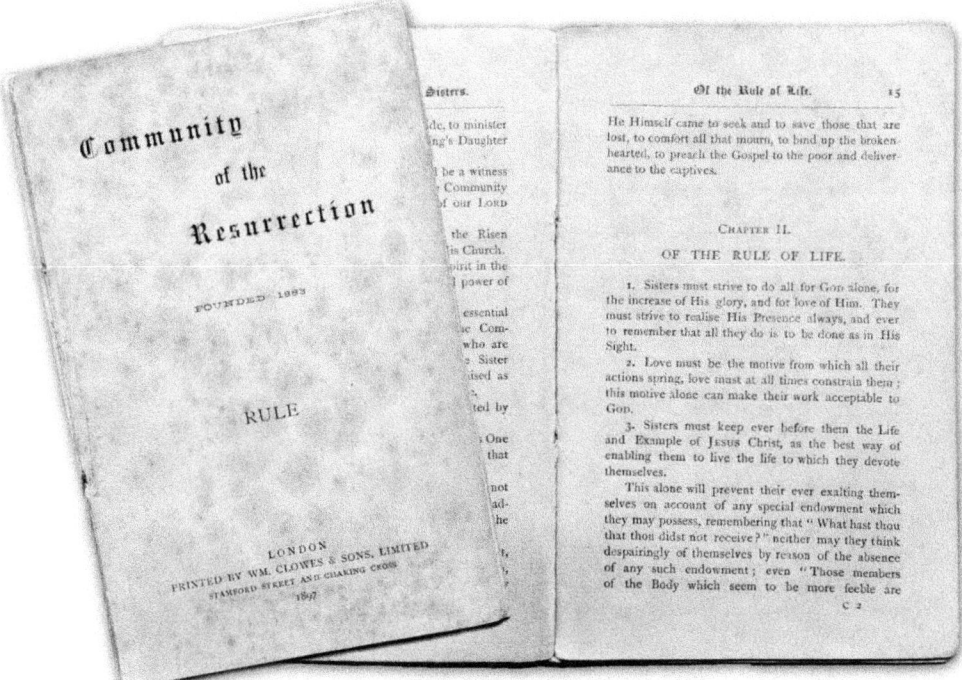

Constitution and Rule, 1897

community and to be available to hear any appeals from Sisters in the event of dissent. In addition, the Visitor was responsible for installing the Warden and Superior, considering and agreeing on all amendments to the Constitution and Rule, and consecrating Sisters when they took their solemn professional vows.[36] Although a remote figure, the Visitor's position and presence anchored the community within the diocese and he was held in much respect by the Sisters. Charles Cornish had been appointed the fifth Bishop of Grahamstown, succeeding Bishop Webb, in August 1899. Therefore, he assumed the position of Visitor for the first eight years of Margaret's association with Grahamstown until his retirement in 1915 and replacement by Bishop Phelps.

The novice mistress was the second most crucial Sister in the community. It fell to her to survey all around, keep her eyes and ears alert and stay in tune with prevailing opinions. Moreover, the Constitution required her to attend every formal meeting alongside the Superior and act as her principal aid. Under Mother Florence, the procedures and expectations for postulants and novices had become more ordered, as she brought experience from her training in the great Anglo-Catholic convent at Clewer to bear.[37]

---

36 CR, *The Constitution and Rule, Book II: The Rule* (1914), pp. 4–5.
37 A Sister of the Community, *The Story of a Vocation*, p. 19.

'Instructions for Postulants', c.1910

As a postulant, Margaret now adhered to the community's purpose 'to live wholly to the glory of God, in entire self-surrender and whole-hearted loyalty to Jesus Christ'.[38] She was also required to observe the Rule of Life through which she must 'strive to do for God alone; be weak in herself, but strong for Christ': to 'cultivate a spirit of continual prayer and thanksgiving', 'strive to overcome all selfishness', 'cultivate a true spirit of mortification', 'be ready

---

38 CR, *The Constitution and Rule, Book II: The Rule* (1897), p. 13.

to suffer with a good heart', and 'be ready to be thrown into the realities of life'.³⁹ The Rule of Life also set expectations that she would 'accustom herself to speak as a member of the Community', 'look upon every act of submission as an opportunity for rendering love', 'study the Rule prayerfully and strive to keep to it both in letter and spirit', and much else.⁴⁰

Postulants lived in their part of the noviciate at St Peter's Home, separate from the Sisters' rooms, where they had their common room and sleeping quarters. Postulants wore a plain long black dress with a white lace collar and a white lace-trimmed bonnet. A small photograph of Margaret so dressed found its way back to England and into her sister Ethel's album.

Maggie as a 'possy' (postulant), South Africa, 1908

As a postulant, life was simple with the daily rhythm set by frequent services, silences, prayer and time for reflection. The Rule of Silence, which applied to all in the community, was 'to be taken as opportunities for continual remembrance of the holy presence of God'.⁴¹ Silence was observed for two periods each day, with the Greater Silence lasting between 8 p.m. and 8 a.m., which was never to be broken except in an emergency. The Lesser Silence lasted four hours each morning when Sisters were permitted to talk sparingly about their work. Silence was also kept when the chapel's bells rang for the daily cycle of communal prayers known as the Offices, as well as at mealtimes and at all times in the bedrooms and passages. The Rule of Silence was considerably eased on Sundays, Christmas, Ascension, and other high festival days when more talking was allowed.

The rising bell for Lauds, the first Office each day, was usually at 5.30 a.m., in time for the dawn service at 6 a.m. However, owing to the early sunrises in high summer, Lauds was sometimes said the night before. Then, Prime and a service of Eucharist, usually presided over by the Warden, followed at 7 a.m. After breakfast, the Lesser Silence commenced, during which everyone in the

---

39 CR, *The Constitution and Rule, Book II: The Rule* (1897), p. 13.
40 CR, *The Constitution and Rule, Book II: The Rule* (1897), pp. 15–20.
41 CR, *Rule Book* (1933), p. 54.

community set about their work. The Silence was interrupted by Terse at 9 a.m. Sext followed at 12.30 p.m., after which there was lunch. Conversation was permitted during the afternoons, and from one account, given the joyful spirit at St Peter's, chatting and laughter rang out. The service of None was at 3 p.m., followed by Vespers, generally at 6 p.m., after which there was supper. 'At 8 p.m., the Silence bell rang, and we adjourned to our individual tasks till Compline at 8.30, followed by "late supper", more work for some of us, and bed.'[42]

Aside from involvement in the daily cycle of prayer and instructional classes, Margaret would have undertaken household duties, helping in the kitchen, cleaning, serving meals and more:

> Postulants cleaned the Chapel brasses and fetched the post and blew the organ. We all had to take turns at washing up when the servants were off. There was a scale of jobs. Newcomers meant a step-on for those above them. I was soon put on to blow the organ. The one vacating the post showed me how to work the bellow handle without labouring it and keep the indicator steady and supply the right amount of wind. I managed fairly well. But once or twice, a foot came round to stir me.[43]

Although other postulants wrote about their uncertainties during this stage of preparation, notably their dilemmas of being partly attracted to the religious life yet daunted by the immense and irrevocable commitment required, Margaret left no intimation about how she felt.[44] She would have understood that she was entering as a neophyte and would have to accept what she found. 'Any spirit of criticism should be laid down outside' as she was assumed into the community.[45] This aspect of the discipline, which all postulants and novices would have had to submit to, was to some degree at odds with the community's need to draw in agile and enquiring minds who would be able to help advance its work and spiritual mission, without challenging or disturbing the status quo.

Fraternisation with Sisters and novices was discouraged. Postulants were equally discouraged from discussing concerns between themselves, even in the privacy of their own common room.

> As a rule, the beginning of the Postulancy is comparatively easy. The Aspirant has been moved to the depths of her being by the greatness of the Call, and the first fervour of her response will usually carry her safely over the initial difficulties of her new life. The complete change of surroundings and

---

42 CR, Sister Margery's Reminiscences.
43 Naylor, *South Africa: My Venture*, ch. III.
44 Naylor, *South Africa: My Venture*, ch. III.
45 A Member of the Community, *The Religious Life*, p. 12.

the freshness of everything help all unconsciously to give a zest to what she undertakes. But the real test comes when the novelty has worn off, and the Postulant finds that in spite of the Call, she is still the same person she was before she heard it, and that the old faults she thought were got rid of are now beginning to stir to a new life in a different setting.[46]

The expectation was for the postulancy to last six months to allow a proper course of instruction on the rules and ways. With the grounding received from her father, Margaret would have readily picked up many of these expectations, though there would have been some areas where she had less experience. Some candidates decided during this trial that the religious life was not for them and left. Others fell short of expectations and were encouraged to leave. Keeping a close eye, the novice mistress alone would decide when and if a postulant might progress to take her next step of being clothed as a novice and making her first simple vows.

Under the Constitution, the six-month postulancy could last longer if the Superior and Warden saw fit. Later, a twelve-month limit was introduced. However, Margaret's duration was quite different, as records show that she remained a postulant for twenty-one months. While no explanation has been found for her extended period, it is likely that she was unwell or, having completed her initial six months, she was not ready to enter the noviciate and sought to delay. Even at thirty, and perhaps with few alternatives available, she faced a daunting decision. To enter the religious life would be an enormous undertaking by anyone, all the more so by someone of her age and experience, as it would curtail any other aspiration. The novice register reveals that she was not alone in having a less than straightforward way into the religious life and in seeking more time.

Margaret would, undoubtedly, have received every kindness and loving support from the novice mistress at the time, on whom it fell to help advise doubting minds. Sister Edith, who entered as a postulant in 1891 and made her profession in 1893, had been installed in this capacity in 1907, the same year Margaret had arrived.[47] Through her strong spiritual personality, combined with 'common-sense and a great sense of humour', she held the office with 'great distinction' and helped prepare many Sisters for the religious life.[48] With her experience from being eleven years older and an enforced separation from her own family after her father was consecrated Bishop of St Helena in 1899, she must have understood Margaret's desire to return home.

---

46 A Member of the Community, *The Religious Life*, p. 14.
47 CR Remembrance Book, Mother Edith CR (1868–1966).
48 CR Remembrance Book, Mother Edith CR (1868–1966).

Sister Edith CR, novice mistress between 1907 and 1911 (n.d.)

Margaret's sister Dorothy had written about their mother's frail state of mind following their father's sudden death on New Year's Day in 1906.[49] With the loss of her family home and ecclesiastical income, and without the close support of her children, who, like Margaret, had dispersed, Margaret Lockhart had returned to London by 1910. An equally likely reason for Margaret wanting to return home was simple and practical, as once she took the next step into the religious life and entered the noviciate, it would be out of her hands when she could see her family again. Her eldest brother, Frederick, most likely supported her decision to return home, as she would have needed to write to him to ask for the passage fare.

Trusting that it might ultimately be beneficial for Margaret to go, Sister Edith gave her consent. Therefore, unlike other postulants who decided to leave, for whom exit was definitive and bluntly entered in the register with a leaving date, Margaret had her postulancy significantly extended.[50] For her, the words 'Went to England' were recorded against her name.[51] There seemed, however, no particular hurry for Margaret to return to England as she did not leave until December 1909. This delay may have been because she became involved with the myriad activities at St Peter's, which required a great deal of supervision. Over the Easter weekend in 1909, the Community 'contributed a contingent of over two hundred children and students to the Three Hours' Devotion on Good Friday. Then, on Easter Monday, an autumn picnic expedition took place:

A College Wagon Picnic

> The wagons were ordered for 6.30 am, and (which is rather an unusual circumstance, as the oxen have a way of getting lost when they are wanted) at 6.30 punctually they arrived. The food had all been stored … and took very little time to pack into the wagons.

---

49 Dorothy Watson, letter to Basil Watson, 22 April 1912, Watson family papers.
50 CR Register of Novices [from] 1908.
51 CR Register of Novices [from] 1908, entry 110.

CHAPTER 3 | PREPARATION FOR GOOD THINGS

Preparing for a 'wagon picnic'

At 06.40, the College bell was rung, and the students came flocking from the different houses; as soon as they had had some coffee and something to eat, we started, about 70 riding in wagons and about 30 walking. There is no difficulty keeping up with a wagon, as the average rate at which the oxen go is a good deal slower than a brisk walking pace.

The place chosen was Howson's Poort, a charming spot about seven miles out from Grahamstown. It is a narrow valley surrounded by hills, which, though picturesquely rocky, can be climbed without great difficulty, and through it runs a stream of fresh, clear water, a very important item for so large a party. The ride out was lovely; the air was still fresh, and the sun had not been up long, and it is one long decline nearly all the way, so that the oxen did the whole distance in an hour and a quarter.

As soon as we arrived the four native boys on the wagons lighted a fire and boiled the water, while some of the students unpacked the things and got breakfast ready. Most of us were very hungry, but a few energetic people went out for a scramble on the hills first, only returning when we had nearly finished breakfast. We were hungry, and we did eat – twelve loaves, each about two feet long, disappeared, and other things in proportion.

After breakfast, nearly all the girls scattered in parties of four or more, some to sketch, some to botanise, and some simply to scramble. A few stayed in the valley and cut up meat for dinner, as we had brought the big joints with us, and the boys washed up all the breakfast things, which meant plates, cups and saucers, knives and teaspoons for a hundred people; this the four boys did of their own accord after each meal. They ate very little themselves all day, as they preferred to keep the food given to them, to eat at night when the day's work is over.

At about one the different parties came in, somewhat tired but very happy; we had dinner, and then most of them rested a bit, while the energetic, artistic ones seized the opportunity and practised figure drawing.

Once in the morning it seemed as if there was going to be a heavy storm; thunder rumbled and large drops of rain began to fall, but to our intense relief it passed over, and we had fine weather all the rest of the day.

At 5.30 we had tea, and directly after started homewards, the walkers going on ahead. The walk was a rather wonderful one, in spite of the three- or four-mile-long hill which had to be climbed. About a quarter of an hour after we started it began to get dark, so that quite half the distance was tramped in the dark, the only light there was coming from the lightning which was playing on the hills round; there was a breeze, otherwise everything was very quiet, and there was no other human being, so far as we knew, for some miles around us.

The lights of Grahamstown suddenly came into sight, and they were a welcome sight, as we were beginning to get tired. The walkers all got in by 8.15, the front ones arriving at 7.45, and were ready to receive, not without a suggestion of superiority in their manner, the sixty-odd who had come in the wagons.

Margaret must have witnessed the construction of the Mother Cecile Memorial Hall on a plot adjacent to the Training College at St Peter's. Funds had been raised in England to provide a 'fitting memorial to her whose life was so generously given'.[52] 'It had been a wish that the building, with all its sacred associations, would be a worthy tribute to the bright memory of Mother Cecile, and the Community was not to be disappointed with what was built.'[53] A Gothic-style structure arose to serve as a dining hall or concert space with kitchens, all associated rooms and a lofty oak hammer-beamed roof worthy of an Oxbridge college. Mother Florence wrote: 'It will be a beautiful building; I do not think that we shall be wrong in considering it the finest building in Grahamstown.'[54]

---

52 CR Quarterly Letter, July 1908, p. 7.
53 CR Annual Report [for 1906], January 1907, p. 8.
54 CR Quarterly Letter, July 1909, p. 2.

In early July, the Governor and Lady Hely-Hutchinson inspected the nearly completed hall before it opened at the end of the month.

Margaret's eventual departure in mid-December corresponded with the end of the school year. Then, after the campus below St Peter's Home had quietened, she left Grahamstown before the Christmas festivities and made her way to Port Elizabeth. On Friday, 10 December, she was taken out into Algoa Bay on a lighter to commence her voyage home. This time, she travelled on a lesser vessel of the Union-Castle Line, SS *Dover Castle*,[55] one of three sister ships built simultaneously in 1904 for an entirely

Mother Cecile Memorial Hall under construction in 1909

Mother Cecile Memorial Hall, alongside Canterbury House, after completion in 1909

---

55 Board of Trade, Inwards Passenger Lists, Class BT26, Piece 369, UK National Archives.

SS *Dover Castle*, D-class 'intermediate' vessel of the Union-Castle Line, built in 1904

new 'intermediate service' between Great Britain and the Cape, which called at additional ports. Their passenger accommodation was more limited than the faster mailships that sailed directly to England. Consequently, Margaret and another single lady who embarked with her at Algoa Bay were given a first-class cabin. After calls at Cape Town, Las Palmas, Tenerife and Plymouth, they arrived at Southampton on 6 January 1910.[56]

During the three years that Margaret had been away, her brother Arthur had been ordained priest in 1908.[57] He had married his sweetheart Olive Courtenay that year,[58] before moving in 1909 to the parish of St Peter and St Paul, Wantage, as curate.[59] Their second child, Mary Monica, was born on 17 January,[60] just a few days after Margaret returned. Margaret attended Monica's christening on 19 February in Arthur's Wantage church and became her godmother.[61]

There were other family events for her to attend. After Frederick returned from his first consular posting at Valparaíso in Chile, he married Mary Durrell at Fulbourn, near Cambridge, on 3 August 1910.[62] This union between the Durrell and Watson families was a grand society event, and many who knew

---

56 Board of Trade, Inwards Passenger Lists, Class BT26, Piece 369, UK National Archives.
57 *Crockford's Clerical Directory* 1935, p. 1496.
58 Register of Marriages for the Parish of East Horsley, Surrey, 1908, UK National Archives.
59 *Crockford's Clerical Directory* 1935, p. 1496.
60 Wantage Parish Register, 1911, Berkshire Records Office.
61 Wantage Parish Register, 1911.
62 Venn and Venn, *Alumni Cantabrigienses*, p. 369.

the Watson family from Cambridge were present, including Dr and Mrs Caldecott. Margaret joined with her sisters to give the newlyweds a travelling clock.⁶³

Christopher also married in 1910 before going to live at Higham in Norfolk. Of her other brothers and sisters, Ethel was training as an artist in London; Dorothy was with families in France and Germany; Basil went to Argentina to work for the boilermakers Babcock and Wilcox; Grace turned nineteen in February 1910; and Margaret's godson John was at preparatory school. He had his twelfth birthday in March.

Margaret reached the age of thirty-one on her birthday on 31

Grace Watson (Margaret's youngest sister) with Mary Monica Watson (Margaret's niece and goddaughter), c.1912

May 1910. She was to remain in England for almost seventeen months. Again, it is uncertain where Margaret stayed or how she passed her time, as her mother had previously given up the family home and moved from Cambridge. However, on 2 April 1911, according to the census, Margaret and Ethel were living with their mother in an apartment at 31 Cromwell Road, in West London, with both sisters registered as art students.⁶⁴

Margaret later wrote that during her time in London, she 'had been fortunate enough to go through a course of fresco painting with Mr Frampton, a well-known fresco painter, whose work was delicate and cultured'.⁶⁵ This artist was E. Reginald Frampton, who had received much acclaim for his church fresco designs. 'Frampton was a consummate colourist' whose richly decorative landscapes and symbolic portraits were in the Pre-Raphaelite style.⁶⁶ He took a fresh approach to frescoes by emphasising the need for preparing and grounding the plaster to be over-painted with stabilising media to ensure longevity for his work.

For this, he developed a petroleum-based spirit-fresco medium of his own. Then, his practice was to cover the whole area to be decorated in monochrome

---

63 'Interesting Weddings Watson-Durrell', *Royston Weekly News*, 4 August 1910, p. 7.
64 The National Census, 2 April 1911.
65 Sister Margaret, *Chapel of St Mary and All the Angels*, p. 2.
66 *The Studio*, vol. 36 (1906), pp. 346–349.

Cromwell Road, Kensington, London, from a postcard in 1910

before lightly applying overlaying colours and building up. His work in churches was 'marked by a thorough knowledge of suitable church designing and a sympathy with the significance attached to church work generally, if it is to raise itself to be worthy of the purpose'.[67] Margaret would have learned from him the importance of preparing the plaster on which any fresco was to be placed.

Brook Green, where Reginald Frampton had his studio, in 1912

---

67 *The Studio*, vol. 36 (1906), p. 346.

CHAPTER 3 | PREPARATION FOR GOOD THINGS

Serene on the eve of her return to Grahamstown, Margaret with her family at Bognor on the Sussex coast in the summer of 1911

Frampton worked from no. 1 Brook Green Studios in Hammersmith, which was easy for Margaret to reach by the Metropolitan Railway from Kensington. She wrote that he had been 'interested to know that I hoped to come out to a Religious Community and spared no pains to put me through the whole course, including making the spirit-fresco medium'.[68]

Photographs of Margaret dressed as a postulant in mid-1911 confirm her intention to return to the community in Grahamstown. Although opportunities for women of her standing may have widened since she first left for the Cape in 1907, it was said that 'nowhere would Anglican women experience more opportunity than in the mission field'.[69] Seemingly, she had decided to do just that and enter the religious life. Before leaving, however, she enjoyed an outing to the seaside at Bognor in Sussex with her mother and sisters and her schoolboy brother John. Wearing her long postulant's dress with a crucifix, she appeared serene while admired by her sisters on the shingle against the groyne. Exciting but apprehensive for Margaret, sad but glad for her mother and sisters, this must have been a bittersweet moment for them, uncertain as they must have been when they would meet again.

The Union-Castle steamship service to the Cape departed every Saturday. In due course, Margaret made her way back to Southampton Docks. Then, on 17 June, she sailed for Port Elizabeth on the SS *Durham Castle*, another 'intermediate' vessel built to serve smaller ports. This voyage took Margaret to Tenerife, then Walvis Bay, before Cape Town and Algoa Bay. This time, she travelled third class, with 'nil' entered as her profession on the passenger manifest, a status that would soon change.

---

68 Sister Margaret, *Chapel of St Mary and All the Angels*, pp. 2–3.
69 Maughan, *Mighty England Do Good*, p. 33.

Bognor in Sussex, where Margaret visited with her family before her farewell, from a postcard, c.1911

SS *Durham Castle*, D-class 'intermediate' vessel of the Union-Castle Line, built in 1904

Margaret returned to a new nation. During her absence, on 31 May 1910, the former British colonies combined with the former Boer republics to form the Union of South Africa, a self-governing dominion within the British Empire. No doubt, she was warmly greeted when she reached the shore. There are many accounts of the kindness women received and the joy they felt as they were greeted at Port Elizabeth, especially so for Margaret after nineteen months away: 'Once landed, all discomforts vanished. There was old Sister Charlotte, Irish to the marrow, fluent in commands and kindness, come to speed us through the customs and carry us for the day to the mission house. We were to go up by the evening train to Grahamstown.'[70]

---

70 Naylor, *South Africa: My Venture*, ch. II.

Chapter Four

Bestowal of the Habit

※※※

MARGARET RETURNED TO Grahamstown in mid-July 1911. She did not then wait long before taking her next step into the religious life, as on Tuesday, 1 August, she was clothed as a novice in the Community of the Resurrection. Entering the noviciate was Margaret's invitation to prepare herself for a period of profound self-examination. Assuming she would get through the challenge of her noviciate, the expectation was that she would be invited to undertake her first temporary vows after two years, and then, after a further four years, finally profess through the undertaking of permanent vows. A lot lay ahead.

To be accepted into the noviciate so swiftly after her twenty-one-month absence in England implied that Margaret and the novice mistress were both confident about her suitability and successful passage. Those empowered must have decided that Margaret had given 'adequate signs of a definite purpose to give herself to God' and that no further probationary period was required.[1] Her father's credentials as an Anglo-Catholic clergyman in Cambridge would have helped, as many women entering communities came from clergy families, including Sister Edith, the novice mistress. There was, however, a change in the community at this time, for Sister Edith, who had held the position since Margaret first arrived in Grahamstown in 1907, was sent to Bulawayo in

---

1 Advisory Council on Religious Communities, *Guide to the Religious Communities of the Anglican Communion*, p. 13.

what is now Zimbabwe in June 1911 to take charge of the community's new responsibilities there. In her place, Sister Gertrude was appointed.

Gertrude Hill had come to Grahamstown in 1889, followed shortly afterwards by her military family from India. As free spirits, 'Gertrude and her sister used to electrify, if not shock, the staid people of the Cathedral City by the pace in which they rode down the High Street and over the veldt'. However, it was not long before Gertrude was 'led to give up her life in the world and its enjoyments and to offer

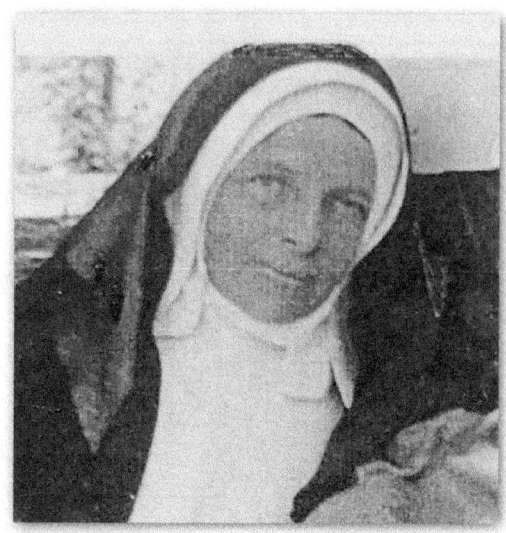

Sister Gertrude CR

herself to our Lord in our Community'. Having done so, she devoted herself unsparingly to the work of the community and did what she could to help advance it spiritually. Although her active life was curtailed by illness, rendering her unable to 'do much walking or much regular work', for a while between 1911 and 1913 she served as novice mistress, coinciding with Margaret Watson's return. During her tenure, Sister Gertrude was 'counted far more than what she did, for she was very spiritual, prayerful, and very selfless – and really saintly in character'.[2] Her tragedy most likely served as an inspiration for Margaret and others in the noviciate. Sister Gertrude was recalled as wonderfully joyous, fresh and original. 'Her religion seemed so spontaneous and free – a realisation of the glorious liberty of the children of God.'[3]

At the end of June 1911, just a few weeks before Margaret returned, six novices had been elected to the sisterhood, making room in the noviciate for Margaret to join seven others already in training. As she took this step, Margaret now assumed her name 'in religion', which would have been chosen for her by Mother Florence. Although this usually corresponded with a novice's Christian name, that was not necessarily the case if other Sisters used the same name. For Margaret, however, the choice was clear. As there had been a previous Sister Margaret, Margaret Isabel West, the third sister to enter the community, each subsequent Margaret who joined had been given an additional name to distinguish them, such as Margaret Faith in 1901, Margaret Evelyn in 1906, and Margaret

---

2 CR Remembrance Book, Sister Gertrude CR (1860–1918).
3 CR Remembrance Book, Sister Gertrude CR (1860–1918).

The Reverend Francis Robinson Phelps, Warden, 1909–1915, and Visitor, 1915–1931

Constance in 1907.[4] However, as the original Sister Margaret left the community in 1905,[5] her name in religion was vacant and was given to Margaret Watson unembellished.

Whatever the mix of influences that had readied Margaret's mind to enter the noviciate to test her vocation for a religious life, none is likely to have been enough on its own. Others have described the 'calling' they received as a persistent notion that, although possibly suppressed or delayed, ultimately triumphed. Their 'callings' provided overwhelming certainty about entering the religious life. 'No one, whatever her natural or acquired gifts might be, could possibly make a good Religious unless God had called her to His life. The Call is an absolute essential; equally essential is the continual whole-hearted response.'[6]

Grace Eleanor Wood had also reached this stage.[7] Like Margaret, she initially came to the community as a worker but decided to return to England before committing further. Thus, at the evening service of Vespers on Tuesday, 1 August 1911, both sat in the front row just below the chancel in their black postulant dresses and white caps. Then, while the Sisters sang '"Ye have not chosen Me," He saith, "but I have chosen you"',[8] the order of service called for Mother Florence to lead Grace and Margaret to the altar steps, with the novice mistress following.

At the altar, the Warden, the Reverend Francis Phelps, asked the Reverend Mother whether the two postulants had been rightly instructed. He sought assurance that they fully understood the objectives of the religious life and that they had been led to it by the love of Christ.[9] Satisfied with this, he spoke

---

4   CR Profession Register, entries 3 & 35; & CR Register of Novices for 1906 & 1907.
5   CR, 'A Record concerning the Chapel of the Resurrection at St Peter's Home, Grahamstown'. Sister Margaret transferred to the Community of the Epiphany in Truro, England, where she was admitted into the community on 19 September 1905 and admitted into the noviciate on 18 March 1906 (Register of the Community of the Epiphany).
6   A Member of the Community of the Sisters of the Church, *The Religious Life*, p. 22.
7   CR Register of Novices [from] 1908, entry 109.
8   John 15:16. 'Ye have not chosen Me', He saith, 'but I have chosen you.'
9   CR Office Book, pp. 3–8.

the words of admittance. Having received their habits, Grace and Margaret would have retired to the antechapel to put them over their postulant's dresses. Then, back at the altar, they each received from Mother Florence a white veil to wear under their novice caps to distinguish them from professed Sisters. Next, they received a brass cross in the community's Celtic design to wear from their necks before being blessed and led to their chapel stalls. For all present, the entry of Grace and Margaret into the noviciate would have been a joyous day.

Brass novice cross as supplied by Moore & Son of Jermyn Street, London

Having made solemn promises to obey the rule of the community and all who bore authority, Margaret was now bound. Her clothes and possessions would have been boxed up and put in the attic for storage in case she decided to leave. Devoid of everything except for her copy of *The Cloud of Witness* from Baldersby and a book of verse, Margaret would henceforth have needed to ask for any personal items she required. Then, towards the end of her training, she would have prepared a will to dispose of everything she owned, including valuables and money, to the community. For some, this caused anguish in their families, especially about jewellery and heirlooms they sought to have returned. Wills were not enacted until after final profession, in case the Sister decided to retract.

The black habit they would now wear served to remind novices that they had pledged to do nothing that would reflect poorly upon 'her Master's honour'.[10] For Margaret, the habit was henceforth an expression of her resolve to stand apart from the secular world and a sign that she had invested instead in the quest for a spiritual purpose to her life. The uniformity of her garments also served to remind her that there was no place for self in the community and that self-interests needed to be set aside.[11]

Now apprenticed to the great counsels of poverty, chastity and obedience, Margaret was required to study her obligations. She would have attended classes on the sacraments, liturgy and theology, with her knowledge tested by written

---

10 A Member of the Community of the Sisters of the Church, *The Religious Life*, p. 16.
11 A Member of the Community of the Sisters of the Church, *The Religious Life*, p. 17.

examination.[12] The Warden held classes alongside the Superior and the novice mistress. Phelps once wrote:

> The poor Novices (or some of them) have found my lectures very hard, I fear! At least Sister — tells me. But they are very diligent in taking notes and then she [the novice mistress] looks over them. So they won't come to any harm I hope! I tried to make it as simple as I could, but I felt it must be very difficult for some, and I felt sorry for them![13]

Novices also received practical instruction from the sacristan. Each was allocated a companion Sister to understudy. Every Monday, novices joined the community for choir practice.[14] In the chapel, novices sat on chairs between the choir stalls in the aisle. They also served and waited at table during meals, as they would have done as postulants. In the refectory at St Peter's, Sisters sat according to seniority by profession date, starting at the Superior's table, positioned across the room. Two other tables were arranged parallel to each other, longways down the room, and a table for novices and postulants lay across the lower end of the room. On entering or leaving, everyone made a reverence towards the crucifix. At other times, an inclination offered suitable humility when passing any crucifix.[15]

Novices resided in their own separate wing at St Peter's Home, where each had a simple cell, furnished with a bed, chair, prayer desk, and locker. Novices were responsible for keeping them in 'scrupulous order', 'leaving nothing lying about'. Nothing but a crucifix was allowed on the wall, and only two devotional books were allowed on the prayer desk.[16]

With eighty women in the community in 1911, including two postulants, eight other novices, sixty-eight Sisters, and one Sister aged over seventy, St Peter's was busy, even though many were out at branch houses. Novices were expected to stand back as other Sisters passed in the corridors. The rules of deference also required all to rise and curtsey when meeting the Warden or Reverend Mother or when entering or leaving a room in which they were present. There were similar rules of deference towards the Assistant Superior and the novice mistress when they took charge.[17]

Novices were permitted to write to their family whenever they desired and one additional letter a week. As an economy, ink was watered down, and

---

12 CR, *The Constitution and Rule, Book II: The Rule*, p. 30.
13 Letter to a Religious, 28 February 1910, in Phelps, *Some Letters and Counsels of Francis Robinson Phelps, Archbishop of Cape Town 1931–1938*, p. 31.
14 Sister Margery's Reminiscences.
15 CR, *The Constitution, Rule and Customary* (1933), p. 75.
16 CR, *The Constitution, Rule and Customary* (1933), p. 75.
17 CR, *The Constitution, Rule and Customary* (1933), pp. 70–71.

the writing paper was almost translucent in its economy. Scraps of paper were salvaged and kept for use as notes during the Greater Silence.

Sister Margery wrote a description of her experiences passing through the noviciate a decade after Sister Margaret:

> Saturday afternoons brought some relief, as we went out for good walks, sometimes for the whole afternoon, taking tea with us, sometimes for an hour or so. It was glorious to be out in the open, stretching one's legs, breathing the air of Mountain Drive; sometimes, we under-estimated our distance and had to rush back. One Novice was said to have run from the top of Mountain Drive to the Home in ten minutes, arriving just in time to walk demurely into supper! On Saturday evenings we continued our non-stop programme – Novice choir practice, reading by the Novice Mistress, quick cleaning of shoes and polishing of crosses, then Compline followed by Lauds. Sundays were equally non-stop; no 'Day of Rest' for us. We got up a little later certainly, then to Prime, down to Mass, up (in procession, of course) to breakfast. Then quiet, tea, meditation, copying of notes, etc., till dinnertime. (All notes of classes had to be taken down as fast as we could make it and copied neatly into a special book to be corrected by the Novice Mistress. It seemed to take hours!) In the afternoon, some were fortunate enough to have a rest; others went at 2 p.m. to teach at St Clement's Sunday School, returning hot, sticky and tired – we walked, of course – to snatch a cup of tea and be in time (just) for Recreation taken by the Mother. We sat on low chairs in a circle, she on an easy chair, with the Senior Novice on her right. She read letters from Sisters in Branch Houses, commented on them and told a bit of Community news, read a poem from 'The Christian I Am', and the bell went for Vespers at 5.30. Thence to supper. Once a month, we Novices went on duty in the kitchen clearing supper, laying breakfast, seeing to late supper and carrying upstairs several trays for Sisters who went to bed early.[18]

Mother Cecile had written that one's time in the noviciate was meant to bring out character faults by confronting all that had been wrong in life before.[19] 'We learn painfully that sin is our fault and not that of circumstances.'[20] She held that knowledge of oneself was acquired not just to deepen an indebtedness to Christ, but to help 'more than anything to understand others and give them a helping hand'.[21]

---

18 Sister Margery's Reminiscences.
19 A Sister of the Community, *Mother Cecile in South Africa*, p. 235.
20 A Sister of the Community, *Mother Cecile in South Africa*, pp. 269–270.
21 A Sister of the Community, *Mother Cecile in South Africa*, p. 285.

There could be no place for any unrealistic ideas about the Sisterhood. Any sense of glamour needed to be dispelled to ensure that a novice had a genuine call. Nor could there be any thoughts that this period was just a passing phase. On the contrary, the noviciate was a dress rehearsal for the enduring discipline of a religious life.

The novice mistress held high expectations for those under her charge and would have used all her skills and empathy to help, encourage, love and understand. She needed to be available to listen to and guide every novice so they could work through their doubts.[22] Mother Cecile had written for those struggling: 'I have passed through it, and believe that most do.' She shared her belief that the reward for all the soul searching would be a life 'tenfold more real than years spent without anything to draw you out of yourself or make you strong in the Lord'.[23]

Any novice who fell short could be asked to leave or could decide to go for any sufficient reason.[24] The mechanism was straightforward and abrupt: those leaving were reunited with their belongings, brought down from storage in the attic, and assisted with the fare home. Such departures were not uncommon, as during Sister Margaret's time in the noviciate, five of the twenty-eight she coincided with left. They faced a lonely exit, being taken to the station without delay and put on the next suitable train.

> Our numbers varied. We were generally about a dozen; all very human, ready for a bit of fun, but were seriously feeling our way. Life was more interesting, warmer and fuller than in the workers' bare little room. Some took to the life more readily than others. There was, for instance, A, who always had her chapel places ready and could prompt the reader with a memorial and keep a wobbly antiphon going. B, on the other hand, was unsuited to the life and found it cramping. It was whispered that she had 'failed her vocation', and when she left, none of us saw her off.[25]

Novices were required to maintain unbroken residence in the novice house for their first full year, preventing visits to branch houses or outlying missions. However, in the second year, this was relaxed to allow them to work at branch houses, provided they returned to St Peter's for the final three months, to enable the other Sisters to form an opinion of their suitability to take their temporary profession vows.[26] By 1912, distant outposts under the care of the community

---

22 Sister Janet CSMV, *Mother Maribel of Wantage*, p. 51.
23 A Sister of the Community, *Community of the Resurrection of Our Lord*, p. 237.
24 CR, *The Constitution and Rule, Book II: The Rule* (1914), p. 30.
25 Naylor, *South Africa: My Venture*, ch. III.
26 CR, *The Constitution, Rule and Customary* (1933), p. 28.

CHAPTER 4 | BESTOWAL OF THE HABIT

The noviciate in 1912 in the ground of St Peter's Home with Sister Gertrude (centre, third from left) and novice Sister Margaret (second from right at the back)

had increased to include St Monica's House of Mercy for unmarried mothers in Queenstown, and St Peter's Diocesan School for Girls and St Gabriel's Home in Bulawayo, in addition to the already established institutions in Port Elizabeth and at Keiskamma Hoek.

As Margaret entered her final six months in the noviciate, the novice mistress would have begun to collect reports from those who had overseen her, covering both practical capabilities and her suitability to profess. Assuming that everything was favourable, the Warden and Superior would have met to consider Margaret's suitability under the guidance of the novice mistress. Only after they had decided would her name have been put forward for other Sisters to consider. The Rule called for voting in the chapel by secret ballot at a celebration of Holy Communion, with a two-thirds majority required.[27] If unsuccessful, Margaret would likely have left the community immediately unless the novice mistress thought she needed more time.

Margaret's noviciate lasted for just under two and a half years, from 1 August 1911 until her election in January 1914. Then, following a month-long silent retreat to prepare, she was again led to the Sisters' Chapel altar during a service of Vespers. On Tuesday, 22 January, in the presence of all available Sisters gathered as witnesses, she dedicated her life to God and the service of his Church through the community.[28] Two other novices had also reached this point: Margaret Cobden, who had been given the name in religion of Sister Leila Margaret, and

---

27 CR, *The Constitution and Rule, Book II: The Rule* (1914), p. 32.
28 CR, *The Constitution and Rule, Book II: The Rule* (1914), pp. 32–33.

Pocket-sized Hours of Prayer containing the liturgy of the Hours

Millicent Helen Willett, who became known as Sister Millicent. This day was the one they had longed for, yet at times they may have thought that they would not reach it. All that had gone on before in their lives was the lead-up. All that counted would follow their profession.[29]

Professions were the 'high festivals in Sisterhood life', bearing some resemblance to a marriage service, as, through their vows, the novice candidates were to commit to a spiritual marriage.[30] The custom therefore was for novices to come to the altar adorned in a wedding dress as the 'ideal Bride full of humble clinging dependence'.[31] Then, after taking their vows, they would change into the black habit of a professed sister, with a black veil to replace their white novice veils. In addition, each newly professed Sister received a silver cross to exchange for their brass ones, a full-length scapular as an outer garment, and a girdle of light linen rope to symbolise chastity and protection. They also received a copy of the breviary and a small pocket-sized volume containing the service liturgy. These books passed through the generations, handed from Sister to Sister and increasingly embellished with pencil notes recording anniversaries and reminders.

Although their profession was a happy occasion and a cause of great satisfaction, newly professed Sisters still had five years before they might make their final vows. The custom was for new Sisters to be sent to branch houses to work away from Grahamstown, and no doubt this was what Sister Margaret was expecting. The Superior decided where each went, considering what the novice mistress thought would be best and what the community's needs were.

Since assuming the role of Superior in 1906, Mother Florence had sought to strengthen the institution and was ready to face difficult decisions if needed.

---

29 A Member of the Community of the Sisters of the Church, *The Religious Life*, p. 20.
30 Mumm, *Stolen Daughters*, p. 29.
31 A Sister of the Community, *Mother Cecile in South Africa*, p. 270.

CHAPTER 4 | BESTOWAL OF THE HABIT

Sisters' Chapel of the Resurrection at St Peter's Home as it was at the time of Sister Margaret's profession in January 1914, after construction of the chancel in 1901 but before further alterations in 1917

She had to balance the ever-widening calls for more Sisters to enter work against who was available. Although active Sisters had increased from sixty-eight in 1912 to seventy-five in 1914, none were to spare.[32] She would have known that Sister Margaret had trained as an artist and muralist in London and hoped to offer these skills, but Mother Florence had other priorities. Therefore, when Sister Margaret's turn came, she was sent to St Monica's Home of Refuge for unmarried mothers in distant Queenstown. Sister Margaret may have been hoping for such an opportunity to make a difference away from Grahamstown, and, if so, she would have been rewarded for all her preparatory work.

---

[32] CR Profession Register.

Chapter Five

St Monica's Home

ONE HUNDRED AND thirty miles north-east of Grahamstown lies the important settlement of Queenstown (now called Komani). The town was initially founded as a military post in 1853 and named after Queen Victoria, who, had she visited, would have been reminded of Scotland by the surrounding mountain scenery. In the following sixty years Queenstown's white settler population had grown close to five thousand out of about ten thousand souls all told. A contemporary report gives some idea of its character and self-image:

> Despite its romantic origin and historic associations, Queenstown had not been content to dwell in the past, dreaming of glories that had gone. On the contrary, the town marched abreast, and sometimes ahead, of the times, developing its commercial, agricultural, and educational resources and striving to maintain a high level of communal and municipal welfare. With its broad, sun-kissed, wind-swept streets lined everywhere with shady trees, with mountains serving as a majestic background, Queenstown represents the best type, and upholds the finest traditions and characteristics, of a South African town.[1]

The community was already working with the African population around Queenstown when, in early 1909, Sister Bessie was approached by a white

---

1   *Queenstown, Cape Province, South Africa* (1924), pp. 3–4.

Queenstown from Bowker's Kop

Cathcart Road, Queenstown postcard, c.1920

girl needing help.² Her response was prompt, as was Mother Florence's. The community decided to open a small House of Mercy to support this girl and other unmarried mothers.³

Since early in the nineteenth century, there had been growing recognition

---

2   'St Monica's Home, Queenstown' (c.1955), Queenstown Historical Society Archive.
3   'St Monica's Home, Queenstown'; & *Church Weekly*, vol. 1, no. 24, 12 December 1935, p. 42, 'Sanctuary: The Story of St Monica's Home, Queenstown'.

in English society of the vulnerabilities that young unmarried mothers faced.[4] Mother Florence had first-hand knowledge of providing this challenging work of care from her training with the Community of St John Baptist at the Clewer House of Mercy. Initially, the Sisters of the Community of the Resurrection rented a tiny cottage on Green Street in Queenstown, followed by a second to provide staff quarters. Then, with space for the young women and babies still cramped, a third cottage was rented in April 1909.[5]

As word began to spread, enquiries started to come in from across the eastern districts of the Cape. The community soon concluded that the cottages could never offer enough space. Furthermore, being on a residential street, they lacked the necessary seclusion. Instead, a significantly larger and adequately equipped building was needed, positioned away from the residential part of Queenstown. In response, the Queenstown Town Council provided a stand to the north-east, on higher ground overlooking the pretty frontier town, and fundraising began. Magistrates and doctors testified for the need, one writing: 'The home will fill a great want and do excellent work for these parts.'[6] A generous donation from an East London merchant enabled the community to approach the architectural practice of Herbert Baker, Kendall & Morris in Cape Town for plans, and soon construction commenced.

Bishop Cornish laid the foundation stone on 27 September 1911, and by early 1912 the Warden was able to describe the new building:

> There is to be first a two-storied building to accommodate about twenty persons and second a nursery cottage, the latter not yet begun. St Monica's has a small entrance hall with a refectory and Community-room on one side, and on the other a tiny visitors' room and office, the kitchens being beyond. On either side of the passage stand four good-sized rooms, to be used as refectory, workrooms, laundry, etc. Upstairs, besides the sleeping and bathrooms, is the Chapel, built over the community room and hall. It promises to be very well proportioned and is to have a good ecclesiastical window fitted with toned glass.
>
> We look forward to it being a most helpful centre of the whole house.[7]

On 7 April 1912, Easter Day, the Warden and the Reverend Canon Edward Hext, the parish priest, opened the newly completed St Monica's Home. The following year, a nursery cottage was built a few yards away from the house,

---

4 Magee, *Anglican Sisterhoods*.
5 A Sister of the Community, *The Story of a Vocation*, p. 39.
6 CR Quarterly Letter, April 1910.
7 CR Annual Report [for 1910], January 1911, pp. 7–11.

The Reverend Canon Edward Hext, vicar of St Michael and All Angels, Queenstown, 1906–1916

which 'answers its purpose very well'.[8] With these greatly improved facilities, the Sisters were able to take in more young women and carry out their work 'in an infinitely more simple and satisfactory manner'.[9]

By late 1913, there were ten occupants just before Sister Margaret arrived. The number rose to seventeen the following year.[10] Sister Bessie, who had come to Queenstown after her profession in 1908, had been instrumental in setting up St Monica's. 'She could truly be called a "great soul" and she was a great friend of the poor and needy and all in distress. Her tender love for the small babies was beautiful and she absolutely sacrificed her own comfort for the care of them all.'[11]

Under Sister Bessie, Sister Margaret would have found well-established routines, starting at 6.30 each morning. All girls were required to help with the cleaning, meals and care of the children. There were also housekeeping duties each afternoon. In addition, there was always a lot of laundry and needlework to get through, as the Sisters took in orders from the town to augment their income.[12] Not having been trained as a nurse or a midwife, Sister Margaret took charge of the laundry,[13] and, with unreliable helpers, had to bear the brunt of this heavy work.

The girls could participate in a band, attend dressmaking and shoe-mending lessons, or join a Bible reading group for evening recreation.[14] On Saturdays, they were taken on long walks. There were opportunities to help in local Sunday Schools either as teachers or as interpreters.[15] Or they might go to a service at

---

8 CR Annual Report [for 1913], January 1914, p. 49.
9 A Sister of the Community, *The Story of a Vocation*, p. 43.
10 CR Annual Report [for 1914], March 1915.
11 CR Remembrance Book, Sister Bessie CR (1867–1945).
12 CR Annual Report [for 1919], January 1920, pp. 3–5.
13 Sister Margaret, *Chapel of St Mary and All the Angels*, p. 2.
14 CR Quarterly Letter, October 1913.
15 CR Quarterly Letter, October 1913, p. 48.

The parish church of St Michael and All Angels, Queenstown, as completed in 1923

the parish church of St Michael and All Angels, where they sat separately in the Lady Chapel out of concern about not being recognised.

The Sisters' work was challenging as each girl taken in had suffered a personal tragedy. Some were sent to St Monica's by the magistrates, for whom the home was to serve as a penitentiary, while others came in need of a refuge from trauma and violence at home.[16] Some gave 'very little' trouble and were anxious to make a fresh start.[17] However, there could also be great difficulties, and the Sisters had to be ready to cope with extreme behaviours. A Sister at the community's House of Mercy in Port Elizabeth recorded that the girls they took in had 'much to learn and unlearn'. On occasions, the Sisters found that they were no match for the girls' destructive rages, attacks and acts of revenge.[18]

Confinements took place in the nursery cottage where a qualified midwife was stationed.[19] A 'very necessary rule' was that the girls should stay a whole year; otherwise, it was feared that St Monica's would do more harm than good.[20] Earlier in 1914, an account had been written about the work and challenges by

---

16 CR Annual Report [for 1917], January 1918, pp. 4–6.
17 'St Monica's Home, Queenstown'.
18 A Sister of the Community, *Mother Cecile in South Africa*, pp. 18–19.
19 'St Monica's Home, Queenstown'.
20 CR Quarterly Letter, October 1913.

St Monica's Home with entrance doorway and small first-floor chapel, Queenstown, in early 1913

a Sister who had recently arrived; quite likely, therefore, these words were from Sister Margaret's hand:

> After two months' work at S. Monica's, one feels qualified to give to any who may be interested, some account of the place, its surroundings and the work carried on within its walls.
>
> First of all – a description of the Home itself. There are two houses, one at either end of the garden, the Home proper and the Nursery. The former is a rectangular building housing the sisters, staff, and the majority of girls.

Chapter 5 | St Monica's Home

A Sister tends to infants at St Monica's Home, c.1920

Attached is the laundry where much work is turned out. Here also is the Chapel, the centre of the life and work of the establishment, but more of that later on!

By way of a 'mealie patch', the nursery is approached, and here we find the children – tots of varying ages, and tiny babies cooing or crying as they feel inclined! One Sister and the nurse live here in addition to some half dozen young mothers. The nursery boasts a spacious stoep [verandah] where may be seen the tinies' cots and often the small toddlers playing with toys sent by many friends. From this stoep, a beautiful view may be enjoyed both day and night – the latter, of course, provided there is a moon! To the writer this view is ever an inspiration. It speaks of the 'wideness of God's mercy' and also of courage and steadfastness – two things needed so sorely for the work.

In addition to this view, there is music as soon as the sun sinks. Crickets and such like things, and sometimes winged creatures which bite!, combine to produce a volume of sound which seldom ceases.

Below S. Monica's, and about fifteen minutes' walk across the veld is Queenstown. It lies in a hollow, clustering round the square towering church of S. Michael and All Angels, and away beyond are the wonderful mountains again, rising and falling as far as the eye can see.

St Monica's Home in 1926

The work at S. Monica's is essentially a work of prayer. As was said above, the Chapel is the centre of the life here. The Rector of Queenstown very kindly comes to us for Mass and also Evensong once weekly. In addition, there are, of course, the daily Offices, and morning and evening prayers for the girls are read here too. One feels that all power is drawn from the Altar, and continuous offering of Praise and Intercession bears one's own efforts with it. And the work amongst the girls and children needs every bit of the grace which comes from Communion with Him Who came to seek and save. These girls come to us with very different ideas of life and happiness. Some are hopeless, some despairing, others again seem to care little for their own souls or for the new life for which they are responsible.

Ours is the struggle, the privilege, the suffering, the joy – that they may win new hope and be restored to the fuller life and glorious liberty of the children of God.

Often it seems ours must be the fight and theirs the victory. We must stand and fight with them, left alone they will turn and flee, and they have not yet learnt to lean on their own strength. It is ours to teach them, to struggle with and for them, and send them on their way lifted up – with new hope and faith.[21]

Soon after Sister Margaret came to St Monica's, news of the outbreak of war with

---

21 CR Quarterly Letter, November 1915, pp. 5–6.

Chapter 5 | St Monica's Home

Sisters and a novice with infants at St Monica's Home in 1926

Germany on 4 August 1914 reached the community in Grahamstown and rapidly spread to the branch houses. Although there was no immediate effect, Mother Florence reflected that people were unsure how to react in South Africa, aside from being bewildered. War in Europe 'did not directly touch Africa's people as a whole. Volunteers joined up and many had the anxiety of knowing that their brothers and friends were in danger, but the life of the country went quietly on and the Community's work was not interrupted.'[22]

Sister with infant in 1926

In the coming months, three of Sister Margaret's brothers joined the forces: Christopher and Basil, both being commissioned into the Army, and by 1915 Henry, who had qualified as a master mariner with his tugboat 'Starston', returned from Prince Rupert in British Columbia to join the Inland Water Transport Corps in France. Later, after leaving school in 1917, Margaret's youngest brother and godson, John, went

---

22 A Sister of the Community, *The Story of a Vocation*, p. 46.

Father William E.C. Frith, Warden, 1916–1923

straight from school into the Royal Flying Corps and served in France. Ethel returned from Canada to volunteer with the Women's Land Army, Dorothy took a position in an Admiralty signal department, and Grace served in a military catering unit. Luckily, all came through the conflict and later resumed their lives in 1918, much as before.

Finance was an enduring concern at St Monica's during the war years, especially as the income earned from laundry and needlework was insufficient to cover the cost of food.[23] Therefore, there was pressure to take in additional work from the town, with orders sought for dyeing, cooking, stitching, and fancy needlework. The need to increase St Monica's income placed even more pressure on Sisters Bessie and Margaret and the third Sister working there.

The usual pattern was for the Warden to visit most branch houses late each year to be able to write about them in his annual report. In his report written in late 1919, the Reverend William E.C. Frith, who had been installed as the Warden of St Peter's Home in October 1916 following his predecessor's elevation to the episcopate, shared some anxiety about St Monica's. Frith recognised that the Sisters were struggling 'both financially and emotionally as they gave their very best to make the mission work'. Also, despite their efforts, earnings from work taken in were inadequate to cover expenditure, which 'proves we are not self-supporting, and we never shall be'.[24]

By Christmas 1918, Sister Margaret was approaching the moment when she might expect to make her final profession. In preparation, Mother Florence would have alerted the other Sisters to the possibility that her name was to be put up for election so that they could begin to form their views. Then, as before, the matter was determined by ballot. The Rule stated that voting would occur in the chapel at the end of three and a half years, with the usual two-thirds majority required. If not elected, then at the discretion of the Warden and Superior, Sister

---

23 CR Annual Report [for 1920], January 1921, pp. 3–5.
24 CR Annual Report [for 1920], January 1921, pp. 3–5.

Sisters at St Monica's Home

Margaret might have a second chance the following year. Otherwise, just as in the earlier stages, it would be best for her to leave straight away.[25]

In late 1918, most likely before Advent, voting took place. Sister Leila Margaret and Sister Millicent, who also made their first professions alongside Sister Margaret in January 1914, were put up. All three were successfully elected.[26]

Just as they had done before their first professions, the elected Sisters would have spent a month on a silent retreat to 'bring a lasting grace and strength to the soul'.[27] They were thus required to spend three weeks before and one week after taking their vows in seclusion at St Peter's Home.

Mother Florence CR at St Monica's Home, Queenstown, during her visit in 1920, following her re-election as Superior

---

25 CR, *The Constitution and Rule, Book II: The Rule* (1914), p. 34.
26 CR Profession Register, entries 110, 123 & 124.
27 CR, *The Constitution and Rule, Book II: The Rule* (1914), pp. 34–35.

Sisters' rings and silver cross, such as Sister Margaret would have received on 18 March 1919

During this period, meals were solitary, and time was set aside for reading, sitting in the garden and long walks. Each morning, their isolation was interrupted by the novice mistress, who conducted classes to ensure they understood the magnitude of making permanent vows. After her classes, it would have been usual for them to spend time in the Sisters' Chapel to reflect.[28]

This pause gave Sister Margaret time to ponder the all-important question about her readiness and willingness to irrevocably profess before the service on Saturday, 18 January 1919, which was to be conducted by the Visitor, Bishop Phelps.[29] Although she left no account of her determination or feelings, one of her contemporaries, Sister Kate, recorded that when giving out the typed service script, the novice mistress said of the promise: 'You understand this is for life.' Across the community, the occasion of a final profession was treated as a 'double feast', a special celebration day, when antiphons were sung at all the Offices, and the Rule of Silence was relaxed at dinner time.[30]

By 1920, Sister Margaret's sixth year at St Monica's, as many as twenty-four deeply troubled young women were at the home. Despite what they had to cope with the Sisters gained great encouragement from turning around troubled lives, especially when their charges left to take up positions in domestic service or returned to their families at the end of their stay.[31] In April 1922, routines

---

28 CR, Sister Valerie, long retreat timetable.
29 CR Profession Register, entries 110, 123 & 124.
30 CR, *The Constitution and Rule, Book II: The Rule* (1914), pp. 16 and 19.
31 CR Annual Report [for 1920], January 1921, pp. 3–5.

at St Monica's were interrupted by a visit from Princess Alice of Connaught, wife of the Governor General of the Union of South Africa, who came to see the work and offer encouragement.[32] Her interest, and the work of the Men's Advisory Board set up the year before to encourage local support, had begun to draw in donations. The home's finances were also helped by subsidy payments from the local council for each girl taken in.[33]

However, any relief for Sister Margaret from her arduous work in the laundry came too late, as sometime in 1921 she became seriously ill. She may not have known about the 'family disease', a hereditary heart condition that was the cause of her father's death, nor realised that prolonged heavy laundry work in Queenstown's summer heat was to have a lasting effect.[34]

Miss Letitia Hart was one of the well-intentioned and well-to-do women in Queenstown who did their bit to support the Sisters at St Monica's Home by visiting and bringing gifts. Having worked as a teacher, she very likely appreciated the difficulties Sister Margaret faced.[35] 'She mingled with and knew of all those connected with the Anglican Church, and she, of all people, would have known about St Monica's and Sister Margaret's being unwell.'[36] Miss Hart often stayed with her brother, Mr Donald Hart, and his wife Win. They lived at Everton Farm in the hills about six miles north-east of Queenstown, overlooking the Bongolo Reservoir. Donald had returned from England in 1919, having served with distinction in the Great War, and began a custom of inviting children from the Queenstown orphanage to stay on the farm during the school holidays.[37]

When Donald Hart heard about Sister Margaret's illness through his sister Letitia, he was inclined to invite her to stay as well. Letters reveal that he was a decisive man and had no hesitation in writing to the Reverend Mother in Grahamstown to seek her consent. Mother Florence agreed that it could only be good for Sister Margaret to be away from the stresses at St Monica's. Accordingly, she permitted her to recuperate at Everton Farm.[38] Mr Hart's daughter Shirley recalled that Sister Margaret stayed for a 'very fair period of time, possibly some months, six months'.[39] She also recalled that on discovering that Sister Margaret was an artist, her father voiced his opinion that he thought it a great pity that she had not used her talent for art as it was an 'awful waste' of her gift. He believed

---

32 CR Annual Report [for 1921], March 1922.
33 CR Annual Report [for 1920], January 1921, pp. 3–5.
34 Dorothy Watson's childhood reflections.
35 Letter from Mrs Shirley Hunter to Prof. F.G. Butler, 21 December 1997, Amazwi South African Museum of Literature.
36 Letter from Mrs Shirley Hunter to Prof. F.G. Butler, 21 December 1997.
37 Letter from Mrs Shirley Hunter to Prof. F.G. Butler, 21 December 1997.
38 Letter from Mrs Shirley Hunter to Prof. F.G. Butler, 13 November 1997.
39 Letter from Mrs Shirley Hunter to Prof. F.G. Butler, 13 November 1997.

Paintbox and materials purchased by Donald Hart for Sister Margaret's use in 1922 with tubes of Winsor and Newton oils, photographed in 2022

Bongolo Reservoir, which was overlooked by Everton Farm from the right-hand (south-east) shore, on the banks of which Sister Margaret painted poplar trees in 1923. Image published in 1924.

CHAPTER 5 | ST MONICA'S HOME

'The Hangklip from Nonesi's Nek' on Everton Farm by Sister Margaret CR, 1922, oil painting, approximately 20 by 28 inches

it would be beneficial for Sister Margaret to be able to paint as it would be therapeutic. Again, Donald Hart wrote to Mother Florence for her consent; he would provide the materials. Mother Florence assented.[40]

With this agreement, Donald Hart purchased an easel, paintbox, paints, palette knives and brushes for Sister Margaret to use, with an assortment of canvasses, all from the very best supplier of artists' materials, the Winsor and Newton Company in London. Shirley described how Sister Margaret went out most days, spending hours at a time working on her paintings and enjoying what she was doing in the outdoors, the sun, the countryside and nature.[41]

Sister Margaret took the opportunity to paint at least four works. The most striking was an oil painting of the Hangklip, a dramatic outcrop of rock painted from a remote ridge on Everton Farm, which was described as a 'large and arrestingly spacious work and gentle in tone'.[42] Donald Hart's daughter Shirley explained that the painting depicted the 'huge valley and plains and prominent was the "crouching lion" (our name for this mountain) behind other distant mountains'.[43] 'The story attached to it is that Mr Donald Hart needed to take Sister Margaret up to Nonesi's Nek in the gig and leave her there for a few hours,

---

40 Butler, *The Prophetic Nun*, p. 22.
41 Letter from Mrs Shirley Hunter to Prof. F.G. Butler, 13 November 1997.
42 Butler, *The Prophetic Nun*, p. 22.
43 Letter from Mrs Shirley Hunter to Prof. F.G. Butler, 13 November 1997.

Sister Margaret's painting of 'The Hangklip from Nonesi's Nek', prominently hung in the hall at the Everton home of Mr and Mrs Donald Hart

providing her with a large umbrella etc. While there, a rain shower came up and Sister Margaret went on painting; hence, the rain pools in the foreground.'[44] The painting was given to the Harts, who hung it in the hall at Everton 'directly opposite the front entrance where it could be seen by all who stepped in'.[45]

Other significant works included a view from Nonesi's Nek in the opposite direction, overlooking Glen Grey Valley.[46] Also, in the first months of 1923, Sister Margaret completed a watercolour of autumn poplars from the top of the Bongolo Reservoir dam. In addition, there was a similar scene of poplar trees standing prominently at the back of a field with small fruit trees in front.[47] Neither Donald Hart nor Sister Margaret could have anticipated the change in her life as a result of his intervention and enthusiasm, or the success that her works would have. Nor could he have known that by allowing Sister Margaret to recover her artistic skills, he may have prepared Mother Florence to agree to another artistic suggestion she was to receive.

Although in her humble position in the laundry at St Monica's, Sister Margaret was unlikely to have attended the consecration of the community's newly built Chapel of St Mary and All the Angels in Grahamstown in October 1916, she would have known about it. However, she could not have known that the building contained a flaw or that the recent chain of events would create an enormous opportunity for her.

---

44 Letter from Mrs Margaret Hodges to Prof. F.G. Butler, 20 April 1998.
45 Letter from Mrs Shirley Hunter to Prof. F.G. Butler, 13 November 1997.
46 Letter from Mrs Margaret Hodges to Prof. F.G. Butler, 20 April 1998.
47 Letter from Mrs Shirley Hunter to Prof. F.G. Butler, 13 November 1997.

Chapter Six

St Mary and All the Angels

AFTER THE COMMUNITY purchased Eden Grove in 1884, a chapel for the Sisters became an early priority. Accordingly, plans were drawn up for a building adjacent to St Peter's Home to serve the Sisters' needs. Bishop Webb laid the foundation in June 1886. Five months later, on St Thomas's Day, 21 December, the Bishop consecrated the chapel to the accompaniment of Handel's 'I Know That My Redeemer Liveth'.[1]

With its Norman style of stone construction and simple bench seating, the building had been designed to serve the Sisters rather than hold hundreds of students and girls from the community's expanding schools. A chancel was added in 1902, but the extra space was nowhere near adequate for the whole family of orphanages and schools under the Sisters' direction, let alone the extensive Training College. Considerably more space was needed. However, the limitations of the chapel's site against the rising ground of the city's Botanical Gardens ruled that out.

The community discussed whether the building should be further enlarged, which would have required complete reconstruction, or whether it would be better to look forward to a new, ampler replacement. 'It was agreed that it would spoil the Sisters' Chapel to meddle with it. We would wait.'[2] In 1909,

---

1 'A Record concerning the Chapel of the Resurrection at St Peter's Home, Grahamstown', p. 1; & CR Quarterly Letter, October 1936, pp. 2–3.
2 Naylor, *South Africa: My Venture*.

Sisters' Chapel of the Resurrection as originally completed in 1886

the Warden wrote:

> We especially want a new Chapel. I speak most feelingly, for owing to the smallness of the Chapel, services constantly have to be duplicated, even triplicated. Not half of the Community can get into the Chapel at once. Surely, St Peter's Home is deserving of a bigger Chapel than at present. We cannot have a more beautiful one, but it would be of inestimable use as a place of private prayer and devotion.[3]

The project received serious consideration two years later, and an appeal commenced in 1912. Mother Florence wrote in 1915 that 'it seemed most desirable that we should put the work in hand at once' despite the onset of war.[4] The commission went to Messrs Herbert Baker, Kendall & Morris, the Cape Town architectural practice that had previously designed St Monica's Home in Queenstown. They were also responsible for the impressive new set of buildings for Rhodes University College, completed in 1904, immediately adjacent to Eden Grove. In contrast to the simple Norman style of the Sister's Chapel, their proposal was for an Italian basilica-style structure, which was considered 'so well suited to the brilliant sky and the landscape usual in South Africa'.[5] The new

---

3   CR Annual Report [for 1911], January 1912, p. 9.
4   A Sister of the Community, *The Story of a Vocation*, p. 47.
5   CR Annual Report, January 1917, p. 7.

CHAPTER 6 | ST MARY AND ALL THE ANGELS

A view across to the Sisters' Chapel of the Resurrection (left), adjoining St Peter's Home from the Training College grounds, before the chancel was added in 1902

chapel was to lie on a north-south axis on the lawns below St Peter's Home, adjacent to the Training College. With a capacity for five hundred worshippers, it was substantial and would include a half-domed apse above the sanctuary, with lancet windows to light the altar.

The foundation stone was laid by Lord Buxton, the Governor General, on 2 June 1915. Sixteen months later, on 4 October 1916, the magnificent building was 'transformed from an edifice into a church'[6] when consecrated by Bishop Phelps. He 'had done so much towards the beginning of the chapel, and as Visitor had given so much careful supervision to its completion and its furnishing'.[7]

> Externally, the outstanding features are the campanile at the 'northwest' corner and the 'west' front, with its stone pillars and arches, and its semicircular spread of red steps. The walls stand on a grey stone plinth, and the whiteness of the rough cast stucco above is diversified by lines of brick and sets of tiles. Inside, the light is pleasantly subdued by the thick cathedral glass, and the rays falling across from three large windows in the clearstory give beautiful lights and shades on the five white stone pillars opposite and on the red brick arches above them. The fine proportions of the building and its spaciousness strike all who enter, as does the harmony of colouring – the dark brown roof, the

---

6   CR Annual Report, January 1917, p. 7.
7   CR Annual Report, January 1917, p. 7.

red of the walls, the white of the columns, and of the ceiling of the Apse. The lower part of the Apse is screened off as a sacristy, and the Sanctuary stands out in the body of the Church, raised by two shallow steps above the communion level. To complete the architect's design, the steps, rail, paving, and reredos are to be of white marble, and already gifts of money are coming in for this. From roof to floor, and from porch to Apse, the whole structure is marked by an almost severe simplicity, by a wonderful restfulness, and by a workmanship and care for detail which reflect great credit on all responsible for the building.

Sister Margaret explained that Bishop Phelps chose the chapel's dedication to St Mary and All the Angels after visiting Assisi. He was attracted by the name of the little chapel where the Franciscan Order began. 'The legend was that St Francis heard angels singing there one night when it was empty and uncared for and named it the "Chapel of St Mary and All Angels" and spared no pains to make it a fitting place of worship.'[8]

Despite all the accolades, most unexpectedly, the building contained a flaw that Sister Margaret would be asked to help put right. The fault only became apparent several years later during a visit by Father Noel, a priest of the Society of St John the Evangelist. His order was one of the first for men following the revival of Anglican religious communities in England, having been founded in Cowley in 1866.[9] The 'Cowley Fathers' had begun work in Cape Town in 1883. Their links with the Grahamstown Sisters deepened in 1904 after taking charge of St Augustine's Mission, Tsolo, in the 'native reserve' of the Transkei, which included boarding schools and clinics. Henceforth, the Cowley Fathers regularly stayed with the Grahamstown Sisters when they travelled between their principal missions of St Cyprian's in the Cape and St Cuthbert's. In addition, over the years several Cowley Fathers were invited to lead the Sisters' annual retreats in Grahamstown, with Father Noel doing so in January

The Chapel of St Mary and All the Angels, Grahamstown, soon after completion in 1916

---

8   Sister Margaret, *Chapel of St Mary and All the Angels*, p. 3.
9   Anson, *Call of the Cloister*, p. 74.

1910 and then again in early 1914.[10]

For several months during early 1922 while the Warden, the Reverend William Frith, was on leave in England,[11] Father Noel stayed at St Peter's to officiate at their Lent and Easter services.[12] Frederick Noel had worked as a civil servant in London and on his retirement sought ordination. He was greatly interested in church architecture, making detailed studies of English and Continental cathedrals as a labour of love. His pen and ink drawings reveal his critical observations of the effects of sunlight as it fell on architectural features and monuments. It was this aspect that he found unsatisfactory in the new chapel at Grahamstown.

Father Noel SSJE

Father Noel's three-month stay with the Sisters provided ample opportunity to admire the new Chapel of St Mary and All the Angels. Whilst doing so, he became increasingly troubled by the inclusion of the four high lancet windows in the apse above the altar. He considered that the shafts of bright light that fell from them were an unwelcome distraction from the altar. He therefore proposed that the windows be blocked up. Furthermore, he suggested that a marble altar, reredos, screen and pavement be installed in the sanctuary to create a more dignified and beautiful setting for worship.[13] These aspects had formed part of the architect's original design but were omitted in 1916 due to the constraints of the Great War.[14]

> At the age of seventy-nine in early 1922, Father Noel had no hesitation in speaking his mind. He had a long-standing acquaintance with the community, and Mother Florence accepted his advice. Sister Margaret described how her involvement stemmed from them.

---

10 CR Annual Report [for 1910], January 1911, p. 31; & CR, Sister Edith, 'Notes on Retreat Address by Father Noel, SSJE', January 1914.
11 CR Annual Report [for 1921], March 1922, pp. 3 and 4.
12 CR Annual Report [for 1922], March 1923.
13 CR Annual Report [for 1922], March 1923.
14 CR, 'Notes on the Chapel of St Mary and All the Angels'.

Interior of the Chapel of St Mary and All the Angels as completed in 1916, with four lancet windows in the apse

It was because of his advice that a scaffold was put up, and the windows blocked, and the ceiling of the Apse was covered with a smooth white plaster with a fine finish, which was of great service later on.

The next step was that Father Noel[15] said to the Mother 'Haven't you got a Sister who could go up there and paint?' The Mother's answer was 'Yes, we have a Sister trained for Art, but she is in St Monica's, Queenstown, at present helping in the laundry!'

In due course, the Sister (myself) was brought home and introduced to Father Noel. Well I remember that meeting. The Father had a half-sheet of notepaper and began to scribble down ideas as an artist would – Our Lady and the Holy Child in the Centre, angels here and there, and two above Our Lady's head bearing a crown (actually the only bit of the design still existent), and Saints to fill in the picture; and all the time Father Noel talked and explained.

Very soon I found myself launching forth on designs and all the necessary studies. I had been fortunate enough to go through a course of fresco painting with Mr Frampton, a well-known fresco painter, whose work was delicate and cultured and spared no pains to put me through the whole course, including making the spirit-fresco medium. So, when Mother Florence asked me if I could do the painting, I could truthfully say that I knew what to do from beginning to end; but whether I should do it was another matter! 'Well,' said

---

15 Noel incorrectly set as Noël in Sister Margaret's printed text.

CHAPTER 6 | ST MARY AND ALL THE ANGELS

Pen and ink drawing by Father Noel SSJE, revealing distraction caused by over-intense sunlight in the high altar setting of an unknown Continental church

The exposure setting of this photograph reveals Father Noel's concern about the amount of light from the four lancet windows, distracting from the altar

Mother cheerfully, 'we can always white-wash it over if we don't like it!' And so I began.[16]

As it was twelve years since Sister Margaret had trained under Reginald Frampton in London, this was an extraordinary opportunity, especially as it was to be her first undertaking. However, it was also twelve years since she entered the community in August 1911 and she was entitled to six months of home leave. The timing of her return to England should have allowed her to discuss her forthcoming commission with her tutor, Mr Frampton, and seek his assistance with the design and purchase of stabilising materials. His sudden death in Paris, where he had been making sketches for a large picture of Notre Dame Cathedral, on 5 November at the age of fifty-three, shocked the British artistic colony in Paris and the art establishment in London. He died eleven days before Sister Margaret sailed, denying her the opportunity to seek his advice on her first enormous commission.[17]

An additional desire to return may have been an equally shocking family tragedy. On 4 August, her brother Basil died unexpectedly from an infection after routine surgery at Birmingham General Hospital at the age of thirty-four. His two infant children included Geoffrey, Margaret's second godchild. Despite

---

16 Sister Margaret, *Chapel of St Mary and All the Angels*, pp. 2–3.
17 *Belfast Telegraph*, 10 November 1923.

RMS *Arundel Castle* preparing to get under way

these upsetting circumstances, it must have been with some excitement that she began her journey home twelve years after last sailing from Southampton. Emigration records confirm that Margaret Watson, listed as 'Sister of Mercy', embarked on RMS *Arundel Castle* of the Union-Castle Mail Steamship Company at Algoa Bay on Friday, 16 November. The voyage north took eighteen days, sailing first to Cape Town, then Madeira, before arriving at Southampton on Monday, 3 December. As was the norm for members of the community, she travelled third class. The passenger manifest shows 69 Sumner Place in London as her destination, where Ethel and Dorothy lived in the mews with their mother.

While travelling at sea and staying away, Sisters were subject to the Rule for Intercourse with the Outer World. This instruction made clear that community matters were not to be discussed and that they must be careful not to seek friendships for their benefit. Their correspondence was to be governed by the principles of loyalty, truthfulness and charity.[18] The rule also spoke of self-restraint in speech, looks and general demeanour. It stated that the hour for rising remained at 5.30 a.m., and it regulated sleep and meals.[19] The customary for travelling set further expectations, requiring Sisters to show cheerful readiness to share compartments with others but be careful not to be seen without habit, cap and veil. 'When travelling by sea Sisters must avoid being involved in the social activities of the ship.'[20]

---

18 CR, *The Constitution, Rule and Customary* (1933), pp. 58–59.
19 CR, *The Constitution, Rule and Customary* (1933), pp. 59–61.
20 CR, *The Constitution, Rule and Customary* (1933), p. 75.

Arriving on 3 December, Sister Margaret was reunited with her family well in time for Christmas. She was to stay in England until the following July. By the time of her return to England, Frederick, her oldest brother, had been promoted to HM Consul General in Philadelphia. Henry had returned from Prince Rupert in British Columbia to take on the Pandora Inn at Restronguet near Falmouth, and Arthur was at his Berkshire parish. Christopher was joint headmaster and proprietor of St Cuthbert's Preparatory School in Malvern, and John left for Rangoon in 1922 to work for the Indian Railways as a civil engineer. Of her sisters, Ethel was an art mistress working at a preparatory school in London, while Grace had established a cottage industry that made jams and preserves. Meanwhile, after working through an apprenticeship with Dora Lunn at the Ravenscourt Pottery in Hammersmith, Dorothy founded her pottery studio in 1921. As space in her London mews was inadequate, she was to purchase three small cottages at Beauworth in Hampshire during Margaret's stay and moved her Bridge Pottery there in 1924.

Sister Margaret CR, passport photograph, c.1923, when she was forty-four

'That photo does do her justice. She was a lovely, holy, gentle, humble person. She is wearing the kind of habit all Sisters were wearing at that time, nothing extra.'

(Sister Dorianne CR, Letter to Prof. F.G. Butler, 2 February 1995)

Their clergyman brother Arthur had been appointed to the parish of St Mary the Virgin, Aldworth, Berkshire, in 1918. His family moved into the Victorian vicarage from his previous parish in Wantage. When Margaret visited, Arthur's second child, Monica, then aged thirteen, was keen for her godmother to arrive. She awaited with some anticipation, as her siblings' godparents had a reputation for giving extravagant presents. So it was that Monica was invited to her aunt's room to receive her present – half an hour of praying.[21]

---

21 Richard Torrance, 'Notes on the Family of (Rev.) Frederick Watson and Margaret Lockhart Adam', Watson family papers.

Arthur's parish church of St Mary the Virgin, Aldworth, Berkshire, from a postcard dated 1938

Monica Watson, aged thirteen, at the time of her godmother's visit in 1924

Sisters on leave in England were sometimes invited to talk about the community's work at public meetings arranged by the English Helpers Union to raise funds and support. Sister Margaret most likely contributed where she could, as, in addition to being held in the smart drawing rooms of Knightsbridge, meetings regularly took place in Lincoln, Norwich and Cheltenham.[22]

Refreshed by her visit, Sister Margaret returned to Southampton on 20 June 1924 with her painting supplies packed up.[23] This time, her voyage was on the RMS *Edinburgh Castle*, which, when completed in 1910, had been the largest vessel in the Union-Castle fleet.[24] She reached Grahamstown in mid-July. On arrival, she would have seen the other parts of Father Noel's plan to enhance the Chapel of St Mary and All the Angels, which had been dedicated a month earlier, on

---

22 CR Annual Report, May 1919.
23 Board of Trade, Outwards Passenger Lists, BT27, UK National Archives.
24 Mitchell and Sawyer, *The Cape Run*, p. 40.

CHAPTER 6 | ST MARY AND ALL THE ANGELS

RMS *Edinburgh Castle* of the Union-Castle Line

Ascension Sunday, 1 June 1924.[25] An altar of cream and green marble stood before a new white reredos on a raised podium paved with alternating green and white marble squares.

However, she was also in for a surprise, as, while she had been away, Bishop Phelps had developed other ideas about the decoration of the apse. He was concerned that Sister Margaret did not have the necessary experience to complete such essential work and preferred a mosaic. He had seen such work in Assisi and thought it would complement the Sicilian marble already installed. Furthermore, the bishop thought Italian craftsmen would best do this work and intended to arrange for them to come to Grahamstown during his forthcoming holiday in Italy.

While Sister Margaret politely wrote that this was a 'glorious idea – but rather impracticable', Mother Florence was less happy about employing expensive foreign workmen.[26] Accordingly, she instructed Sister Margaret to get up on the scaffolding and start painting before the bishop returned, and, for a while, nothing became of the Italian workmen or the mosaics.

---

25 A Sister of the Community, *The Story of a Vocation*, p. 56.
26 Sister Margaret, *Chapel of St Mary and All the Angels*, p. 4.

Chapel of St Mary and All the Angels

With such a name, there could be little doubt what the subject of the painting should be; and given a free hand, I made numerous sketches – the Blessed Mother must take a prominent place with angels round about. Finally, I settled down to a careful charcoal drawing of Our Lady holding the Holy Child, feeling that ideas would grow as I worked.

I made some sketches of a tall, graceful girl from our Woodville Home, who posed for me with one of the smaller children on her knee. Church vestments provided the draperies (draped on a patient lay-figure), from which I made the needful studies. At that time, we were using blue vestments at the Mother House, with Bishop Webb's permission, and the delicate colouring gave me just what I needed. But the faces! That was going to be something that mattered very much; I could get the outer shell, as it were, from my models, but there must be far, far more than that.

I sent the models away and worked on, trusting to prayer and much thought. I fetched a large photograph of Mother Cecile from our Community Room feeling that the dark, expressive eyes would help, and the general feeling: and did begin to get something of what was needed, and as the Mother's face grew, so her attitude towards the child changed. She must be no longer the young mother, caressing and possessive. She is offering Him, holding Him out to the world, and so her eyes are to be looking outward, not at him, as she holds the child securely on her knees. But, meantime, her thoughts are busied with Him, and as I worked and prayed, I grew to know that the Mother I was trying to portray was no longer the young Bethlehem mother but the wonderful present Mother who is now with her Son. The Mother who has wept and anguished and suffered all through her Son's life and has finally come through the joy and certainty of His Glorious Resurrection. She is pondering all things in her heart, not only

The image of Mother Cecile used by Sister Margaret to represent the Virgin Mary

His holy infancy; but the solemnity of that made me afraid. It was then that the picture itself helped me, not just the design, but the growing picture as I worked on it.[27]

Shortly after Sister Margaret made a start, Bishop Phelps came to have a look. By then, she had already outlined Mary's robes and had practised the application of paint.

I heard voices below the platform and made myself as small as possible. Afterwards, Mother Florence told me that Bishop Phelps was quite content that we should go forward with the work: he had heard no more of the Italian workmen. She added kindly, 'I think the Community would be glad that one of themselves should do the painting.' After that, I felt more especially that the Community prayers were behind me.[28]

Sister Margaret combed Grahamstown, looking for the ideal little boy model for the Christ child before settling on Burt Pinnock, a blond curly-haired three-year-old. She took him to the chapel, put him in a high chair to pose, and gave him paints and brushes to keep him quiet. 'A few years later, Sister Margaret gave his parents a portrait of him painted from the fresco itself – apparently in lieu of model fees!'[29]

Aside from the central figures of the Virgin Mary, modelled by a graceful girl from Woodville who posed with the Christ child on her knee, images of saints were to form the background. These included St Michael and St Gabriel, for whom she had prepared initial cartoons. She also sketched Bishop Phelps's head for a possible St Peter. However, when she tried them on the wall, the 'perspective of the curved apse made them look far too big and they dwarfed the central figures'. Therefore, the sketch of Bishop Phelps was not used, and chapel servers posed for other characters instead.[30]

Father Noel visited periodically and took great interest.[31] Once he had approved her small-scale design drawings, she moved on to full-scale drawings for use as templates on large sheets of cartoon paper. Scaffolding was erected behind a temporary altar at the head of the nave.[32] The next stage was for full-sized tracings of the design to be secured in position so that the outlines could be transferred by pricking the lines onto the plaster of the apse. 'A careful outline

---

27 Sister Margaret, *Chapel of St Mary and All the Angels*, pp. 3–4.
28 Sister Margaret, *Chapel of St Mary and All the Angels*, p. 6.
29 Brand, 'Sister Margaret's Fabulous Fresco'.
30 Sister Margaret, *Chapel of St Mary and All the Angels*, p. 7.
31 F.G. Butler, notes from interview with Sister Maryan CR, 7 April 1996, Amazwi South African Museum of Literature.
32 Sister Margery's Reminiscences, p. 10.

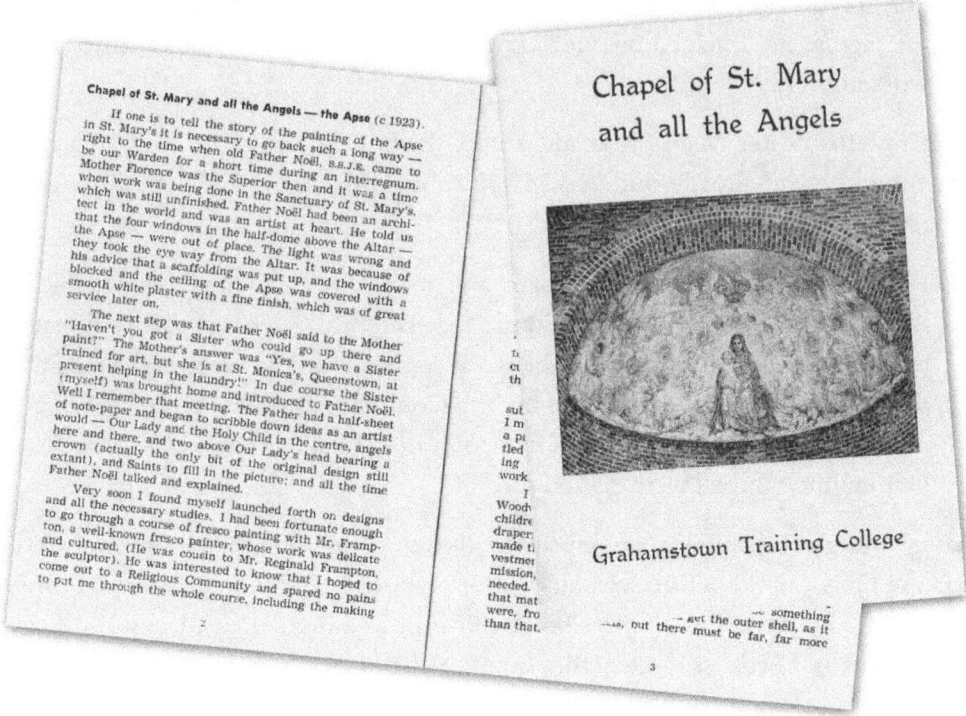

Sister Margaret's account of her decoration of the apse at St Mary and All the Angels, c.1960

was painted over the dotted lines with a thin brush.'[33] 'I had to get help from a Sister to manage the unwieldy sheets! My instructor said "Once you have a trustworthy outline, keep to it, and paint inside. Do not try to change it high up on the wall." So, comparatively quickly the main outlines of the central figures were up.'[34]

After all her preparations, Sister Margaret was ready to start painting in 1925.[35] Reginald Frampton had taught her to select a palette carefully to paint in her colours as directly and simply as possible.[36] Symbolically, on 18 October 1924, the festival of St Luke, the patron saint of artists, Sister Margaret began to apply the prominent blues and pinks of Mary's robes. 'The colours were powder colours, which I had bought in England, mixed rather wet with spirit-fresco medium on a huge palette, with a special broad, strong palette knife. They were used semi-fluid, more like water colours and were delightful to work with and very bright and clear.'[37]

---

33 Brand, 'Sister Margaret's Fabulous Fresco'.
34 Sister Margaret, *Chapel of St Mary and All the Angels*, p. 5.
35 A Sister of the Community, *The Story of a Vocation*, p. 58.
36 *The Studio*, vol. 36 (1906), pp. 346–349.
37 Sister Margaret, *Chapel of St Mary and All the Angels*, p. 5.

By the end of 1924, Father Noel's plan had steadily progressed, with the 'central figure of Our Lady, enthroned and holding the Holy Child, with His arms outstretched' nearing completion. By then, the 'clouds of angel heads above, and the saints and angels in adoration on either side' had also been sketched, allowing some hope that the work would be nearly completed by the time of the Training College reunion at Michaelmas the following year.[38] Completion, however, would not occur for another four years.

Work was slow owing to the routines at St Peter's Home and frequent use of the chapel, which interrupted progress given the time it took to prepare the spirit-fresco recipe. Getting the beeswax, spike oil, gum arabic and turpentine to the right temperature and consistency often took two hours before they could be poured into vacuum flasks and carried onto the scaffold. Sister Margaret was, however, in no hurry, and only slowly did her work evolve. Progress was also interrupted by visitors, including the Governor General, the Earl of Athlone, who inspected the grounds and buildings in early March 1925.[39] His visit was followed a few days later, on Friday, 15 March, by the Prince of Wales during his tour of Grahamstown. The Sisters prepared for days to make sure his visit was successful.

> On the Monday we got together the company that was to meet the Prince, and a goodly number it was: 600 pupils including 260 of the Training College, and with staff, workers, Sisters etc., we were 800 in all. The rehearsal went well and showed plenty of enthusiasm, and every thing was ready for the welcome at 11 o'clock on Friday …

> The cheers that burst out on the arrival of the Prince at the [convent] gate were loud and joyous: and red, white and blue handkerchiefs were waved enthusiastically. The Rev. Mother and the Warden were down at the gate to meet the Prince. The Mayor of Grahamstown accompanied him, and presented the Mother who then presented The Warden, and Sister Dora [acting principal of the Training College] brought him up to the Chapel steps … The Union Jack was flying from its post overlooking the steps down to college while S. George's flag waved over his head from S. Mary's campanile. Altogether the setting of the whole scene was most attractive. Meantime the cheering had gone on growing in volume but at a given signal it ceased and the College Orchestra which stood opposite the Prince struck up the hymn for S. George's Day.

---

38 CR Annual Report [for 1924], March 1925, p. 13.
39 CR Quarterly Letter, October 1925.

Grahamstown: view from the railway station on the eve of the Prince of Wales's visit in 1925

The Prince of Wales's visit on 15 March 1925

> A beautifully illuminated card with the words and music and a little sketch of St Mary's was presented to the Prince by the Head Girl [of the Training College] and His Royal Highness graciously accepted it and shook hands with her.[40]

After a week of interruption, work on the apse resumed. Unfortunately, the painting was far from ready for the Training College Old Girls' reunion on Michaelmas, 29 September 1925. However, the Warden could report that the work had been favourably received. 'I think the real appreciation shown by the Old Girls … made us realise more and more than ever what St Mary's stands

---

40 C.R. Quarterly Letter, June 1925, pp. 1–2.

for in the life of the College, the Centre, as the Bishop reminded us, for all our work.'[41] By then, the central figures were practically complete, revealing the Christ child stretching out his arms 'to draw all into the embrace of His Love'.[42] But much else remained to be done.

Another diversion occurred because of the community's decision in 1924 to build a temporary oratory chapel for their large boarding school in Bulawayo, St Peter's Diocesan School. The brick rondavel was to serve temporarily until the time came for a new permanent chapel. The result was a space of charm and simplicity as well as quietness. However, the cream walls, the white ceiling with its brown crossbars, and the altar made of native Rhodesian hardwood 'are almost severely plain', reported a Sister to the *Rhodesian Church Magazine*. Sister Margaret was asked to see what she could do to add a sense of awe to the chapel. This led to a painting being sent from Grahamstown to hang above the altar.[43]

> The Madona and Child gives a permanently needed touch of colour in the beautiful robes of Our Lady. The picture gives more than that, for the Little One standing on His Mother's knee, holding out His little arms, expresses wonderfully the eternal attractiveness of the truly human child, and something of the marvellous appeal of Incarnate Love Divine. In every way the picture fits our Oratory of the Epiphany, and evidently means much to our children.[44]

This description of the Holy Child standing on his mother's knee, as distinct from the image painted in the apse of St Mary and All the Angels where the Holy Child is sitting, corresponds with Sister Margaret's preliminary sketch for the apse. The picture sent to Bulawayo thus seems likely to have been a superseded preliminary study. Given the urgent need to improve the severely plain oratory before the girls returned from their summer break in January 1925 and Sister Margaret's preoccupation in the apse, recycling her discarded work was evidently prudent.

In early 1927, Father Noel revisited Grahamstown to view progress in the apse before being called back to Cowley for a final time. He had become increasingly agitated at the time it was taking Sister Margaret to complete her work. 'He had wished her to stop at various stages', yet, somewhat to his concern, she went on and on 'developing and refining the work for four years'.[45] He urged her to finish, but, being more guided by prayer than temporal pressures, she resisted and was still developing fresh ideas, even in the latter stages of completion.

---

41 CR Quarterly Latter, October 1925, p. 14.
42 CR Annual Report [for 1925], March 1926, p. 14.
43 CR Quarterly Report, October 1925, p. 7.
44 CR Quarterly Report, October 1925, p. 7.
45 F.G. Butler, notes from interview with Sister Maryan CR, 7 April 1996.

Fully realised design for the sanctuary of St Mary and All the Angels, photographed c.1928

> The students of the day and the artist decided that the College buildings must have their own place up there under St Mary's robes, just to show that they had the right to be up there sheltered by their own Madonna and very close to her. So they are – Canterbury and Lincoln and a bit of Bangor – enough to show that they represent all the College houses … The tower of St Mary's is indicated too, and also the belfry of the Sisters' Chapel of the Resurrection – are all included.[46]

In early 1928, the community took on a sixteen-year-old school-leaver, Camilla Reppert, to help Sister Ellen with the housekeeping at St Peter's Home. Camilla had regularly visited her extended family in Grahamstown, where her uncle was a doctor. While working at St Peter's, Camilla came across Sister Margaret, and they occasionally spoke and prayed.[47] Camilla was twice taken up to the apse to assist. On the first occasion, Sister Margaret asked her to sit as a model, holding her arm across her chest. Later, when the work was nearing completion, she was taken up the scaffold by Sister Innes to help paint some of the gold lettering of the Magnificat: 'My soul doth magnify the Lord and my spirit hath rejoiced in God my saviour'. 'I only painted "Spirit",' she later wrote.[48]

---

46 Sister Margaret, *Chapel of St Mary and All the Angels*, p. 11.
47 Cecily Camilla Bannister, letter to Prof. F.G. Butler, 30 July 1988, Amazwi South African Museum of Literature.
48 Cecily Camilla Bannister, letter to Prof. F.G. Butler, 23 August 1988.

Sister Innes was one of the great characters in the community. 'Everybody was her friend.'[49] She was of the same generation as Sister Margaret, a few weeks older, and joined the noviciate in March 1907.[50] She had spent her life teaching. Described as 'undoubtedly eccentric', she was also 'very gifted, with a very deep love of people, especially children'.[51] With her and Margaret's lives bound in common purpose, each must have been both proud and interested in the other's unfolding achievements, especially the beautification of their beloved Training College chapel.

Finally, after four years of work, Sister Margaret was satisfied and, in August 1928, concluded her work.

The Warden, the Reverend Charles E. Thornley, on the steps of St Mary and All the Angels

It had been an extraordinary accomplishment, especially as it was her first substantial work. Constrained and framed by the apse's brick construction, which helped draw people's sight into it, the painting made a profound statement. Six months later, on 2 February 1929, the Feast of the Purification of Our Lady, the completed fresco was blessed by the Warden, the Reverend Charles Thornley.

Sister Margaret recorded that he said some simple prayers at the end of Mass that day. Then, the censer was brought in, and the mural was censed from below.[52] The community recorded its satisfaction that the removal of the ugly scaffolding made possible the full realisation of Father Noel's scheme: 'The marble Altar, reredos with its lovely new silver crucifix and candles, and the apse roof painting standing out in all its simple majesty.'[53]

---

49 CR Remembrance Book, Sister Innes CR (1879–1971).
50 CR Profession Register, entry 100.
51 CR Remembrance Book, Sister Innes CR (1879–1971).
52 Sister Margaret, *Chapel of St Mary and All the Angels*, p. 11.
53 CR Quarterly Letter, June 1929, p. 2.

Sister Margaret's mural as part of the fully realised design for the sanctuary of St Mary and All the Angels, photographed c.1928

CHAPTER 6 | ST MARY AND ALL THE ANGELS

Detail of Sister Margaret's completed painting in the apse of St Mary and All the Angels, photographed in 2018

We see our Lady seated in the centre with the Holy Child on her knees, holding out His tiny arms as He leans back on His Mother's breast, welcomes us to Himself yet content in human frailty to depend on others. Our Lady's magnificent blue robe stands out against a golden halo of a beautiful sweet-faced Cherub, while beyond are adoring Angels representing the fifteen mysteries, their symbols anticipating the glorious and sorrowful events of the thirty-three stupendous years which lay before the Mother and Child. Low down, under the rays cast by the seraphic glow, we see a miniature sketch of S. Mary's Chapel, Canterbury House and the Home Chapel. The whole stands out in striking contrast to its red-brick surroundings.[54]

---

54 CR Quarterly Letter, June 1929, p. 2.

Chapter Seven

A Life of Prayer without Ceasing

AFTER SHE COMPLETED her fresco in the Chapel of St Mary and All the Angels in August 1928, there was to be a ten-year gap before Sister Margaret embarked on her next substantial work. During this period, she continued to live at St Peter's Home, where she contributed as an artist to further the community's work.

By 1930, the community had increased from sixty-nine women in the year of her arrival in 1907 to a hundred and was to expand to over a hundred and fifty in later years.[1] In 1930, sixty-four Sisters lived at St Peter's Home, with a further thirty-seven at branch houses.[2] There were also twenty-one lay workers helping in Grahamstown that year, contributing their nursing, teaching or caring skills as aspirants to the religious life or simply from a desire to help. Some came with established skills and professions, drawn to the challenge in Grahamstown, while others, like Sister Margaret, came searching for a new life. All were welcomed for longer or shorter stays, without any commitment or necessarily any assumption that their involvement might lead them to enter the religious life.

The community had grown into a sizeable organisation under Mother Florence's superiorship since 1906, with significant work and building expansions. These included a new Sisters' wing at St Peter's Home, an extension to the infirmary, and the opening of a rest home for the Sisters to use at Stones

---

1 CR Profession Register.
2 CR Logbook, 1931–1938.

St Peter's Home, Grahamstown, in the 1930s

Hill, a few miles south of Grahamstown. On the lawns below St Peter's, a range of accommodation halls had been completed for the Training College, making a 'lovely group of buildings amidst green lawns and flowering trees'.[3] Elsewhere in Grahamstown, there were new buildings for Woodville School and Orphanage, the Queen Alexandra Home for Infants, and the Good Shepherd School. In Port Elizabeth, St Francis Xavier School had opened for Chinese children, adding to the community's existing mission in the parish of St Mark in the city's North End.

Further afield, in Southern Rhodesia, the community had opened a small mission in 1927 in Salisbury, where Sisters helped in the cathedral parish. The community had also been invited to found two large institutions in Bulawayo, St Peter's Diocesan School for Girls, which was to grow to become a large boarding school for all ages of white girls, and St Gabriel's Home, which provided the colony with its only orphanage for white children. To the south-east, close to the border with Portuguese East Africa (present-day Mozambique), a hundred and sixty miles from Salisbury, a few Sisters had started working alongside the CR Fathers to take care of the girls at the large mission station of St Augustine's, near Penhalonga. Others had similarly begun serving at St Faith's Mission, Rusape, which required a five-day journey from Grahamstown.[4]

Being described as 'quiet and retiring' and not in the strongest health, Sister Margaret most likely did not help at any of these distant places. However, she

---

3 CR Remembrance Book, Mother Florence CR (1855–1950).
4 CR Annual Report 1918, The Warden's Letter, 2 January 1918, pp. 5–6.

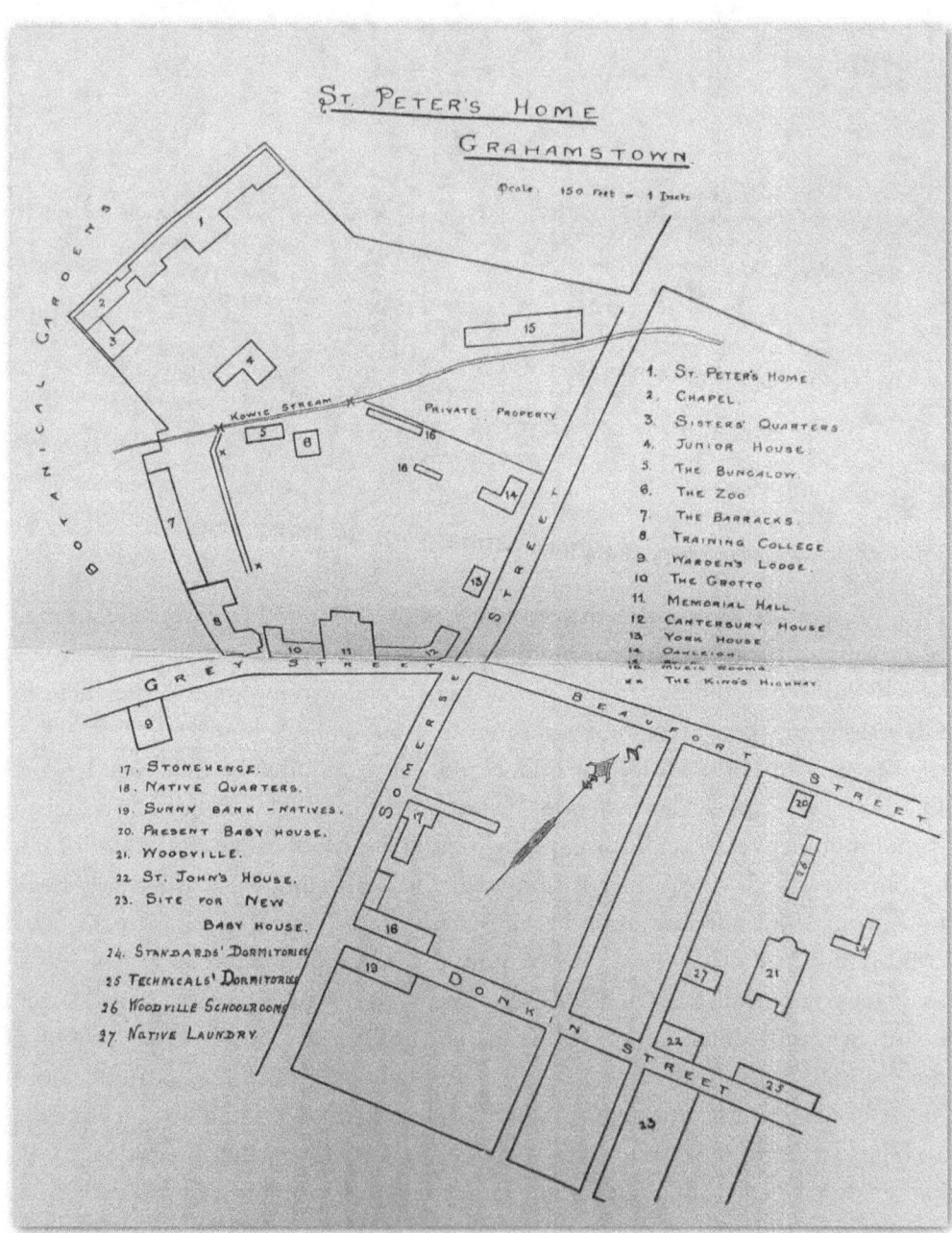

Location of the community's works in Grahamstown

Chapter 7 | A Life of Prayer without Ceasing

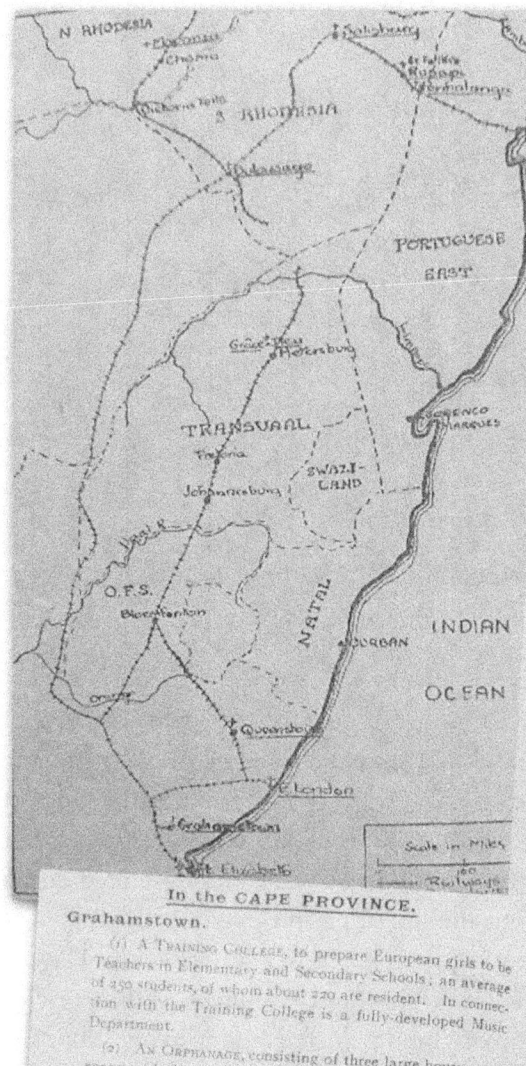

'The Works of the Community in 1929', CR Annual Report [for 1928], March 1929

Driveway from the convent gates to St Peter's Home (right) with St Peter's School (left) and the city's Botanical Gardens extending on the high ground beyond

visited a few of the community's outlying houses and was to paint for several more.[5] At St Peter's Home, no one could have avoided being swept up in the activities of the large Training College or St Peter's School, both cornerstones of the community's primary purpose to educate. After all, Mother Cecile had felt sure that it was through education 'that the forces of the Catholic Creed could find their easiest and fullest channel into the life of people'.[6]

By 1930, Mother Florence was nearing the end of her superiorship. Having arrived in 1887 and been the fiftieth to profess, and having served as novice mistress and then Assistant Superior before being elected Superior in 1906, she was one of the 'foundation stones'.[7] Re-elected Superior in 1913, 1920 and 1927, she had been at the helm for almost twenty-five years.[8] However, with each additional piece of work that the community took on adding to her burden, Mother Florence was 'worn out' by the end.[9]

Responsibility for electing a Superior fell to the Chapter, the body entrusted with governing the community and voting on the most critical issues, which

---

5   Sister Dorianne, letter to Prof. F.G. Butler, 27 January 1995, Amazwi South African Museum of Literature.
6   A Sister of the Community, *Mother Cecile in South Africa*, p. 176.
7   CR Profession Register, entry 6; & CR Remembrance Book, Mother Florence CR (1855–1950).
8   CR Profession Register, entry 4.
9   CR Remembrance Book, Mother Florence CR (1855–1950).

Chapter 7 | A Life of Prayer without Ceasing

View from St Peter's Home towards the Training College buildings below and to the south

View of St Peter's Home from the Training College buildings, with the roof of the adjacent Sisters' Chapel and Sisters' wing (left)

Mother Edith CR, third Superior of the Community of the Resurrection of our Lord, in December 1930, with Bishop Webb's episcopal cross, which had been presented to the community after his death in 1907 to be worn by the Superior

Mother Edith CR, with her predecessor, Mother Florence CR, after her installation as Superior on 31 December 1930 by Bishop Phelps

required a two-thirds majority for any motion.[10] As required under the Constitution, the Chapter met on 13 December 1930 to vote for a new Superior. Sister Edith was elected. Eighteen days later, on New Year's Eve, she was blessed and installed in the Sisters' Chapel by the Visitor, Bishop Phelps, and took her place as the third Superior.[11]

Edith Holmes had come to Grahamstown at the age of twenty in 1888 when her father gave up his parish of Sydenham in London, having been appointed the Cathedral's Dean. She used to walk with her sister from the Deanery to St Peter's Home every day to help Mother Cecile darn the orphans' clothes, and she therefore possessed a direct link with the foundress.[12] Through this link, Mother Edith was able to bring a 'fresh spirit of adventure' to the community as the Superior, and over the years since they had first been acquainted, Sister Margaret and Mother Edith became devoted friends.[13]

---

10 CR, *The Constitution, Rule and Customary* (1933), pp. 17–21.
11 CR Remembrance Book, Mother Edith CR (1868–1966).
12 CR Remembrance Book, Mother Edith CR (1868–1966).
13 CR Remembrance Book, Mother Edith CR (1868–1966).

There were other changes to the community's oversight at this time, as in May 1929 the Reverend Charles Thornley, who had replaced the Reverend William Frith as Warden in 1923, resigned and returned to England.[14] By October, the services of a most devoted churchman were secured to replace him, when the Right Reverend Wilmot Lushington Vyvyan was installed. He had just retired as Bishop of Zululand. His move into the Warden's Lodge with his wife Edith brought to the community a couple who were to take great interest in its 'multifarious and widely scattered projects' and provide the Sisters with much loving support. Edith Vyvyan was also to take great interest in and provide much encouragement for Sister Margaret's work.[15]

In 1931, Bishop Phelps was consecrated Archbishop of Cape Town and assumed his new position as Primate of the Church of the Province of South Africa. In his place, Archibald Howard Cullen was enthroned as the sixth Bishop of Grahamstown and assumed the role of Visitor to the community, which he held until 1950. Having served as Warden of the nearby St Paul's Theological College in Grahamstown since 1926 and being a frequent visitor, he was already known.[16]

As for her own work, as far as it is known, Sister Margaret was asked to take on sacristan duties for the Sisters' Chapel.[17] Given the chapel's centrality in the community's life, this role suited her creativity and intellect, and was constantly demanding. With seven daily Offices and frequent festivals and thanksgivings, there was plenty to arrange and oversee, and all had to be just right. The gentle and reflective way she carried out these duties and conducted her religious life gave rise to the description by college girls that hers was 'definitely a life of prayer without ceasing'.[18]

In February 1930, Sister Margaret produced a little booklet in which she recorded her thoughts on retreat. Her 'Meditations on the Life of the Blessed Lord' provide a glimpse into the depth of her thoughts on the subject through their orderly arrangement of concepts.[19] Retreats were a regular part of community life. The Sisters' annual retreat took place early in each new year to coincide with the time when many serving in distant missions came to Grahamstown over Christmas for a break during the summer heat. Retreats provided opportunities for Sisters to step back from their temporal responsibilities for four or five days and benefit from seclusion, inspiration,

---

14 A Sister of the Community, *The Story of a Vocation*, p. 107.
15 Butler, *The Prophetic Nun*, p. 33.
16 *The Times*, London, 28 October 1931, p. 11.
17 Sister Dorianne, letter to Prof. F.G. Butler, 2 June 1995.
18 Sister Dorianne, letter to Prof. F.G. Butler, 2 June 1995.
19 CR, Sister Margaret, 'Meditations on the Life of the Blessed Lord'.

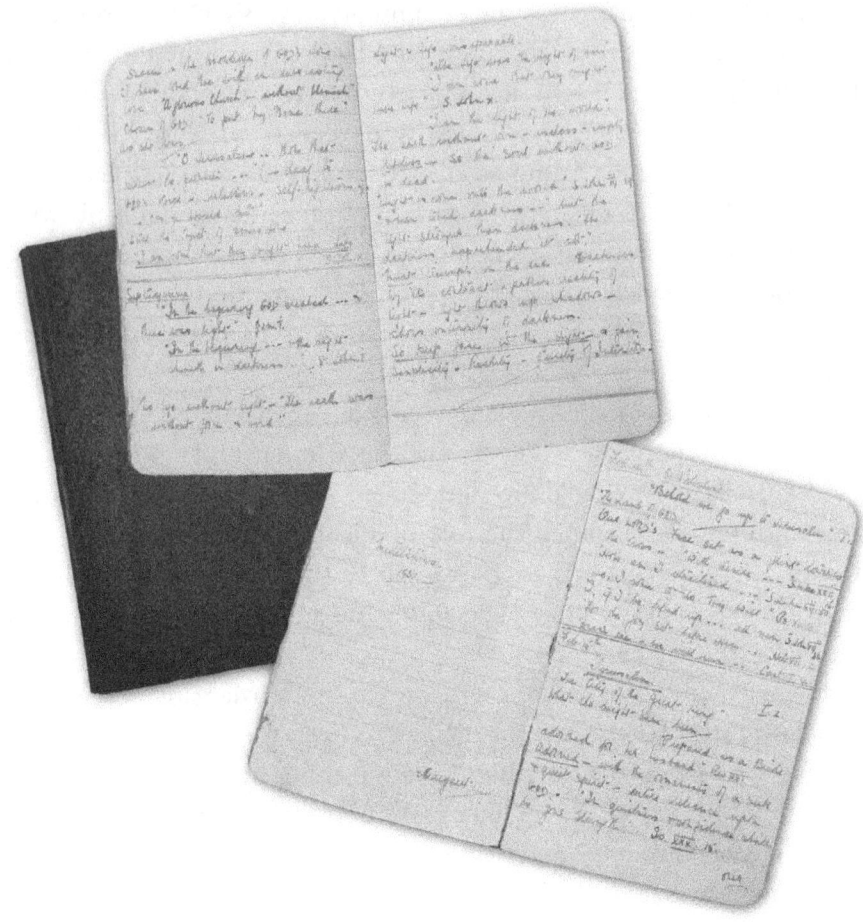

'Meditations on the Life of the Blessed Lord', by Sister Margaret CR, February 1930

meditation, fellowship and prayer. These were large gatherings: in January 1932, for instance, seventy Sisters were able to attend.

During the 1930s, Sister Margaret also continued to paint when instructed and undertook many commissions either as gifts from the community, to adorn its chapels and halls, or to be sold to raise funds for the community's programmes. Her works included 'Our Lord' and a second large canvas, 'The Flight into Egypt', for the refectory at St Peter's Home.[20] Another work was a life-sized picture of Christ with a shepherd's crook holding a lamb, which was placed in the Bethlehem Orphanage in New Street.[21]

One of her most striking works from this period was 'Walk to Emmaus' on three panels, set into the altar of the small oratory at the Sisters' Home of Rest

---

20 Butler, *The Prophetic Nun*, p. 37.
21 Butler, *The Prophetic Nun*, p. 37.

CHAPTER 7 | A LIFE OF PRAYER WITHOUT CEASING

The refectory at St Peter's Home set for Christmas dinner with 'Our Lord' by Sister Margaret hanging above the mantelpiece, mid-1930s

at Stones Hill.[22] For the St Francis Xavier Mission in Port Elizabeth, where the community worked among Chinese families, she produced 'A Missionary Saint Stepping Ashore', probably depicting St Francis Xavier, which was painted with a pagoda and junk in the background to 'suggest the East'.[23]

Before assuming her new responsibilities as Superior in 1930, Mother Edith had served as Sister Superior in Southern Rhodesia. She had assumed responsibility for the community's growing works there, helping to build up St Peter's Diocesan School in Bulawayo. Although her travel details are uncertain, Sister Margaret is thought to have visited several of the community's houses during this time and travelled at least to Salisbury and Bulawayo. Most likely, Sister Margaret also visited Victoria Falls, where she completed some sketches for a magnificent canvas depicting the Falls.

In September 1931, Mother Edith shared in her weekly letter sent across the community that the '"Falls" picture is framed and looks beautiful. It seems to be the general opinion that she should put 100 Guineas on it, of course, there have been expenses for materials, and she will have to employ an agent in Cape

---

22 Mother Joanna Mary, Occasional Letter to Associates and Friends, 6 August 1964, CR Archive.
23 Butler, *The Prophetic Nun*, p. 36.

Town.'[24] With a sale opportunity identified, the picture was packed up and sent to Cape Town by rail. However, rather than accompanying it, Sister Margaret set off in the opposite direction on 13 November, travelling to St Monica's Home in Queenstown. She needed to collect a young woman with her child and escort them to the Cape.

With her duty discharged, Sister Margaret then went to stay with a friend of the community, Mrs Holmes, in Wynberg. The following day, she returned to Cape Town and made her way to the docks to meet up with Sister Ivy, who had sailed there from Port Elizabeth on her way back to England on leave.[25] Unfortunately, Sister Margaret and her 'Falls' picture encountered a double dose of bad luck, as out of 600 entrants, only 250 pictures were selected, not including hers. 'Hers was rather large,' wrote Mother Edith. 'I daresay they considered space.'[26] Somehow, while being manhandled, the frame became damaged, which delayed Sister Margaret's return so that she could arrange the repair. Nonetheless, she returned to Grahamstown on 23 December, just in time for Christmas, having dropped off her charges in Queenstown.[27] With the frame repaired, Mrs Holmes kept the picture for a little while 'to show people as opportunity serves'.[28] Evidently, it did not sell and was returned to Grahamstown and hung in one of the Training College lecture rooms.[29]

By the early 1930s, Sister Margaret had established her studio in the novice wing at St Peter's Home, which she used as an intimate place for work and prayer. However, owing to the expansion of the noviciate, Mother Edith needed to move her out to make two more novice cubicles in that space.[30] She was provided with another room with views from its high garret window over the Sisters' gardens to the trees and high ground to the west. 'It was right on the top floor and when you reached the top you turned right, overlooking the Botanics. As Novices, we were told not to go into the room, because Sister Margaret did a lot of painting there and spent much time praying there as well over her pictures and our Novice Mistress didn't want us to disturb her.'[31]

Undisturbed in her own space, Sister Margaret completed a succession of panels and paintings for installation in churches across South Africa. By March 1932, it was recorded that she had 'done a good bit on the Reredos picture

---

24 Mother Edith, Logbook entry, 28 September 1931.
25 Mother Edith, Logbook entry, 16 November 1931.
26 Mother Edith, Logbook entry, 12 December 1931.
27 Mother Edith, Logbook entry, 20 December 1931.
28 Mother Edith, Logbook entry, 1 March 1932.
29 Camilla Bannister, letter to Prof. F.G. Butler, 23 August 1998.
30 Mother Edith, Logbook entry, 1 March 1932.
31 Sister Dorianne, letter to Prof. F.G. Butler, 30 May 1995.

recently working at the two figures of Our Lady and St John on either side'.³² This report referred to a 'Christ on the Cross' for the small church of St James the Less at Sidwell in Port Elizabeth, which was to be the first of at least five altarpieces eventually completed for churches in Port Elizabeth. As was her custom, Sister Margaret would have visited Sidwell at least once to determine requirements, then completed the picture in her studio, and most likely returned to oversee its installation. She was to repeat her 'Christ on the Cross' composition a decade later when asked to paint for the rural church of St Andrew's, Chilton, in the Cathcart district.

'Christ on the Cross' installed at St James the Less, Sidwell, after installation, c.1932

Her study of the crucifix was to take a more lifelike form the following year when Mother Edith asked her to attend to one of the community's most cherished possessions: a life-sized crucifix from Bavaria. The community had been given this carving by Sister Catherine's mother and brother, who had visited Oberammergau in August 1914 for the Passion plays. The crucifix had been sent directly to Grahamstown from Bavaria in two packing cases and arrived safely just before the outbreak of war.

'Christ on the Cross' at St James the Less, Sidwell, Port Elizabeth, above a new altar dating from 1951

The crucifix was placed in more than one temporary position at St Peter's Home until finally being hung in the novice room. However, following her appointment as Superior, Mother Edith asked Sister Margaret to paint the figure of Jesus in flesh-like tones before she had it installed in the Sisters' Chapel of the

---

32 Mother Edith, Logbook entry, 1 March 1931.

An image of the Oberammergau crucifix which had been painted in flesh tones by Sister Margaret as a devotional card

Resurrection. This move was possible as, after the completion of St Mary and All the Angels for the use of the Training College and schools in 1916, the Sisters' Chapel reverted to its intended purpose. With less seating required, a reordering occurred in 1917, with the altar moved towards the choir, which enabled the space behind to be screened off to create a separate chapel.[33] Mother Edith had the crucifix mounted in this space, slotting into a stone from the Anglican Cathedral of St George in Jerusalem, let into the wall to form a support. The crucifix, mounted on the 'north' wall, 'at once gave its name to the Chapel', and became a powerful image which Sister Margaret repeatedly returned to in her work.[34]

The year 1934 was to be eventful. After attending the Sisters' retreat and

---

33 'A Record concerning the Chapel of the Resurrection', pp. 5–6.
34 'A Record concerning the Chapel of the Resurrection', pp. 5–6.

CHAPTER 7 | A LIFE OF PRAYER WITHOUT CEASING

The Sisters' quarters with their small chapel at St Mary's Mission, Grace Dieu Diocesan Training College, in 1934

annual Chapter meeting in early January, Sister Margaret left for a holiday on the rugged coast at Sea View, just south of Port Elizabeth.[35] All Sisters could expect an annual holiday, albeit strictly governed by the community's rules while away.[36] At the time of her visit, several boarding houses and tea shops had been built at Sea View, together with a tidal swimming pool, owing to the construction of a metal road. Later that year, a large and luxurious hotel opened, further enhancing the Sea View esplanade.[37] Sisters were usually invited to stay by friends of the community, and Sister Margaret was away for two weeks, returning at the start of February.[38]

In May 1916, the Bishop of Pretoria asked Mother Florence if Sisters might be available to help at the Diocesan Training College at Grace Dieu. This institution, founded in 1906 as the only college in the diocese to train African teachers to serve in Anglican mission schools, was located sixteen miles from Pietersburg (now Polokwane), on the highveld a hundred and sixty miles north of the capital of Pretoria. The college and its elementary school drew in trainees and children from South Africa and Southern Rhodesia.[39] The principal, Canon Woodfield, was an old friend of the community. He needed the Sisters to take charge of

---

35 CR Logbook, 1931–1938.
36 CR Rule Book (1933), p. 56.
37 McCleland, 'The Seaview Hotel', in *Port Elizabeth of Yore*.
38 CR Logbook, 1931–1938.
39 'Grace Dieu Diocesan Training College 1906–1969', Historical Papers, Wits University.

the girls' boarding department and teach all branches of housekeeping.[40] 'The work and opportunity seemed a complete answer to prayers offered when the African Industrial School at Grahamstown was relinquished. The call was gladly accepted and in February 1917, three Sisters entered on the works.' They found themselves housed at St Mary's Mission in a 'picturesque group of huts on a little hill about seven minutes' walk from the Church and College Halls'.[41]

An initial task was to oversee the construction of a small rondavel oratory for their use, which was ready by early March and dedicated by the bishop when he visited on 23 August.[42] 'The Chapel Hut is beautifully made and finished. Half-a-dozen little desks and stools are arranged in a curve facing the simple Altar: and you step straight on to the veld – from God's very little Sanctuary to His vast dwelling-place.'[43]

In 1934, an additional structure was completed at St Mary's, a second, larger oratory which was needed for the girls to go to whenever they wished, as until then there had been 'no place to meet their needs as the Sisters' Chapel was too small, and the College Church was half a mile away'.[44] The All Saints Oratory was a simple, rustic, rectangular building, constructed and finished by the students, with white walls, a roof of iron and a 'good supply of windows to make it light and airy'. The furnishings were also 'very simple – a large crucifix with a shelf under it to hold flower vases and candlesticks, and a prayer desk in front of it, a statue of our Lady'. The chapel 'had been long wanted, and many have prayed earnestly and worked diligently for it: it cannot fail to be of great value in the spiritual development of our [African] girls'.[45]

Mother Edith visited Grace Dieu in February, most likely with Sister Margaret in attendance, who agreed that she would contribute three paintings for the new oratory: 'Our Lord', 'The Walk to Emmaus' and 'St Francis and the Birds'.[46] At least one picture was in place by December, with the others following in March.[47] Given that she had already painted each of these subjects, it is likely that these paintings replicated previous compositions.

---

40 'Grace Dieu Diocesan Training College 1906–1969'.
41 A Sister of the Community, *The Story of a Vocation*, p. 50.
42 CR Annual Report [for 1917], January 1918; & A Sister of the Community, *The Story of a Vocation*, p. 51.
43 A Sister of the Community, *The Story of a Vocation*, pp. 50–51.
44 CR Annual Report [for 1934], March 1935, p. 20.
45 CR Annual Report [for 1934], March 1935, p. 20.
46 Mother Edith, Occasional Letter to Supporters and Associates, 27 February 1934; & CR Annual Report [for 1934], March 1935, p. 20.
47 *Grace Dieu Bulletin*, December 1934; CR Annual Report [for 1934], March 1935; & Butler, *The Prophetic Nun*, pp. 35 and 37.

CHAPTER 7 | A LIFE OF PRAYER WITHOUT CEASING

A classroom at St Mary's Mission, Grace Dieu Diocesan Training College

St Mark's Day, 25 April 1934, was the jubilee of the Community of the Resurrection of Our Lord. Fifty years had passed since Annie Cecile Ramsbottom Isherwood had knelt before the altar in the small chapel at Bishopsbourne to take her novice vows in the presence of Bishop Webb. Mother Edith decided to hold a novena before the anniversary to get as many friends as possible to give support through prayer.[48] She also used the novena to petition for the number of vocations to increase.[49] Her appeal was well judged, as, with 119 women present in 1934, the number of Sisters had almost peaked. Although the overall number in the community was to remain at about that level for the following twelve years, Mother Edith had shrewdly foreseen that the community was at the 'top of the hill', as the number of women joining was merely sufficient to replace the elderly. With an increasing burden placed on younger entrants to care for the old, the community was in danger of stagnation.[50]

A celebratory service of High Mass was held for the community and guests on the morning of 25 April, at which 'beautiful new vestments were worn for the first time', followed by a 'very sociable and happy gathering' for refreshments

---

48 Mother Edith, Occasional Letter to Supporters and Associates, June 1933, 'Some Plans for Our Jubilee'.
49 CR, 'Novena for the Community of the Resurrection of Our Lord on the Occasion of Its Jubilee, April 13th–21st, 1934'.
50 CR Profession Register.

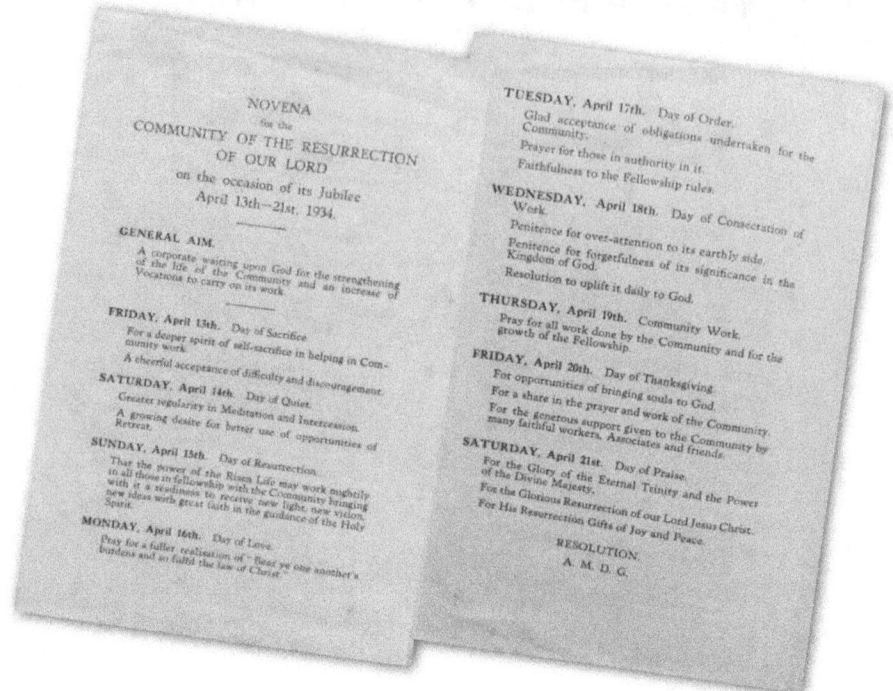

Novena for the Community of the Resurrection on the occasion of its jubilee, 13–21 April 1934

on the Bangor lawn. Masses of flowers arrived to adorn the chapel, which Sister Margaret carefully arranged.[51]

Mother Edith also decided that the jubilee should be marked with the installation of a new altar frontal in the Sisters' Chapel. Again, she turned to Sister Margaret for this work. The design chosen would seem hugely appropriate and symbolic for a community bound by the Catholic creed yet dispersed in its activities across the southern continent. Again, the inspiration was from St John's Gospel: 'I am the vine, ye are the branches' (15:5). The design was executed by the talented and later well-known woodcarver Ernest Mancoba, who had been encouraged to learn his craft at Grace Dieu.[52] 'The design illustrated Our Lord's teaching about the True Vine and its Branches given in St John XV, a passage which forms part of the Gospel for St Mark's Day, the Birthday of the Community … The carving shows painstaking execution of the design as well as a real artistic skill.'[53]

The symbolism of Sister Margaret's design was explained in the community's quarterly letter to English friends and supporters sent out in October 1935.

---

51 CR Quarterly Letter, July 1934, pp. 2–3.
52 Sister Dorianne, letter to Prof. F.G. Butler, 19 July 1995.
53 'A Record concerning the Chapel of the Resurrection', p. 7.

CHAPTER 7 | A LIFE OF PRAYER WITHOUT CEASING

The Warden, Bishop Vyvyan, processes alongside the Chapel of St Mary and All the Angels on 'Jubilee Day', 25 April 1934, proceeded by Father Hill, Warden of St Paul's Theological College, Grahamstown, and Canon Woodfield, Principal of Grace Dieu Training College

Chancel of the Sisters' Chapel with the altar frontal carving 'I am the vine, ye are the branches' designed by Sister Margaret and executed by Ernest Mancoba in 1934; with the Oberammergau crucifix installed on the 'north' wall of the 'Crucifix Chapel of the Lord'

The design for the carving worked out by Sister Margaret represents the Vine and the Branches. This was thought to be a specially appropriate subject as the wonderful passage of St John XV about the True Vine comes to us year by year as the Gospel for the Birthday of the Community, St Mark's Day.

In the centre of the design is a cross, round which the vine-stems twist, forming themselves at its foot into a chalice, the cup-shape being carried out by the leaves and fruit. In the centre of the chalice is seen the Sacred Heart. Round the arms of the Cross is a ring, with the pattern and flames carried out beyond the ring by rays. The circle is intended to suggest that the Sacred Heart of the central panel sets forth the thought of the Eucharist. Life as springing from the union with the vine. Over the Cross broods a Dove.

On each side of the central panel are five smaller panels, divided by knotted vine stems springing from the same root. These are the branches abiding in the vine. These branches, twisted together with those springing from the Cross, form with their leaves and fruit a wide curve that goes from side to side of the Altar.[54]

The dedication of this altar frontal in August 1934 completed the community's jubilee commemorations.[55]

Sister Pauline CR in her element at Grace Dieu

The talent for carving that developed at Grace Dieu had been nurtured by Sister Pauline. Four years younger than Sister Margaret, she trained as a teacher before joining the community in early 1915 and made her profession in late 1917.[56] Although not an artist, she loved company and working with people, and had taught herself woodcarving. Her enthusiasm inspired many young African men to acquire this skill at Grace Dieu, including Ernest Mancoba, who had been taken on to teach Zulu languages. Such was the pool of woodcarving talent that Sister Pauline built up that she constantly

---

54 CR Quarterly Letter, October 1935, p. 5.
55 'A Record concerning the Chapel of the Resurrection', p. 7.
56 CR Profession Register, entry 136.

sought church commissions for pews, furniture and panels to keep them busy.[57]

One of the designs she had previously sought from Sister Margaret was an altar panel for the community's Chapel of St Mary and All Saints in their Salisbury mission house. This work depicted St Mary's visit to her cousin Elizabeth. The need for this design may have prompted Sister Margaret's probable visit to Salisbury in the early 1930s. When complete, the panel was most likely sent to Grahamstown for her to paint the relief of each figure in her studio before being sent to Salisbury for installation.[58] Another collaboration, 'according to hearsay', was a panel depicting an entwined vine with fruit, 'likely to have been executed by Mancoba in the latter half of 1935, after he completed the "vine and branches" altar front'.[59]

Early in 1936, Sister Margaret again took up her entitlement to six months of furlough and returned to England. Eleven and a half years had passed since she last saw her family in June 1924. She departed by train for Port Elizabeth on 9 January.[60] Facilities had greatly improved since her last sailing in 1923, as there was now a deep-water quay for the mailships to berth against, doing away with the need to trans-ship goods and passengers by lighter across the rough waters of Algoa Bay.[61] She was to sail on another 'intermediate' vessel of the Union-Castle Company, the MV *Llangibby Castle*, which had been built to serve the South Atlantic Islands route between England and the Cape. Her passage would therefore have been longer and more varied than usual as, after Cape Town, the voyage proceeded across the South Atlantic to Jamestown on the small Crown Possession of St Helena. The usual practice was for passengers to have the opportunity to go ashore by lighter while cargoes were trans-shipped, to visit the Church of St James and climb up to Napoleon's residence 'Longwood'. Then, the voyage proceeded to the isolated volcanic Crown Territory of Ascension Island for a brief pause to land passengers. However, as the island was virtually the preserve of the Eastern Cable Company, it was only usually possible to go ashore at their invitation.[62] The next stop was Las Palmas on the Canary Islands, before reaching Southampton on 1 February.[63] Sister Margaret was at sea on 20 January 1936 when the death of King George V was announced.

---

57 Sister Dorianne, letter to Prof. F.G. Butler, 19 July 1995.
58 Butler, *The Prophetic Nun*, pp. 37–38.
59 Butler, *The Prophetic Nun*, p. 51.
60 Sister Dorianne, letter to Prof. F.G. Butler, 30 May 1995.
61 McCleland, 'The Three Eras of the Historic Port Elizabeth Harbour', in *Port Elizabeth of Yore*.
62 *The Newsletter*, supplement to *Church News* [of the Diocese of Grahamstown] , October 1961, p. 364.
63 *The Newsletter*, supplement to *Church News* [of the Diocese of Grahamstown] , October 1961, p. 364; & Board of Trade, Incoming Passenger Lists BT26, UK National Archives.

MV *Llangibby Castle* of the Union-Castle Mail Steamship Line, 1924

This time, Sister Margaret's destination in England was 3 England's Lane in Hampstead, North London. This house had become, since 1928, home for Ethel and for Basil's two children, whom she had assumed responsibility for, and for the family's matriarch, Margaret Lockhart, who reached the age of eighty in June 1936. After giving up her pottery in Hampshire in 1934, Dorothy lived there until she found a new studio in Kent. Margaret's family visits included staying with Dorothy at her new Bridge Pottery at Lime House in Rolvenden, where she helped to supervise a dancing party for local children.[64]

In 1929, towards the end of Mother Florence's superiorship, there was considerable strength of opinion that the community ought to have a branch house in England.[65] After withdrawing from Forres in 1901, a small house had been acquired at Rockville in Halifax, which was given up in 1904. Thereafter the community lacked a base in England and thus the means of helping to prepare women for the possibility of entering the religious life before they travelled to Grahamstown. Although there had been some local recruitment of English women from across South Africa, even by 1936 the community remained substantially dependent on the flow of aspirants and helpers from England as well as English support and money. This deficiency needed addressing. A new branch house would also provide somewhere for Sisters to base themselves during prolonged stays in England, as Sister Margaret was

---

64 D.G.W. Barham, childhood recollections.
65 A Sister of the Community, *The Story of a Vocation*, p. 61.

CHAPTER 7 | A LIFE OF PRAYER WITHOUT CEASING

Jamestown, St Helena, from the anchorage, a postcard from the mid-1930s

to experience in 1936.⁶⁶ Accordingly, after considering possible locations, an agreement was reached with the Community of the Sisters of the Church, an Anglican sisterhood, to rent part of a terraced house at 2 Lupton Street, Kentish Town, in North London.⁶⁷

The Sisters of the Church, whose mother house was in Kilburn, had been founded in 1870. No other Anglican religious community had expanded so rapidly, enabling them to undertake work in Canada, India, Australia, New Zealand and South Africa, as well as across deprived parts of London.⁶⁸ Links between the Grahamstown and Kilburn Sisters stretched back to 1906, when the latter took over responsibility for the hostel at the All Saints Mission at Engcobo in the neighbouring

2 Lupton Street, London, c.1936

---

66 A Sister of the Community, *The Story of a Vocation*, pp. 61 and 105.
67 A Sister of the Community, *The Story of a Vocation*, p. 61.
68 Anson, *Call of the Cloister*, pp. 439–441.

Diocese of St John in the Transkei.⁶⁹ From there, their Sisters regularly came to stay at St Peter's for their annual rest.⁷⁰

To support their work in London, the Kilburn Sisters acquired small houses to act as mission centres where they could live and work.⁷¹ A proposal that part of the Lupton Street house should be taken over was 'thankfully accepted' by the Grahamstown CR community on 1 August 1930, whereupon two Sisters were sent to London to take possession.⁷² However, in 1933, the Sisters of the Church withdrew from Lupton Street, leaving it solely as the London base for the Grahamstown Sisters.

Before the jubilee in 1934, Mother Edith had reorganised the community's support network in England, the English Helpers Union, or EHU as it was known, to give greater priority to recruitment. She sought to draw friends and supporters more closely into a fellowship to help secure new aspirants and helpers. Therefore, as well as organising retreats and quiet days for members of the new fellowship, the Sisters at Lupton Street were to help and encourage aspirants. Here Sister Dora was in charge. Given all the activities to support the new fellowship in England and recruitment and training, Lupton Street would have been an intriguing base for Sister Margaret to stay in 1936 and contribute her experience.

In August 1936, Sister Margaret's brother Arthur left his parish of Aldworth in Berkshire to become the rector of St Andrew's at Ufford, near Stamford in Northamptonshire.⁷³ Three weeks after his installation, the Watson family gathered at his parish for the marriage of Arthur's eldest daughter, Margaret Elizabeth, on 3 September.⁷⁴ This happy family reunion was to be Sister Margaret's last, as, after she sailed for the Cape four weeks later, none of her family would ever see her again.

The Reverend Arthur and Olive Watson at the time of Sister Margaret's visit in September 1936

Sister Margaret travelled on the MV *Dunbar Castle* for her return voyage, taking another circuitous

---

69 *A Valiant Victorian*, p. 146.
70 CR Annual Report [for 1946], March 1947, p. 3.
71 The Sisters of the Church, *A Summary of their Life, Work and Rule*, p. 24.
72 A Sister of the Community, *The Story of a Vocation*, p. 62.
73 *Truth*, London, 8 July 1936, p. 44.
74 *Mercury and Guardian*, 4 September 1936, 'Rector's Daughter, Pretty Scenes at Ufford'.

'Pretty Scenes at Ufford, the Bridal Group', *Mercury and Guardian*, 4 September 1936

MV *Dunbar Castle* of the Union-Castle Mail Steamship Line, 1929

route. After sailing from the East India Docks in East London on 9 October, the vessel called at Tenerife, Lobito in Portuguese West Africa (now Angola), and Walvis Bay in South West Africa (now Namibia) before reaching Cape Town.[75] Finally, she reached Grahamstown on 3 November, after three and a half weeks of travel.[76] She brought with her two aspirants from Lupton Street, Miss Helen Price and Miss Winifred Mitchell. Both were to enter the community as postulants the following February 1937.[77] Her homecoming was joyous.

Grahamstown Revisited

> Early morning, and through the window of the train we see the grassy hills with well-wooded ravines, and farmsteads in the valleys, and then, yes, Grahamstown nestling among its hills, with its Cathedral spire, looking just as it did the first time we saw it, unchanged in character in this ever-changing world, its very appearance suggesting calm and repose.
>
> Quiet? Yes, though motor-cars now pass along the broad streets in place of the lumbering ox-wagons. Quiet, but not inactive, for Grahamstown goes to school. Or more truly, the eager, vivacious youth from many parts of the Eastern Province, and indeed from much further afield, gather within the walls of its schools and colleges. There with the bright alertness of the modern young person, with all modern methods and aids at their disposal, they are developing. Behind them is a back-ground, an atmosphere, of graciousness, dignity, stability – the peace of the everlasting hills, the security of the family life of those who have made their homes here since Grahamstown began to be, the sound of church bells and all that implies of prayer, or worship, of devotion.[78]

Safely back after a ten-month absence, Sister Margaret resumed her life of prayer at St Peter's. The following August in 1937, on the 26th, the community suffered a shock when, as Mother Edith wrote, 'Our Warden, Bishop Vyvyan, has left us'.[79] He had been recovering in hospital from an operation but unexpectedly died the day before he was due to go home. The community had lost its spiritual father, 'one who gathered all into his wide charity'. As sacristan, Sister Margaret had much to prepare for his requiem and funeral the next day.

---

75 Board of Trade, Outwards Passenger Lists, BT27, UK National Archives.
76 CR Logbook, 1931–1938.
77 CR Profession Register, entries 226 and 228.
78 CR Quarterly Letter, July 1939.
79 CR Quarterly Letter, October 1937, p. 2.

CHAPTER 7 | A LIFE OF PRAYER WITHOUT CEASING

Sister Margaret (back row, second from right) with Mother Edith (centre, second row) and other Sisters on the steps of St Peter's Home, undated

CR logbook listing Sisters present at St Peter's on New Year's Eve 1937, with Sister Margaret listed 39th in seniority

The Warden, Bishop Vyvyan, with Mrs Vyvyan on his left and Mother Florence on his right, with helpers and Sisters having attended a fellowship breakfast at St Peter's Home in 1936

> All through the morning, wreaths [about eighty] and crosses poured in with messages of affection, and by 11 o'clock, flowers lined both sides of the Chancel to the ante-chapel. When the procession of clergy – two Bishops and twelve priests – came in for the Burial Service, the little Chapel was crowded with those who had come to show their love and gratitude.[80]

Through her arrangements, Sister Margaret brought great beauty to the occasion, with lilies in the chapel, spring flowers from the garden on the coffin, and more flowers lining the sides of the chancel. Narcissus lined the grave, and bunches of arum lilies stood beyond it to bring a little cheer. The shocking suddenness of the Warden's death made his burial a raw occasion for the community. 'It is impossible to say how much we miss him,' wrote Mother Edith.[81]

---

80 CR Quarterly Letter, October 1937, p. 6.
81 CR Quarterly Letter, October 1937, p. 6.

Chapter Eight

Christ the King

THE YEAR 1938 began with seventy-six Sisters, including Sister Margaret, and three novices at St Peter's Home.[1] As was the custom, they were soon joined by others from outlying missions as they gathered for their annual retreat. Branch house Superiors came first, as Mother Edith had invited them for tea on the lawn on New Year's Day.[2]

The retreat commenced after Vespers on Wednesday, 5 January, with 'sacrifice' as the theme.[3] As was also a custom, a senior clergyman led the retreat. This year, Mother Edith had invited Father Runge of the Community of the Resurrection from their priory at Rosettenville in Johannesburg. He was to stay for five days and was assisted by the acting Warden, the Reverend Canon Arthur Hill, who had stepped in the year before following the death of Bishop Vyvyan. The retreat was recorded as 'very helpful and beautiful' in the community's logbook.[4] Father Runge's presence was especially significant for Sister Margaret. During his stay, he would have had time to enter the Chapel of St Mary and All the Angels and admire the bright and moving fresco which had been her work.

Of Anglo-German descent, Carl Runge had followed his father into banking before serving in the British Army in the Great War. After ordination, he was

---

1 CR Logbook, 1938–1944.
2 CR Logbook, 1938–1944.
3 CR Logbook, 1938–1944.
4 CR Logbook, 1938–1944.

Grahamstown 'bird's-eye view' postcard, 1939, from the north with Rhodes University and St Peter's Home campus (beneath the right-hand tree), tower and spire of the Cathedral Church of St Michael and St George (centre), and the ridge before Stones Hill in the distance

admitted during 1924 into the Community of the Resurrection at Mirfield in Yorkshire.[5] This society of missionary priests, founded in 1892, was only the second order established for men in the Anglican Church since the Reformation. Although similarly titled as the Grahamstown sisterhood and with a similar commitment to education, the two communities were independent from each other but linked through their overlapping purpose to serve as educators across the full spectrum of society in South Africa through the Anglican diocesan structure.

The Mirfield Fathers had been active in the Transvaal since 1903, when the Bishop of Pretoria asked them to help rebuild his diocese after the devastating Anglo-Boer War. In response, three Fathers arrived to work among the rough gold-mining encampments on the Rand. During 1905, the Fathers took charge of St John's College, a private fee-paying boys' school which prospered under their leadership. Father Runge was appointed headmaster in 1931. In 1934, however, the Fathers withdrew from St John's College to return to their primary missionary purpose of helping to educate the poor.[6] Following his exit from the college, Father Runge was appointed Provincial Superior for the Community of the Resurrection in South Africa with its headquarters in Rosettenville, south

---

5   Archive of the Community of the Resurrection, House of the Resurrection, Mirfield.
6   Wilkinson, *The Community of the Resurrection*, p. 221.

of Johannesburg. In this capacity, he came to Grahamstown in January 1928 to lead the Sisters' retreat.[7]

The CR Fathers' work took another momentous turn in 1934 when the Bishop of Pretoria asked them to take over the parish of Christ the King in Sophiatown. This new township on the western edge of Johannesburg had become home to many thousands of African and immigrant workers drawn to Johannesburg by the rapid industrialisation of the Rand. Over time it became a grossly overcrowded shantytown. In 1927, a strong-minded and well-connected English woman, Dorothy Maud, daughter of the Suffragan Bishop of Kensington, arrived in South Africa. She had been sent by the Society for the Propagation of the Gospel, having first learned to speak Zulu under Bishop Vyvyan in Zululand. Dorothy Maud soon realised that to help most effectively, it would be necessary to live among the people in Sophiatown. So, with support from friends in England, a 'stand' was acquired, and in 1929 the Ekutuleni Mission House opened – the Place of Peace.[8] Women and girls were encouraged to learn domestic skills at the new facility, and many men benefited from similar opportunities to improve their lives.

Father Raymond Raynes CR, who arrived to take charge of the parish of Christ the King, began to work closely with Dorothy Maud.

> Raynes and Dorothy Maud accepted the challenge. In six years, they built three churches, seven schools, three nursery schools, and had over six thousand children under their care. They expanded the hospital and built a swimming bath: they raised all the money for this themselves. In the township they got water, lighting, sanitation and roads. They fought for the poor and persecuted in the courts, the police station, and in the Town Council. They became known to a whole generation of Africans as white people who would go to outstanding lengths to help them. And they became known as Christians, people who practised what they preached, whose beliefs and way of life were worth following.[9]

The Fathers had taken on the small, run-down mission church of St Mary Magdalene close to Ekutuleni.[10] However, it was inadequate for the hundreds of worshippers attracted to their services, and they had no room for Sunday School or any other activities they sought to provide. Father Raynes and Dorothy Maud agreed on the need for a large new church. They had already obtained another 'stand', close to Ekutuleni on a rocky outcrop at the highest point, and set about

---

7 Mosley, *The Life of Raymond Raynes*, p. 115.
8 'The Apartheid Years', p. 1, Community of St Mary the Virgin Archive.
9 Mosley, *The Life of Raymond Raynes*, p. 72.
10 Mosley, *The Life of Raymond Raynes*, p. 74.

Sophiatown, c.1943

raising funds. A generous donation soon made construction possible.[11] The diocesan architect, Frank Fleming, who was a partner in Herbert Baker's firm, drafted plans for a church with room for a thousand worshippers.[12] However, with the requirement for the structure to be so large, working within the modest funds available, he warned that he would only be able to design what would look like a garage, 'a huge and holy garage'.[13] Construction commenced in April 1933, and after rapid progress, the church was consecrated on 8 September. When completed, the church's high brick walls and red tin roof made it seem as substantial as a cathedral. A clocktower, which greatly improved the austere profile, was added in 1936.[14]

Despite being well proportioned and brightly lit, the church's interior revealed the tight budget on which it had been built, with large expanses of unembellished brick. Father Raynes had the ceiling above the high altar painted blue to signify the presence of the Virgin Mary and bring some dignity, but much more needed to be done to make it a fitting place for worship.[15]

---

11 *The Watchman*, December 1942, p. 5, 'James Smith Friend and Benefactor'.
12 Mosley, *The Life of Raymond Raynes*, pp. 74–75.
13 Mosley, *The Life of Raymond Raynes*, p. 75.
14 Mosley, *The Life of Raymond Raynes*, p. 76.
15 Mosley, *The Life of Raymond Raynes*, p. 75.

Having stayed at St Peter's Home for five days to join a retreat in November 1922, Dorothy Maud was familiar with the Grahamstown Sisters. She returned for four days in March 1928 when Sister Margaret was completing her fresco work.[16] Having seen, like Father Runge, what might be possible to improve the austere east end of Christ the King through the application of plaster and paint, as at St Mary and All the Angels, she most likely helped Father Raynes decide on a similar approach. Her father, John Maud, Suffragan Bishop of Kensington, who had previously acted as commissary to the Bishop of Pretoria, was familiar with what the Sisters had achieved in Grahamstown. Through his visits to the Fathers in Sophiatown, he may also have provided impetus for the beautification of Christ the King by Sister Margaret.[17]

Christ the King, Sophiatown, after its tower was added in 1936

Shortly after Father Runge returned to Rosettenville after leading the Sisters' retreat, Mother Edith was asked if Sister Margaret might be spared. The CR Fathers had in mind an enormous work that would dwarf the fresco at St Mary and All the Angels. With the matter agreed upon, Sister Margaret set off for Johannesburg for a preliminary visit, making the journey of 650 miles by train.[18]

With the benefit of her training under Reginald Frampton in London, Sister Margaret knew that she would need to insist on a great deal of preparation of the walls before she could start. She had kept up to date with the latest scientific and practical techniques for fresco painting through the publication of Professor Max Doerner of the Academy of Fine Arts in Munich, *The Materials of the Artist and Their Use in Painting*. Accordingly, she knew she needed to persuade Father Raynes to prepare the walls carefully before starting. Any bricks that had 'bloomed' from the over-absorption of salts in their firing would need replacing. Then, a layer of buttery lime plaster, up to an inch and a half thick, would need

---

16 St Peter's House, Visitors Book, 1922 and 1928.
17 CR Annual Report [for 1906], January 1907, pp. 15–18.
18 CR Logbook, 1938–1944.

Christ the King with the Ekutuleni House (centre right) and St Cyprian's School (centre), Sophiatown

to be applied. Father Raynes also needed to realise that her palette was limited to colours that did not react to the lime's alkalis and that her work on the walls would commence from the top.[19] Having made her proposal, Sister Margaret was back in Grahamstown by 12 March.

At their Chapter meeting on 21 June, the CR Fathers agreed to pay for a scaffold and have the walls prepared with a preliminary layer of plaster.[20] When that was complete, Sister Margaret returned to Sophiatown on 10 July, ready for an extended stay.[21] She was invited to stay at St Joseph's Home, an institution built as a home for orphaned 'coloured' children, as a memorial to 'coloured' servicemen from the Cape and the Transvaal who had given their lives serving in Palestine with Imperial forces during the Great War.[22] Frank Fleming, the diocesan architect who later produced the plans for Christ the King, designed the first building. A second, larger building was finally completed in 1939, allowing eighty-five children to be taken in.

St Joseph's offered Sister Margaret much familiarity, as it was in the care of Sisters of the Society of St Margaret from East Grinstead in Sussex, who had

---

19 Doerner, *The Materials of the Artist*, pp. 265–270.
20 Community of the Resurrection, Sophiatown Minute Book, 1934–1942, 21 June 1938, Historical Papers, Wits University.
21 Sister Dorianne, letter to Prof. F.G. Butler, 30 May 1995.
22 Welham, *Hope Blossoms in Sophiatown*, p. 2.

Chapter 8 | Christ the King

St Joseph's Home, Sophiatown, after completion of the main building in 1939

Sisters' accommodation at St Joseph's Home

A Sister of the Community of St Margaret on the front steps of St Joseph's Home with a child in 1939

first come to serve the Diocese of Johannesburg in 1898 and took on St Joseph's Home in 1918.[23] This would be her home from July 1938 for the next three years, where she joined the three or four Sisters sent from East Grinstead at any given time.[24] From St Joseph's, it was an easy walk of less than a mile to Christ the King and Ekutuleni, the Place of Peace, where Dorothy Maud and her helpers lived.[25]

---

23 Anson, *Call of the Cloister*, pp. 347–355
24 Welham, *Hope Blossoms in Sophiatown*, pp. 10–12.
25 Sister Gabriel, *Doing the Impossible*, p. 48.

Sisters of the Community of St Margaret

For the fresco design, the CR Fathers agreed that the central figure would be Christ, robed as a king, with other figures on either side. With this central aspect of the design settled, Sister Margaret commenced work on a set of preliminary drawings, which required numerous sketches and studies to determine the scale and arrangement. The next stage was for the spirit-fresco media to be applied using a cauldron of hot water to retain the right temperature. Sister Margaret's exacting specification required two coatings of hot turpentine, then three layers of turpentine and copal varnish in a weak solution, followed by two or three applications of coating medium with white zinc.[26] Then came her preparation of a sige (silicon germanium) solution, which needed to be applied to the walls to give a firm, shiny surface that she could paint. Again, this was a multilayered task: firstly, a thin coating of sige, applied hot; next, a layer of a weak solution of sige and whiting; and, finally, a second coat of sige and whiting mixed according to the recipe of one part sige to a quarter part of whiting, well stirred.[27]

Sister Margaret recalled that one day Father Raynes had come by while she was brewing all the spirits and gum, and told her that the 'Africans would really take me for a witch now!'[28] The oil of spike delighted her as it reminded her of spikenard, with which St Mary Magdalene had anointed Jesus on the night

---

26 'To prepare plaster walls for preparation', Sister Margaret's handwritten notes in her copy of Doerner, *The Materials of the Artist and Their Use in Painting*.

27 'Sige preparations', Sister Margaret's handwritten notes in her copy of Doerner, *The Materials of the Artist and Their Use in Painting*.

28 Sister Margaret, *Chapel of St Mary and All the Angels*, pp. 4–5.

Christ the King, Sophiatown, before Sister Margaret commenced work in 1938

of the Last Supper.[29] Initially, she worked on the central section, high above the chancel arch, and the upper portion of the walls on either side. Then, when the surface was stabilised and ready, she began to apply the outline of her decorations using templates prepared on the ground and secured to the walls. She wrote that she had great difficulty getting the perspective right for the central figure of Christ, high above the chancel arch, as she could only view it close-up from the scaffold.[30] Work was slow. For much of 1938, Father Raynes was in England on leave. When he returned at Michaelmas,[31] a large confirmation service interrupted work, as did the celebrations for new buildings at St Cyprian's School the following spring.[32]

Progress was also diverted by an accident that befell Mother Edith in November 1938. On her way back from visiting the Sisters at Grace Dieu, she had arrived in Johannesburg to stay at St Agnes's Hostel in Rosettenville. This boarding house for schoolgirls had only recently been taken over by the Grahamstown Sisters at the request of the CR Fathers. Mother Edith had been due to come on to Sophiatown next to see Sister Margaret's work. 'Unhappily, on the very evening of her arrival, she slipped and fell in the bathroom and fractured her

---

29 Sister Margaret, *Chapel of St Mary and All the Angels*, p. 6.
30 Sister Margaret, *Chapel of St Mary and All the Angels*, pp. 4–5.
31 Board of Trade, Outwards Passenger Lists BT27, UK National Archives.
32 Mosley, *The Life of Raymond Raynes*, pp. 104–106.

hip.' After a very painful fortnight in hospital, she was brought back to St Agnes's Hostel until the 'bone having mended well', she was allowed to travel back to Grahamstown.[33] The accident required her to spend the best part of three months convalescing and being nursed by Sister Muriel Ancilla. Having only made her first profession in January and then been sent to join the staff at St Agnes, Sister Muriel Ancilla was not expecting this burden.[34] Given the difficulties, Sister Margaret came to St Agnes to support Mother Edith over Christmas rather than return to Grahamstown.[35]

The journey to Rosettenville was straightforward by tram. On arrival, Sister Margaret found Mother Edith established in the 'Staff Block' with five bedrooms, a stoep and a small chapel.[36] She wrote about her stay over Christmas when St Agnes was otherwise empty during the summer holidays. 'Midnight Mass in Mother's own room [was] a wonderful experience. Bethlehem seemed so truly with us.'[37] There had been another reason to celebrate over Christmas, as St Agnes had recently been amalgamated with the adjoining St Peter's School for African boys, the school where Oliver Tambo, later president of the African National Congress, was educated.[38] Sisters on the staff had been greatly encouraged by the 'splendid success' of their girls in December's examinations across the newly combined school.[39]

In the new year, Sister Margaret returned to work. By late January 1939, Mother Edith had recovered sufficiently to visit Christ the King before returning to Grahamstown. She wrote:

> It was a great joy to be able to get over to Sophiatown to the Church of Christ the King the day before leaving Johannesburg to see the painting which Sister Margaret is doing over the Chancel Arch and two side Chapels. Her figure of Christ the King in the centre with groups of native figures rather below on each side seems to me to be just what is wanted, and I believe the native people themselves are much pleased.[40]

Father Raynes hoped Sister Margaret would have completed the painting for Easter, 9 April 1939. She had not. One of the reasons he wanted the church

---

33 CR Annual Report [for 1938], March 1939, p. 6.
34 Sister Margaret, letter to Cecily Camilla Bannister, 19 January 1939; Mother Edith, Occasional Letter to Supporters and Associates, 20 February 1939; & CR Profession Register, entry 219.
35 Sister Margaret, letter to Cecily Camilla Bannister, 19 January 1939.
36 Broughton, 'Early Days at S. Agnes' School', Historical papers, Wits University.
37 Sister Margaret, letter to Cecily Camilla Bannister, 19 January 1939.
38 Broughton, 'Early Days at S. Agnes' School'.
39 Mother Edith, letter to English supporters, 20 February 1939.
40 Mother Edith, Occasional Letter to Supporters and Associates, 20 February 1939.

clear was because of the Passion play, which had become a big event each year. It drew people from Johannesburg to see what was going on.[41] Father Raynes had also invited Geoffrey Clayton, the Bishop of Johannesburg, to celebrate High Mass on Easter Day. Unfortunately, the mural was far from complete by Easter, and service arrangements had to thread through the scaffold. With a hint of frustration, the CR Fathers recorded that 'Easter procession will be a bit awkward, for the scaffolding is still athwart the sanctuary, in spite of dear old Sister Margaret's intentions of having it all clear by Holy Week'.[42] Although Sister Margaret admitted that her progress was 'not very fast',[43] as her art was derived from prayer, she would not be rushed and needed time to complete this work.

On 31 May 1939, eleven and a half months after commencing, Sister Margaret celebrated her sixtieth birthday. Work on the painting was still slow, and perhaps during Mother Edith's visit, she admitted she needed help. The burden of climbing steep ladders onto the forty-feet-high scaffold and then having to stand on a platform at the top while painting the figure of Christ the King was daunting, especially given the need to climb down and back up every time she needed something.[44] An assistant was required. This task fell to Marjorie 'Anita' Hudson, one of Dorothy Maud's helpers, who, being eighteen years younger than Sister Margaret, was rather more agile.[45]

Sister Anita CR after making her profession in 1943

Anita, a Methodist, had qualified as a teacher before serving as a missionary in Rhodesia. Several years later, she left for Johannesburg, where she contacted Dorothy Maud and joined her inner circle at Ekutuleni. Anita was a gifted artist herself. 'She spent a lot of time in the church running up and down the ladder, getting things for Sister Margaret.'[46] A 'real spiritual friendship developed

---

41 Mosley, *The Life of Raymond Raynes*, p. 91.
42 CR, Quarterly Letter, no. 146 of 1939.
43 Sister Margaret, letter to Cecily Camilla Bannister, 19 January 1939.
44 CR, Mother Joanna Mary, 'Reflections on the Life of Sister Margaret CR'.
45 CR Profession Register, entry 240.
46 Sister Dorianne, letter to Prof. F.G. Butler, 30 May 1995.

First stage of Sister Margaret's work, completed in August 1939

between them', leading Anita to join the Anglican Church.[47] Later, after the painting had been completed, and presumably to Sister Margaret's great satisfaction, Anita travelled to Grahamstown. She joined the community as a postulant in January 1941 before entering the noviciate in July and taking vows in 1943.[48]

Anita's assistance had an effect, for, by early August 1939, the first stage of the fresco was complete and the scaffold removed. The church secretary wrote to Mother Edith to express the congregation's great appreciation:

> Holy, Holy, Holy, Lord of Hosts, heaven and earth are full of Thy Glory. Glory be to Thee, O Lord of Hosts.
>
> What St John saw on the Island of Patmos has been interpreted by brush and paint on the wall confronting the High Altar of the Church of Christ the King in Sophiatown. The Hosts of Saints of all Nationalities appear to sing the above quotation. Your courtesy in allowing Sister Margaret to draw this most inspiring and worshipful picture has moved the Church Council unanimously to agree that a letter of thanks be sent to you for it. At the same time, the deep

---

47 CR Remembrance Book, Sister Anita CR (1898–1979).
48 CR Profession Register, entry 240.

interest shown by Sister Margaret to the children here demands mentioning. May what we shall behold day by day be the means of opening our inner eyes to see our 'Crucified and Risen Lord'.⁴⁹

Three months later, the new murals caught the attention of the national press when, on 12 November 1939, the *Sunday Express* in Johannesburg published an article.

Sister Revives Dead Art – in Native Church

In a native church in one of Johannesburg's poorest slums, a seven-foot painting believed to be unique in Africa has just been completed – by a woman.

The artist is Sister Margaret of Grahamstown, who came to Johannesburg when the Anglican Church of Christ the King was being built in Sophiatown. She has revived in this African church a European art, which has been dead for hundreds of years – the characterisation of the Christ against a local background, in this case against a panoramic picture of the Transvaal highveld.

The Sister, who trained in Paris with some of France's most famous artists before she joined the Order, started work on the painting over a year ago.

Sister Margaret boiled and made all her own paints. The work was done under enormous difficulty, as much of it was done in the summer, and the unfinished building had no roof.

Sister Margaret will probably return to Johannesburg shortly to do two more paintings in the church.

Man's Gift

Two years ago, the Church of Christ the King was but a small shanty, incapable of housing the growing congregation. With great difficulty, £700 was saved for the erection of a new church. Then came an unexpected gift of £1,000 from a European as a thanks-offering on his golden wedding day.

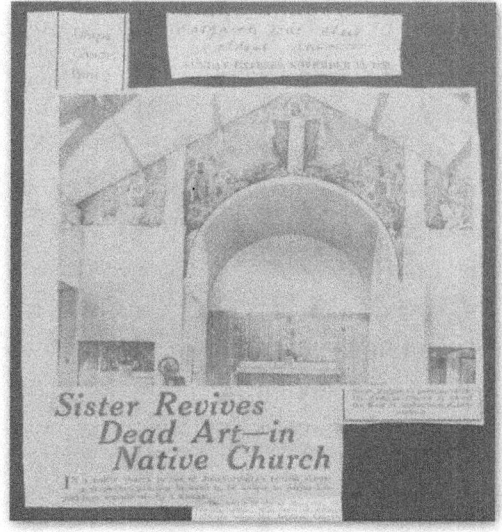

'Unique Church Painting', *Sunday Express*, Johannesburg edition, 12 November 1939

---

49 Mr P.A. Gajaga (parish secretary of Christ the King), letter to Mother Edith, 16 August 1939, in CR Quarterly Letter, October 1939, p. 4.

The new church is built on the head of a koppie, the altar itself being built on a pinnacle of virgin rock. The services are taken in two languages, and the congregation sing the hymns in seven different native languages.[50]

Dorothy Maud recorded her appreciation for 'Sister Margaret's three beautiful frescoes over the Sanctuary'.[51] *The Watchman*, a journal of the Diocese of Johannesburg, also offered more praise:

> Sister Margaret was many months at her task, and besides the trying business of being on the scaffold all day, she boiled and made all her own paints. Some may know that it was the same Sister-artist who decorated the sanctuary dome of the Training College Chapel, Grahamstown, considered by many to be the finest wall painting in South Africa; but her work in Sophiatown is even greater still. Later on she will return to Johannesburg and paint two more panels for the church.
>
> We congratulate the mission on this beautiful addition to their church. – Editor.[52]

A copy of the *Sunday Express* article reached Margaret's sister Ethel in England, who kept it in her family album. Since the outbreak of war in September 1939, Ethel's and Dorothy's lives in Kent had significantly altered. Dorothy had to close her Bridge Pottery as it was not an essential industry. Instead, she took on responsibilities at the Tenterden Food Control Office and spent the early months of the war organising housing for refugees. Ethel remained at home in Rolvenden looking after their elderly mother, while Grace returned to London after giving up her guest house in Minster-in-Thanet. She had been appointed chef at Westminster Hospital, where she remained during the Blitz. Their brother John, who was home on leave from India at the outbreak of war, remained in England and was commissioned into the Royal Engineers.[53]

South Africa was largely untouched by the conflict during the early stage, so the Fathers agreed to invite Sister Margaret back after Easter in 1940 to resume her painting.[54] For the large panel on the south side, the image was of St Francis with an inscription in Sotho: 'Francis mofutsana fa polo e bonolo re rapelle' (Poor Francis makes a simple heart pray, or St Francis prays for me). She depicted him 'kneeling, hands spread, receiving the stigmata among the mine dumps and

---

50 *Sunday Express*, Johannesburg, 12 November 1939.
51 CR Annual Report, 1940, p. 7.
52 'The Church of Christ the King', *The Watchman*, 1940, p. 15.
53 Torrance, 'John Douglas Watson', Watson family papers.
54 Community of the Resurrection, Sophiatown Minute Book, 1934–1942, 29 January 1940.

headgear, and all about him are black children, and – a common sight among the humble homes of Sophiatown – a sheep and a goat'.[55] On the north side, the image was of the Virgin Mary in Sophiatown, surrounded by its people and scenery.[56]

While working at Christ the King, Sister Margaret would have heard that her third brother, Arthur, died in his parish of Ufford on 14 March 1940. He was aged fifty-six. She had last seen him during her visit in 1936. More cheerful was the news that her brother Christopher, having retired as headmaster of his preparatory school in Malvern, had been called to the priesthood and had entered Wells Theological College in Somerset.

By the end of 1940, Sister Margaret's work at Christ the King was nearing completion. She most likely stayed at St Joseph's Home over Christmas as she was not on the list of Sisters in Grahamstown at New Year. Christmas at St Joseph's Home would have brought great cheer, with outings for the children to be overseen, a carol service held in the quadrangle, and decorations to be made for the refectory. On Christmas Eve, the children woke up for Midnight Mass, after which the Sisters crept around distributing stockings. 'Christmas Day was filled with gifts, good food and lots of love, and it was a wonderful time for those children who regarded [St Joseph's] as their home and family.'[57]

By early 1941, after being hidden for months, the painting was complete and unveiled in the presence of Dorothy Maud and Father Raynes.[58] Now that it was free of scaffolding, they could fully appreciate her work and observe how the three panels composed a 'unifying triangle' linking the congregation and priests with Christ himself.[59] Worshippers packed the church to see the image of Our Lady 'with a look of Dorothy Maud, and St Francis with the head of Raymond [Raynes]'.[60] For the unveiling, Father Raynes encouraged women in the congregation to wear bright colours. With the combination of dresses and hats and the church 'full of flowers',[61] Mother Edith wrote about the unveiling spectacle to supporters in England: 'From all I hear, it must have been very beautiful and an inspiration to the people.'[62]

While Sister Margaret worked in Sophiatown in the early years of the war, Dorothy Maud faced difficulties in getting fresh volunteers from England for

---

55 Butler, *The Prophetic Nun*, p. 59.
56 Butler, *The Prophetic Nun*, p. 59.
57 Welham, *Hope Blossoms in Sophiatown*, p. 20.
58 Butler, *The Prophetic Nun*, p. 59.
59 Butler, *The Prophetic Nun*, p. 59.
60 Mosley, *The Life of Raymond Raynes*, p. 90.
61 Mosley, *The Life of Raymond Raynes*, p. 90.
62 Mother Edith, Occasional Letter to Supporters and Associates, 20 February 1941.

Sister Margaret's completed work at Christ the King

the Ekutuleni mission. She concluded that the mission's future would be best secured if it could be passed into the hands of a religious order, with the Sisters from Grahamstown being an obvious choice. Their appointment did not come about, for unknown reasons, most likely owing to the lack of available women. Therefore, the decision was made to hand responsibility to the Community of St Mary the Virgin, the Wantage Sisters,[63] who had been in Pretoria since 1902.[64] They now work alongside the CR Fathers. However, Dorothy Maud could not withdraw until her replacements arrived.[65]

Father Raynes's time in Sophiatown was also drawing to an end, as in 1942 he was called back to Mirfield, having been elected Superior.[66] However, the partnership between Dorothy Maud and Father Raynes had secured significant improvement for the people of Sophiatown. In the closing years of this partnership between the CR Fathers and Dorothy Maud's helpers, Sister Margaret had to enhance the large church and the spiritual experience it offered parishioners. With her work done, Sister Margaret resumed her life of prayer in Grahamstown on 20 February 1941.[67] However, there was shocking news for her after she returned: Torpedoes had hit MV *Incomati*, the Bank Line vessel

---

63 'Ekutuleni Mission', Community of St Mary the Virgin Archive.
64 Page, *The Harvest of Good Hope*, p. 97.
65 'The Community of St Mary the Virgin in Southern Africa, 1948–1994', Community of St Mary the Virgin Archive.
66 Mosley, *The Life of Raymond Raynes*, p. 124.
67 Mother Edith, Occasional Letter to Supporters and Associates, 20 February 1941.

Father Raymond Raynes CR, following his return to England in 1942

carrying the first Wantage Sisters for Sophiatown during its passage off West Africa. Although only one life was lost and the Sisters were rescued from the sea, soaked in oil, it meant further delay before they could start work.

The community must have been dismayed to hear reports of this and similar attacks on their vulnerable link to England and greatly concerned about the war's course. However, aside from all the anxieties about family members in the line of fire, religious communities in South Africa were largely untouched and able to continue with their work to ameliorate deprivation and injustice.

Chapter Nine

The Beauty of Holiness

HAVING COMPLETED HER work in Sophiatown, Sister Margaret returned to Grahamstown in early 1941. During her two-and-a-half-year assignment, the number of novices at St Peter's Home had declined from seven in any year during the 1930s to three.[1] The most apparent cause was the near impossibility of obtaining passage berths for women who wanted to come out from England during the war. As for Sister Margaret, she now entered her most prolific period as an artist, undertaking several long journeys to fulfil distant commissions.

The sole purpose of her church paintings was to add to the beauty and deepness of worship. Her works were thus intended to be placed centrally, at the focal point of worship, usually as part of or immediately behind the altar. In this way, along with all the other accoutrements of rich Anglo-Catholic worship such as flowers, candles, linens, stained glass, priests' robes, music and incense, her works helped create a powerful, colourful and uplifting experience even in the most rustic or utilitarian buildings. Her work also sought to communicate her community's profound respect for indigenous people, following the High Church custom of enhancing the spread of Christianity through local traditions. Accordingly, she strove through her art to represent biblical characters in ways that would readily connect with local congregations rather than impose European representations of the saints and apostles. In this way, Sister Margaret

---

1   CR Profession Register, 1930–1939.

CHAPTER 9 | THE BEAUTY OF HOLINESS

Aerial view of St Peter's Home (lower centre) in 1939 with St Peter's Lodge (lower left), Chapel of St Mary and All the Angels (centre), St Peter's lawns (left of the chapel), buildings of St Peter's School (left centre), and the extensive Training College buildings beyond. Sister Margaret's studio was on the top floor of the Sisters' wing (extreme right of St Peter's Home) in the high gabled roof facing away from the camera, overlooking the gardens and trees to the south (right)

helped celebrate the cultural diversity across South Africa by carefully representing biblical characters in local forms to draw in worshippers.

> Her work always emanated from her prayer and before she painted Our Lord or Our Lady she spent hours in contemplation – then the result of her vision was translated in form and colour.

> She painted in obedience to authority but also in dependence on her inner vision and when the [work] was complete, she detached herself completely from it. It was her offering to Our Lord and did not belong to her at all; but she strove for perfection in every detail, until under obedience she had to leave it.[2]

Requests for her art came from remote missionary settings in deep rural areas as well as established churches and chapels across the Cape. Although the number that she painted for is uncertain, enough is known to be clear that the 1940s and early 1950s were especially busy times.

Mother Edith's office was on the ground floor of the Sisters' wing at St Peter's.[3] There, she would have considered each painting request. Once it

---

2 Mother Joanna Mary, Occasional Letter to Associates and Friends, 6 August 1964.
3 Sister Margery's Reminiscences.

was agreed upon, Sister Margaret invariably made a preliminary visit to assess the requirements. 'She would then return to her studio and paint the picture in oils on canvas or boards, sometimes in sections to be assembled on-site.'[4] Her paintings usually took at least a year to complete, with many of her more significant works taking considerably longer. For some, she needed to return to the church to ensure her composition would be suitable. When finished, her paintings were displayed at St Peter's before being packed up and transported to the church, with Sister Margaret usually following to oversee their installation.

The logbook for St Peter's Home reveals that one of Sister Margaret's first journeys after re-establishing herself in Grahamstown in early 1941 was to Port Elizabeth. On 14 July she travelled there on the 'day train'.[5] On arrival, she inspected the church of St Michael and All Angels, which was then under construction in the Schauder Township, also known as Schauderville.[6] On a windy hillside overlooking the Indian Ocean, this new township had been laid out in 1935 as part of the city's programme to replace the slum areas of the North End. As an integral part of the town plan, the community received a generous central plot of land on which to provide a church, community hall, school and mission house.

Sister Margaret's arrival coincided with the ceremony on Sunday, 27 July 1941, for Bishop Cullen to lay the commemorative stone.[7] Also present at the occasion was Councillor Adolph Schauder, the 'Father of Housing' and enlightened mayor of Port Elizabeth. He was of Austrian Jewish descent, his family having left Europe to establish a new life in the Cape Colony, where he had become a dedicated public servant. Councillor Schauder initiated schemes to remove slums, build new housing, and improve conditions across the city, and the name of this new district had been chosen to honour him.[8] Mother Edith also travelled to Port Elizabeth for the event. At the dedication service, she took the opportunity to 'promise' that she would let Sister Margaret paint a picture for the high altar.[9] Her announcement 'gladdened our hearts', wrote the Sister Superior in Port Elizabeth.[10] However, little did she realise that Sister Margaret would not be able to fulfil the promise for four years because of other demands.

---

4   Butler, *The Prophetic Nun*, p. 78.
5   Sister Dorianne, letter to Prof. F.G. Butler, 30 May 1995.
6   Annual Report of St Mark's Mission, Port Elizabeth, 1941, in CR Annual Report [for 1941], March 1942, p. 4.
7   Inscriptions on the commemorative stone.
8   McCleland, 'Adolf Schauder aka "The Father of Housing", in *Port Elizabeth of Yore*.
9   Annual Report of St Mark's Mission, Port Elizabeth, 1941, in CR Annual Report [for 1941], March 1942, p. 4.
10 Annual Report of St Mark's Mission, Port Elizabeth, 1941, in CR Annual Report [for 1941], March 1942, p. 4.

The community already had two other missions in Port Elizabeth, each with various offshoots and activities. The oldest was in the parish of St Mark in the city's multiracial North End, including the large and successful St Mark's School.[11] A new branch house, built on Elizabeth Street in 1914, was where Sister Margaret most likely stayed.[12] The community also maintained St Francis Xavier's Church and School to serve the Chinese community in the North End, for which Sister Margaret had painted 'A Missionary Saint Stepping Ashore' in 1934. Further work was undertaken in the city at St James's School at Korsten.

While in Port Elizabeth, Sister Margaret also visited the parish of St Gregory at Fairview on the western side. For this parish, she decided to paint three separate images of 'The Risen Christ' for their new hall.[13] The small church of St James at Sidwell in the North End, dating from 1924, also received Sister Margaret's attention. For this church, she was to paint an altarpiece.[14] Gathering the details for all these works took Sister Margaret a month before she was ready to return to Grahamstown on 13 August.[15] Once back, she started on the three pictures for St Gregory's. She returned to Fairview in December 1940 for another look, returning to Grahamstown on the 15th 'by the afternoon train'.[16]

'Elevation of the chalice', devotional card for an unknown Sister

Sometime earlier, Mother Edith had asked her to paint devotional cards for her to give the Sisters. Mother Edith decided which card was most suitable for whom and added a quotation as a personal message.[17] At Easter 1942, Sister Theresa received 'Lift up your eyes to the heavens, your salvation shall be forever'; Sister Beatrice, 'He is Risen as He said'; Sister Eva, 'Grace be unto you and peace'; Sister Rosemary, 'O Receive the gift that is given for you'; and Sister Ethel Maria, 'He is altogether lovely'.[18] Most cards were about five inches in height, making them suitable as

---

11 A Sister of the Community, *Mother Cecile in South Africa*, p. 23; & CR, 'St Mark's School, Port Elizabeth (1887) – 1892 – 1970'.
12 Inscription on commemorative stone.
13 Butler, *The Prophetic Nun*, p. 82.
14 Butler, *The Prophetic Nun*, pp. 79–80.
15 Sister Dorianne, letter to Prof. F.G. Butler, 30 May 1995.
16 Sister Dorianne, letter to Prof. F.G. Butler, 30 May 1995.
17 Sister Dorianne, letter to Prof. F.G. Butler, 3 July 1995.
18 Archive of the Community of the Resurrection of Our Lord, St Peter's Home, Grahamstown.

 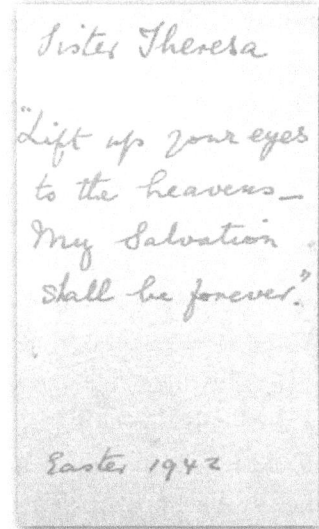 

Devotional cards for Sister Theresa CR (left and centre) and Sister Rosemary (right), Easter 1942

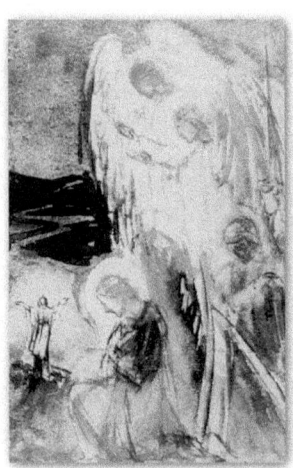

'He shall give His angels charge over thee', devotional card for Sister Jeanette on her birthday, 28 March 1943

'O Lamb of God, who on our behalf was slain upon the cruel tree', Devotional card for Sister Eleanor CR, 14 March 1943

 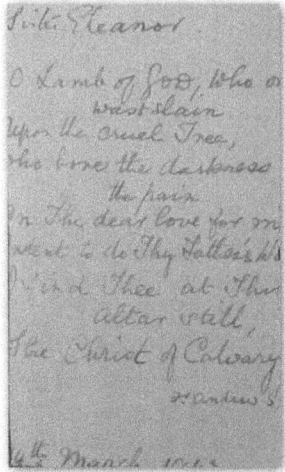

bookmarks or Bible passage markers, which was perhaps part of Mother Edith's intention. Most were on a single sheet of card; some had a simple fold, others a double fold to stand open. These cards were 'greatly valued' and passed from Sister to Sister, just as their prayerbooks and breviaries did, some embellished with further inscriptions.[19]

The next church commission came from an unexpected quarter, the Army Headquarters at Roberts Heights near Pretoria. In 1902, Lord Kitchener had laid the foundation stone for the camp's first Anglican church, which served Imperial forces until 1914. Although there was a second temporary church in the 1930s, it was not until 1940 that the Garrison Church of Christ the King was completed and consecrated by the Bishop of Pretoria.[20] Sister Margaret's work in nearby Sophiatown may have prompted the Chaplain General to ask Mother Edith if her artist might assist.[21] The answer must have been affirmative, as Sister Margaret began to work out designs. Then, on 11 November 1942, she set off for Pretoria by train.[22]

Although Mother Edith had written that Sister Margaret was to paint panels for the Garrison Church, this did not turn out to be entirely correct.[23] Instead, it seems she designed stained glass panels for two windows in the sanctuary as part of the chaplain's desire to 'improve and beautify' that space.[24] While in Pretoria, she stayed at St Mary's Diocesan School for Girls at Hillcrest, which Sisters from the Community of St Mary the Virgin in Wantage had taken charge of since 1903.[25] Under their leadership, the school had grown from strength to strength.[26] Sister Margaret was to remain there for five weeks until after the end of term, returning to Grahamstown on 19 December in time for Christmas 'on the afternoon train'.[27]

Over the years, Sister Margaret most probably designed stained glass panels for several other churches, but there is no existing record. One certainty, however, was her work for St Luke's, Baragwanath, near Johannesburg, where a memorial

---

19 Sister Dorianne, letter to Prof. F.G. Butler, 2 June 1995.
20 'A Short History of the CPSA Congregation and Church in Thaba Tshwane (Voortrekkerhoogte, Roberts Heights)' (n.d.).
21 Mother Edith, Occasional Letter to Friends and Associates, 3 October 1942.
22 Sister Dorianne, letter to Prof. F.G. Butler, 30 May 1995.
23 Mother Edith, Occasional Letter to Friends and Associates, 3 October 1942.
24 'A Short History of the CPSA Congregation and Church in Thaba Tshwane (Voortrekkerhoogte, Roberts Heights)'. The glass was duly installed, but with their design credited to B. Watson, rather than M. Watson, her actual contribution for the church is unclear. Butler, *The Prophetic Nun*, p. 40.
25 Mother Edith, Occasional Letter to Friends and Associates, 3 October 1942.
26 'History of the School', St Mary's Diocesan School for Girls, Pretoria, website.
27 Sister Dorianne, letter to Prof. F.G. Butler, 30 May 1995.

window for Mr Donald Allen, a senior hospital administrator, who died in 1958, has been attributed to her. The window fittingly, depicted St Martin de Porres, patron saint of health workers and all seeking racial harmony.[28]

In January 1943, Sister Margaret participated in the usual Sisters' retreat and Chapter meeting at St Peter's, having been absent the two previous years. The attendance of Father George Scott Dakers of the Society of St John the Evangelist to lead the retreat this year perpetuated a link that went back to the 1920s and to Father Noel. These five days offered her an opportunity to reflect on all that had recently occurred, including her mother's death during the previous May and the ordination of her brother Christopher in the crypt of St Paul's Cathedral in London.[29]

Aside from her church art and devotional cards, Sister Margaret painted watercolours in a lighter style, with the two chapels at St Peter's her most favoured structures, complemented with the lush and colourful foliage of the Eastern Cape. Her works were usually unsigned,[30] although she occasionally placed a discreet M.C.R. on one corner. One recipient of her work was Miss Rollie Beresford when she retired as matron of Bangor House at St Peter's.[31] Other canvasses were completed as wedding presents or sold to help raise funds. In 1942, a brightly lit 'River Scene' with distant mountain ridges was given to Merle Webb, a senior student at the Training College, for her twenty-first birthday. In contrast, Sister Margaret completed a small, sombre line drawing of the 'Elevation of the Chalice' sometime around 1943. Many years later, this was found tucked into a departed Sister's Bible, a place for which it was, most likely, intended.[32]

St Andrew's Church, resting in open countryside adjacent to Chilton Farm in 2022

In August 1943, a request reached Mother Edith for a painting to be completed for the small rural church of St Andrew's, Chilton, on the wayside in open country about a hundred miles north-east of Grahamstown. The church was built by local farming families, of whom the Gibbenses of Chilton Farm, just opposite, served prominently as

---

28 Butler, *The Prophetic Nun*, pp. 41–42.
29 Ethel Watson's diary, 1943, Watson family papers.
30 Beth Denton, letter to Prof. F.G. Butler, 20 September 1995.
31 Mary E. Hall, letter to Prof. F.G. Butler, 9 August 1995.
32 Butler, *The Prophetic Nun*, p. 45.

CHAPTER 9 | THE BEAUTY OF HOLINESS

'Mother Behold Thy Son, Son Behold Thy Mother', installed at the St Andrew's Church, Chilton, in 2022

wardens and caretakers. At the vestry meeting on Sunday, 19 April 1943, the Reverend Father Charles Hill explained that the painting would be a gift from Mrs Lavinia Dell in memory of her parents.[33] With an agreement reached, Sister Margaret most likely travelled to Chilton soon after the meeting to determine what was required. She was to paint an altar panel, to be hung beneath the east window, depicting Christ on the Cross, entitled 'Mother Behold Thy Son, Son Behold Thy Mother'. This work was to be a variation on a composition similar to the reredos picture of 'Christ on the Cross', which she was working on for St James the Less at Sidwell, Port Elizabeth, in 1932. This likeness enabled her to complete the new work surprisingly swiftly, as the following March, Mother Edith wrote about the community's privilege in sending the picture off:

> The subject is of Calvary, our Lady and St John standing at the foot of the cross. The figure of our Lord on the Cross is surrounded by a nimbus (or 'halo of glory' as it was described) painted in greens and blues and oranges such as are seen in dewdrops with the sun shining through them. The idea is that earthly suffering is illuminated and beautified when brought into union with the Passion and seen in the glory of that Perfect Sacrifice. Our Lady is

---

33 Vestry meeting minutes of St Andrew's Church, Chilton, 19 April 1943, St Andrew's Church.

St Gabriel's Home, Bulawayo   St John's Chapel at St Gabriel's Home, Bulawayo

St John's Chapel after restoration in 1945, with the three altar panels by Sister Margaret CR

painted looking upwards, offering her loving desire to share in the redemptive work of her Son, and St John adores in sorrowing love, joining with himself all sufferers.[34]

Given her usual practice, Sister Margaret most likely followed the picture to Chilton by car to oversee its installation. At the following vestry meeting on 16 April 1945, a vote of thanks was passed for the beautiful picture given by Mrs Lavinia Dell.[35]

Another request came in 1944 when Sister Margaret was asked to paint for the Chapel of St John at St Gabriel's Home, the orphanage for white children in Bulawayo. Over the years the material fabric of the chapel had deteriorated and in 1944 a thorough restoration commenced. The walls were stripped back and replastered, three windows in the chancel were unblocked, and a new altar with reredos was installed.[36] The rector of Bulawayo, supported by his bishop, appealed to Mother Florence for help in beautifying the chapel. Sister Margaret's role was to paint three panels for the altar front, which needed to be ready by early June 1945 for the rededication service.

The centre panel, 'Nativity', was the largest, depicting the 'appearance of St Gabriel to the kneeling Virgin Mary who is backed by a tall St Joseph's lily'. The flanking panels, depicting the 'Annunciation' and the 'Resurrection', incorporated angels rejoicing at these events.[37] Sister Bernardine posed as the Virgin Mary, a great kindness and a tribute to this woman who had entered the community as a postulant in 1933.[38]

> She had grown up in the belief that only the best was good enough, as she strove to give her best ... in her life with God. And God had set His seal on her offering for in 1944, just as she seemed to reach the zenith of her powers, she was attacked by a mortal disease – cancer. For long months she bore the weakness and suffered most patiently, keeping her interests ... and praying earnestly ... daily growing nearer to God.[39]

Sister Margaret thus captured an image of this frail and suffering woman before she died four months later.[40] The panels were sent from Grahamstown and installed, 'adding greatly to the beauty of the Chapel'.[41] At the dedication on

---

34 CR Annual Report [for 1943], March 1944.
35 St Andrew's, Chilton, Vestry Meetings Minute Book, pp. 17–18.
36 *St Gabriel's Home for Children, Bulawayo* (1946), p. 13.
37 Butler, *The Prophetic Nun*, p. 85.
38 F.G. Butler, notes from interview with Sister Maryan CR, 7 April 1996.
39 CR Remembrance Book, Sister Bernardine CR (1895–1945).
40 CR Remembrance Book, Sister Bernardine CR (1895–1945).
41 CR, Occasional Letter, October 1947.

19 June, Edward Francis Paget, Bishop of Southern Rhodesia, ended his address with a tribute to all who had contributed to its restoration: 'It [the Chapel] has reached the height of its glory and is established as the central feature of this Home. In this building, re-adorned, beautified and fulfilled, we begin another day, for out of this power-house of the spirit will go forth human lives dedicated to the service of God.'[42]

The community's other establishment in Bulawayo was St Peter's Diocesan School for Girls, which opened in 1911. This school was another large undertaking, with six Sisters on the staff in 1933 and many lay teachers overseeing what was to become a large and successful preparatory and senior school for white girls.[43] As the school grew, its buildings were added to and adjusted. There had been hope in the 1930s that money would be found for a new chapel, as although what they had was 'very nice indeed', it was inadequate.[44] Instead of replacing it, a humbler plan was adopted to enlarge the current chapel, which was originally built as the assembly room. The space was enlarged, and the room was made more church-like by raising the sanctuary floor to form a communion step.[45] A photograph of the altar and reredos from 1937 shows three altar panels. If these were her work, Sister Margaret most likely painted them in Grahamstown and sent them up for installation.[46]

Altar and reredos in the Chapel of St Peter's Diocesan School, Bulawayo, with three panels possibly by Sister Margaret

Some years after his installation as Warden in 1927, Bishop Vyvyan expressed his hope that someday the community would work in his former diocese of Zululand. He wrote: 'This would be a great happiness. At present it is not possible, but dreams come true.'[47] Unfortunately, his wish was not realised before his unexpected death in 1937.

After the Anglo-Zulu War of 1879 and the subsequent civil wars in Zululand, the Anglican Church was determined to 'replant on this

---

42 CR, Occasional Letter, October 1947.
43 Le Tutla, *Bulawayo's Forgotten School*, p. 54.
44 CR Quarterly Letter, October 1930, p. 6.
45 CR Annual Report [for 1935], March 1936, pp. 24–25.
46 Le Tutla, *Bulawayo's Forgotten School*, p. 21.
47 CR Annual Report for [1932], March 1933, p. 4.

CHAPTER 9 | THE BEAUTY OF HOLINESS

St Augustine's Mission Church, Nqutu, as completed in 1902

battlefield'.[48] Among the clergy appointed for this task was the Reverend Charles Johnson, who worked tirelessly to help the local people and established numerous mission stations throughout Zululand. He then turned his attention to building a central church and mission station. The site chosen was called St Augustine's, located about four miles north of Rorke's Drift, site of a famous engagement during the Anglo-Zulu War, for which eleven British soldiers were awarded the Victoria Cross.

Charles Johnson was a 'born builder' and, since 1890, had begun to dream of a noble church that would become the spiritual home of the thousands of Zulu Christians living in the district.[49] He designed an enormous church to hold two thousand worshippers, large enough to allow people from all his missionary outstations to congregate for the principal festivals under one roof as one congregation.[50] For this, he gathered a workforce and trained them in building and construction techniques. In 1901, they set about building the walls out of sandstone under the charge of a carpenter from Grahamstown. The church was completed in 1902.[51]

---

48 Page, *The Harvest of Good Hope*, p. 52.
49 Lee, *Charles Johnson of Zululand*, pp. 122–123.
50 Lee, *Charles Johnson of Zululand*, p. 123.
51 Lee, *Charles Johnson of Zululand*, p. 125.

He had designed a nave 100 feet long by 60 feet wide, with a Chancel and Sanctuary 60 feet long by 40 feet wide. The clerestory was upheld by two rows of massive stone pillars – each 32 feet high – which stand, rugged and grey, along the length of the Nave. The presence of these pillars gave the church its distinctive note of dignified simplicity.[52]

Bishop Vyvyan consecrated the church in July 1903 as one of his first duties following his appointment as the fourth Bishop of Zululand earlier that year.[53] The bishop served the diocese and the Zulu people for the next twenty-six years until his retirement in 1929, when he took up the wardenship at St Peter's Home.

After her husband's sudden death in 1937, Edith Vyvyan was taken in by the community to live in their guest house.[54] Most likely, it was through an introduction of hers that Sister Margaret was asked to paint for the great church of St Augustine. This request came from Mrs Blake, who had lived nearby. She sought to commission a painting in memory of her sister and had an enormous picture in mind which would span the width of the church.[55] Having been instructed, Sister Margaret set off for St Augustine's with Mrs Vyvyan in the spring of 1944. The journey to Nqutu, a settlement close to Rorke's Drift, located about two hundred and fifty miles south-east of Johannesburg, would have been no small undertaking. First, they travelled to Johannesburg by overnight train, covering six hundred and fifty miles. Then, they continued by train to the mining town of Dundee before being taken by car for the final thirty miles, mostly on gravel roads. Although the journey must have been exhausting, Mother Edith wrote that they were 'established' there in October.[56]

Their visit lasted several weeks to allow Sister Margaret time to assess the church, take measurements, and make preliminary drawings. Her challenge was not only the scale of what she would need to paint but to ensure that it stood out in such a large space and that it fitted in with the church's dignified yet rustic simplicity.[57] She also needed to arrange for a sturdy frame to be fixed on the east wall to hold her proposed work high above the altar. In keeping with the substantial proportions of the building, her work was to measure thirty feet wide and ten feet tall and be hung thirty-two feet above the floor.[58] However, the only practical way of achieving this was to paint across five panels in her studio at Grahamstown and then transport them to St Augustine's for mounting on the

---

52 Lee, *Charles Johnson of Zululand*, p. 124.
53 Lee, *Charles Johnson of Zululand*, p. iii.
54 Jean Spence, letter to Prof. F.G. Butler, c.1995.
55 Letter by Edith E. Vyvyan in CR, Occasional Letter, October 1946.
56 CR, Occasional Letter, 23 October 1944.
57 Lee, *Charles Johnson of Zululand*, p. 124.
58 Bishop Peter Harker of Zululand, letter to Prof. F.G. Butler, 22 May 1995.

frame. With all particulars gathered and instructions for the frame agreed, Sister Margaret and Mrs Vyvyan made their way back to Grahamstown and were at St Peter's Home in time for Christmas 1944.

After the Sisters' retreat over the New Year, the Chapter met to elect a new Superior.[59] Mother Edith was by then aged seventy-six and had not been well. The Visitor wrote of his sorrow that she had decided to 'lay aside her great office after fourteen years of abundant labours'.[60] Sister Dorothea was elected as the fourth Superior of the Community of the Resurrection of Our Lord.[61] Born in 1886, she came to the community from St Albans in 1925 and was appointed Assistant Superior in 1938.[62] At the age of fifty-seven, she was the obvious choice, having taken the helm when Mother Edith was incapacitated in Rosettenville in 1938; this gave her some experience of the lonely position she now held. Her qualities included her expert administrative skills and her capacity for finding the best in everyone.[63]

The Visitor, Bishop Cullen, installed Sister Dorothea as Superior on 16 January 1945 in the presence of all the assembled Sisters.[64] He wrote that her appointment marked a new beginning for the community, with much promise. 'May God bless her and all the Sisters committed to her charge!'[65] Mother Dorothea wrote to the Sisters afterwards to say that it had been a most beautiful service and left one with the words 'Who is sufficient for these things?' However, she had the courage to 'go forward in humble dependence on the Holy Spirit and conscious of the great backing of your loving prayers'. Her installation marked a new chapter for the community, not only because it marked the end of Mother Edith's superiorship, which had stretched

Mother Dorothea CR, photographed most likely towards the end of her superiorship in 1962

---

59 CR Logbook, 1944–1949.
60 CR Annual Report [for 1944], March 1945.
61 CR Profession Register, entry 173.
62 CR Remembrance Book, Sister Dorothea CR (1886–1976).
63 CR Remembrance Book, Sister Dorothea CR (1886–1976).
64 CR Profession Register, entry 173.
65 CR Annual Report [for 1944], March 1945.

for fourteen years, but also because she was the first Superior not to have known the foundress.[66]

For Sister Margaret, despite the hope that she might make a start on the enormous task of completing the 'Epiphany' across five panels for St Augustine, she still had other paintings to finish. Most notable were her three panels that were to be framed as a combined altarpiece for St Michael and All Angels in Schauderville, which Mother Edith had promised in 1941. With some urgency, she worked to get it completed. These canvasses may already have been well advanced, as Mother Dorothea was able to write on 25 February that 'Sister Margaret would be going down to Port Elizabeth about mid-Lent to see to the finishing touches'.[67] She wrote again on 5 March to confirm that the paintings had been sent off.[68]

However, before attending to the installation of her works at Schauderville, Sister Margaret's devotion to Mother Edith determined that she should travel with her to East London as a companion during the former Mother's extended absence from St Peter's Home while Mother Dorothea settled in. Mother Edith needed support as, although she was 'well', she was 'but naturally very tired'.[69] They had been lent a cottage by the Wantage Sisters for a rest at 93 Hood Street on the West Bank. Another visitor was Miss Gertrude Holmes, Mother Edith's faithful older sister and friend of the community from when she used to walk up to St Peter's Home with Edith in the 1890s to help Mother Cecile darn clothes. Aside from walking to church, there was little to do in the great heat, thus allowing Sister Margaret to complete yet another painting.

Her commission was for Father Patrick Maekane's church at Masite, set amid the dramatic mountains of Basutoland. As the picture was to hang in the church of St Barnabas, inevitably it portrayed this missionary apostle. Getting to Masite would have required a journey of three hundred and sixty miles by train from East London, travelling first to the border town of Ladybrand, then on by car from Maseru for about thirty miles south on unmade roads.

Father Patrick was a devout pioneer. Having been the first novice of the Mokhatio we Bahlanka ba Kreste, an African brotherhood founded under the auspices of the Modderpoort-based Society of the Servants of Christ (whose name it shared), he was ordained a priest in 1932 and finally professed in 1942. However, his community, which was to serve his native Basutoland, encountered many difficulties, not least a lack of recruitment, leading to it being disbanded

---

66 Mother Dorothea, general letter to Sisters, 16 January 1945.
67 Mother Dorothea, general letter to Sisters, 25 February 1945.
68 Mother Dorothea, general letter to Sisters, 5 March 1945.
69 Mother Dorothea, general letter to Sisters, 16 January 1945.

in 1944, at the very time that Sister Margaret was trying to complete his work.[70]

However, in 1943, a society of local women, the Handmaidens of Mary, Mother of Mercy, had been founded by Father Patrick and another priest at Masite under the guidance of the Community of St Mary at the Cross, a Basotho branch of the Community of St Michael and All Angels in Bloemfontein. With the number of local women rapidly increasing, 'until there were forty of them', life flourished in the parish of St Barnabas.[71] Sister Margaret's painting would have been very welcome after she finished it in East London and had it sent off to Basutoland by train.[72]

Sister Margaret also visited her community's branch house in East London, the House of the Good Shepherd, where two or three Sisters had undertaken parish and children's work since 1917. After a modest start, the community opened its second successor house at 14 Belgravia Crescent in 1935, adjacent to St Saviour's Church.[73] Sister Margaret visited the house for a quiet day at the start of Lent and spent two nights here.[74] Her stay in East London lasted for a month until 12 February, when she travelled straight to Port Elizabeth to oversee the installation of her pictures in Schauderville.[75]

For St Michael and All Angels in Schauderville, she had completed and sent off three connecting panels in oil on canvas to be integrated within a single timber frame. Of the three, the central panel depicted 'Christ Serene' with his right hand raised in blessing, set against a seascape to acknowledge the church's location. On his right, the panel depicted St Michael, and on his left, St Gabriel swinging a censer, to represent the archangel's power to announce God's will to all mankind.[76] When she eventually arrived at the church, Sister Margaret found that Father Burvill 'seemed very pleased' with her work and had brought the framing men out to meet her. As they hoped to have it completed by Easter, she decided to stay at St Christopher's, the Sisters' adjacent mission house, until after Easter, which fell on 1 April 1945.[77]

> Our Lord after His resurrection is depicted standing upon the water flood with His right hand held up in blessing and holding the Host of the Blessed Sacrament in His left hand. On His right hand is the Archangel Michael as

---

70 'Maekane, Patrick Umzimkhulu (1902–1985)' in Akyeampong and Gates, *Dictionary of African Christian Biography*.
71 Sister Theresia Mary, *Father Patrick Maekane MBK*, pp. 10–11.
72 Mother Dorothea, general letter to Sisters, 19 March 1945.
73 Steer, *The House of the Good Shepherd, East London: Twenty-One Years' Work, 1917–1938*.
74 Mother Dorothea, general letter to Sisters, 19 February 1945.
75 Mother Dorothea, general letter to Sisters, 25 February and 5 March 1945.
76 Butler, *The Prophetic Nun*, p. 79.
77 Mother Dorothea, general letter to Sisters, 19 March 1945.

Sister Margaret's completed works for St Michael and All Angels, Schauderville, as installed in 1945

Sister Margaret's completed works for St Michael and All Angels, Schauderville, in 2018

CHAPTER 9 | THE BEAUTY OF HOLINESS

God's Standard Bearer – holding the Cross. On the left hand is the angel Gabriel with a censer typifying worship. A few houses at Schauder Township, with a stretch of Algoa Bay, are incorporated into the picture.

It is hard to describe the vast improvement the pictures have brought into the Church. They are the result of years of prayer and meditation, and we may expect them to be the endless source of teaching and inspiration.[78]

Despite her anxiety to see the panels in position over the altar in the broad and spacious sanctuary, Mother Dorothea was not able to come to Schauderville until early October. When she arrived, she reported how very impressive they were, 'beautifully fitted into wooden panelling which matches the altar and other woodwork in the Church'.[79] Sister Martha, Sister Superior in Port Elizabeth, also came to see the finished work. She wrote: 'It is a lovely church, and I think the painting has improved the East End wonderfully.' She had an eye for beautiful paintings and pressed Mother Dorothea into agreeing that another of the community's missions in the city, St Mark's, would similarly possess one of Sister Margaret's finest works for their chapel.[80] Although the Mother agreed, little did Sister Martha know that because of the backlog of commissions, St Mark's would have to wait for another four years.

After Easter, Sister Margaret returned to her studio and started to work on the large panels for St Augustine's Mission. In the months since her visit to Zululand, Sister Edith Perpetua had stepped in to help with the arrangements, as Sister Margaret had so much else to do. Sister Edith Perpetua had entered the community as a postulant in 1925 and professed in 1928.[81] At forty-six that year, she had a fair advantage over Sister Margaret, who turned sixty-seven in May. Sister Perpetua was keen to ensure that the panels were swiftly completed to Mrs Blake's satisfaction, and visited the church, 'harrying' local timber suppliers to install the wall frame.[82] Aware of the lengthy time that other churches had waited for their art, Sister Edith Perpetua pleaded with Mother Dorothea that Sister Margaret should not get distracted with other commissions. Mother Dorothea agreed and wrote definitively to confirm that the big picture for Zululand 'must be done next'.[83]

Despite all the activities across the community in 1945 and Sister Margaret's

---

78 'St Michael and All Angels', *The Newsletter (Official Journal of the Diocese of Grahamstown)*, May 1945, p. 9.
79 Mother Dorothea, Occasional Letter to Associates and Friends, 19 October 1945.
80 CR Remembrance Book, Sister Martha CR (1884–1969).
81 CR Profession Register, entry 175.
82 Butler, *The Prophetic Nun*, p. 86.
83 Mother Dorothea, general letter to Sisters, 9 April 1945.

preoccupation with her work, VE Day on 8 May must have come as an enormous relief. John, her only brother to have seen active service in this conflict, had been promoted in the Army as a lieutenant colonel. In early 1946, Sister Margaret received the sad news that her eldest sister, Ethel, had died in Kent on 30 January. After the war, Ethel had returned to live with Dorothy at the Bridge Pottery in Rolvenden, where she suffered a stroke. She was aged sixty.[84] More sadness followed on 14 September the following year when her eldest brother, Frederick, succumbed to the family heart disease and died in Philadelphia.

By early August 1946, Mother Dorothea was able to report that Sister Margaret was doing as she said that she would: 'working very hard at the picture for Zululand'. Also, she hoped to get the panels 'pinned up in St Peter's School before it was packed up so that everyone could see it'.[85] Perhaps the Mother had not realised the scale of this work, as, rather than a single picture which could be 'pinned up', space was needed for five panels stretching almost thirty feet across and ten feet tall. In completing them in sixteen months, Sister Margaret had worked unusually fast for such a substantial commission. Evidently, it was not possible to show the entirety of Sister Margaret's work, as only the three central panels were put on display in one of the St Peter's School classrooms over a weekend. Nonetheless, 'many were very glad to have the opportunity of seeing it'.[86] Mother Dorothea wrote: 'Ethelwyn Russell got two very good snaps – we are surprised that it came out so well – but the room was not quite wide enough, so the very nice servers at either end are not included in the photograph.'[87] Mrs Vyvyan wrote to convey her satisfaction:

An Appreciation

> In one of the classrooms at St Peter's School, Grahamstown, on a Saturday and Sunday towards the end of August was exhibited a strikingly beautiful picture painted by Sister Margaret CR. The picture, a description of which follows, has been given as a memorial to her sister Miss Maud, by Mrs Blake who lived at or near St Augustine's Mission, Zululand for many years, and is to be placed in the Sanctuary of the great church there. Its subject is an Epiphany – our Lady and the Holy Child in the centre medallion and a group of worshippers either side. The figures of these worshippers are full of life and of adoration and joy. On the right hand of our Lady stands St Augustine in cope and mitre, the inspiration for this figure having been drawn from an early photograph of Bishop Vyvyan, sometime Bishop of that Diocese.

---

84 Dorothy Watson's childhood account (late 1960s), Watson family papers.
85 Mother Dorothea, general letter to Sisters, 12 August 1946.
86 Mother Dorothea, general letter to Sisters, 2 September 1946.
87 Mother Dorothea, general letter to Sisters, 2 September 1946.

Below him kneels a Zulu Deacon, an acolyte and angels are grouped beyond. The left-hand central figure is that of St Monica, vivid and splendid both in pose and colouring. The kneeling figure of a Priest is strikingly real and reminiscent of the Founder of the Mission and the Builder of the church in which the picture is to be placed: Archdeacon Charles Johnson. Among the worshippers round about Our Lady and the Holy Child are angels with faces representing different nations, African and European. One very beautiful figure on the left side is that of a Zulu girl, quite young, recalling one who was truly a martyr some years ago. During a beer drink in a heathen kraal this small girl was held over a fire and terribly burnt as a punishment for having attended the preaching of a Christian Catechist. The women of the kraal did what they could for her and brought her to the ladies of the Mission at KwaMagwaza, and she was lovingly tended in the hospital there. The injuries were so severe that there was no possibility of recovery, but she lived for about a month, for the last part of which she was sent back to the kraal where the frightened Headman offered to give her anything she wanted. All she asked for was that the Catechist might come to her, and for this she asked repeatedly until at last he was allowed to come and Babazile was baptised before she died. That kraal is now entirely Christian as a consequence of the courage and devotion of Babazile.

This beautiful picture now being placed in the church will carry a message into the heart of Zululand; it is full of the spirit of worship and welcome.

Edith E. Vyvyan[88]

The final task was to get the panels packed up and ready for collection by the hauliers, who were to transport them by road for nearly six hundred miles, a journey which would take them four or five days across mountain roads. Although too frail to undertake the journey to Nqutu again, Mrs Vyvyan insisted on paying Sister Margaret's fare. She was anxious that rather than following by car, Sister Margaret should go the more comfortable but expensive way of travelling via Johannesburg by train. All was well until the carefully made travel arrangements were thrown into disarray when Canon V.A. Hoddinott wrote from St Augustine's asking if Sister Margaret could reach Dundee a few days later than arranged. As the railway booking could not be changed, she set off on 31 August 1946 as planned, but stayed a few days at St Agnes's Home in Rosettenville before travelling on.[89]

---

88 Letter by Mrs Edith E. Vyvyan in CR, Occasional Letter, October 1946.
89 CR Logbook, 1944–1949; & Mother Dorothea, general letter to Sisters, 12 August 1946.

St Augustine's Mission Church, 1902

St Augustine's nave as completed in 1902

When she reached St Augustine's, Sister Margaret found that she could rest, as the panels had not arrived. When they did, she sent a postcard to Grahamstown expressing her great relief and asking for the community's prayers while they were put up.[90] Mrs Hoddinott wrote to Mrs Vyvyan to describe the tense job: 'We had two men out from Dundee on Friday to hang it, and it was a big business even for experts, but it got safely up piece by piece, once or twice we held our breath. However, it was a boiling hot day and very exhausting on top of a high ladder. How I wish you could see it in all its glory!'[91]

Three central panels of the Epiphany for St Augustine's Mission Church, Nqutu, on display before dispatch from Grahamstown

Now that she was able to contemplate her assembled work in its proper setting, the mission's schoolgirls were gathered in the church to be told about its meaning at their service on the first Sunday after the installation. At the blessing the following Sunday morning, two priests thanked Sister Margaret and the community in front of the congregation. One spoke in isiZulu, and the other in English. Canon Hoddinott replied for Sister Margaret and later wrote, 'I think she was somewhat embarrassed, but it seemed right to do some kind of public thanking.'[92] Sister Margaret's recollection of the event included a quote from one of the schoolmaster's speeches in which he said that they 'had never known anybody who had actually done a painting but had always been told that the Europeans flew up to heaven and saw their paintings and then brought them down to earth'.[93] Canon Hoddinott's 'most grateful letter' to Mother Dorothea described the work as a 'glorious addition to our church and an inspiration to all who worship here'.[94] With her work completed, Sister Margaret planned to leave on 30 September.[95] However, Canon Hoddinott sent a wire to Mother Dorothea asking if he might keep her until 4 or 8 October to witness the work of the mission that Charles Johnson had founded, which, in addition to the

---

90 Mother Dorothea, general letter to Sisters, 17 September 1946.
91 An account written for Mrs Vyvyan by Mrs Hoddinott, wife of Father Hoddinott, included in Mother Dorothea's Occasional Letter to Supporters and Associates, 7 October 1946.
92 An account written for Mrs Vyvyan by Mrs Hoddinott, wife of Father Hoddinott.
93 Mother Dorothea, general letter to Sisters, 7 October 1946.
94 Mother Dorothea, Occasional Letter to Supporters and Associates, 30 September 1946.
95 Mother Dorothea, Occasional Letter to Supporters and Associates, 23 September 1946.

Sister Margaret's panels as installed in 1946 above the altar of St Augustine's Mission Church, in 2022

large church and girls' school, included a hospital and dental clinic.[96]

Sister Margaret was back in Grahamstown on 10 October 1946. Having accomplished her third enormous work, she might have expected a rest. However, this was not to be, as after spending Christmas at St Peter's, she prepared to undertake two further substantial pieces of work. The first was for St Mark's, Port Elizabeth, which she began working on in early 1947. The second would involve another lengthy journey, this time deep into the Transkei. However, as she started on them, Grahamstown was electrified by the visit of King George VI and Queen Elizabeth, accompanied by Princesses Elizabeth and Margaret, who came past the community on 22 February. Mother Dorothea reported:

> We had a really good opportunity of seeing the Royal Family, for their car nearly circled round the Home, entering the City by Grey Street, passing

---

96 Mother Dorothea, Occasional Letter to Supporters and Associates, 30 September 1946; & 'Rorke's Drift – St Augustine's Mission', South African National Society newsletter, www.sanationalsociety.co.za.

the College and Home, pausing for a reception in the Botanical Gardens just behind our buildings, and leaving the City again by the same route ... and like South Africans everywhere we were charmed with the glimpses we got.[97]

On 22 July 1947, Sister Margaret set off by motor car for Mount Frere in the Transkei, about three hundred miles north-east of Grahamstown, on her next big assignment.[98] This busy trading settlement on the main road crossing the highlands between Umtata and Kokstad was named after Sir Bartle Frere, High Commissioner for Southern Africa between 1877 and 1880. Having just completed her work at St Augustine's Mission in Zululand, in the great church built by Charles Johnson in the aftermath of Britain's disastrous Zulu War (instigated by Sir Bartle, as it happens), Sister Margaret now turned her attention to a missionary church in the settlement that commemorated his name.

Sister Beatrice travelled with her as far as Umtata, as she was setting out on a 'collecting tour' to raise money for St Monica's Home in Queenstown.[99] First, they were driven to King William's Town and then on to stay the night at Amabele.[100] The next day, their journey took them across the Great Kei River with its rocky scenery and on to Butterworth, named after the Wesleyan mission station founded there in 1827.[101]

> One is now in the Transkei, part of the Native Territories of the Cape Province, which are administered by magistrates working in close collaboration with Native chiefs whom they meet in the consultative council at Umtata, the capital. Ecclesiastically we are in the Diocese of St John's. It stretches for another 200 miles of coastline between the Drakensberg mountains and the Sea. Here are concentrated nearly one-fifth of the Native population of the Union – about a million of them – ... a majority still heathen. It is a country of great beauty, with rolling hills and wide vistas.
>
> Wherever the eye turns can be seen the clusters of round mud huts with their pointed roofs which are homes of the people, and also the long-horned, multi-coloured cattle which are their pride and main source of wealth. Here the Native may own their own land. There are not more than a few thousand white people – traders, farmers, Government servants, and missionaries.[102]

The Transkei was an area that Sister Beatrice knew, having undertaken many

---

97 CR Annual Report [for 1947], March 1948, p. 3.
98 CR Logbook, 1944–1949.
99 CR Logbook, 1944–1949.
100 CR Logbook, 1944–1949.
101 Page, *The Harvest of Good Hope*, p. 113.
102 Page, *The Harvest of Good Hope*, pp. 113–114.

St George's Church, Mount Frere, from the west in 2022

previous collecting tours. She had visited Mount Frere the previous September, staying as a guest of the Reverend Andrew and Mrs Hazelwood at the rectory of St Ninian's, the church which served whites in the district. Sister Beatrice went to see the large mission church of St George 'on the other side' of the main road and viewed three large vacant spaces behind the altar, 'where Mr Hazelwood hopes Sister Margaret will paint a picture soon!'[103]

The community's links with the Diocese of St John's were also secured through Bishop Edward Etheridge, who had retired to Grahamstown to take up the position of Canon Chancellor of the Cathedral. He had become well known to the Sisters by conducting services and standing in for the Visitor.[104] This 'quiet, unassuming prelate' had also led the Sisters' retreat at St Peter's Home in January 1946 and later moved into one of the community's houses when his health failed.[105] Bishop Etheridge had regularly visited Mount Frere to conduct confirmation services as part of his rounds and had written before retiring that he was increasingly troubled by the separation between white and black people in his diocese. He would have undoubtedly encouraged Mother Dorothea to let Sister Margaret undertake the work at St George's, especially given her practice of sensitively using local people and images to portray biblical characters and saints.[106]

---

103 Mother Dorothea, general letter to Sisters, 30 September 1946.
104 CR Logbook, 1944–1949.
105 CR Annual Report [for 1945], March 1946; 'Bishop Etheridge's Memoirs', Historical Papers, Wits University; and Rt. Rev. E.H. Etheridge (obituary), *The Times*, London. 21 September 1954. p. 10.
106 'Bishop Etheridge's Memoirs', Historical Papers, Wits University.

Sister Margaret stayed with the Hazelwood family for several weeks while undertaking preparatory work. The rector wrote: 'As a parish, we are most grateful to her for all her work and abundant interest, while we personally, and the Sunday School children, much enjoyed her visit.'[107] Then, over the next two and a half years, she worked in her studio on three panels needed to carefully fit the three arched recesses built into the wall behind the altar when the church had been constructed in 1935. By early 1950, the panels depicting Christ the King, the Virgin Mary and St George were ready to be packed and sent off. Again, the haulier had great difficulty moving the fragile canvasses up to the Transkei.[108] Nevertheless, they had arrived by the time Sister Margaret reached the Hazelwoods by car on 3 March, and, once fitted, Canon Hazelwood wrote to record his appreciation for the art.[109]

Sister Margaret's works installed at St George's, Mount Frere

> Now that the pictures are in place, we realise how very privileged we are to have some of her work. They light up and beautify the whole church. The central picture is of our Lord triumphant on the Cross with various types of adoring people around Him – on the left is a picture of Our Lady and on the right, St George. It is quite impossible to do them justice in words, they must be seen before one can have any idea of the love and devotion which they express.
>
> We greatly appreciated the privilege of having Sister Margaret with us for nearly three weeks, and the St Ninians's Sunday School children very much enjoyed her visit to them. Our very real thanks go to Sister Margaret for all her loving work, and to the Community for their generosity in giving her to work for us in this way.[110]

---

107 *St John's Chronicle (Supplement to the Church News)*, August 1947, p. 5.
108 Butler, *The Prophetic Nun*, p. 90.
109 *St John's Chronicle (Supplement to the Church News)*, April 1950.
110 *St John's Chronicle (Supplement to the Church News)*, April 1950.

'Christ the King', flanked by 'The Virgin Mary', at St George's, Mount Frere, in 2022

With her work in Mount Frere being the last to require long journeys, Sister Margaret was able to revert to the long-outstanding and closer work that had been promised to the Sister Superior in Port Elizabeth: a painting for St Mark's in the North End. Of the community's works in this bustling industrial city, St Mark's Mission and school for 'coloured' children was their first, having begun in 1886, just two years after their commencing in Grahamstown. The location of St Mark's had moved several times until the community was able to secure a site to build their mission and school on Elizabeth Street.

St Mark's Mission, Elizabeth Street, Port Elizabeth

The mission's chapel, consecrated in March 1927, was central in the Sisters' lives. Here they came to 'renew their faith and find courage and strength to go on in the face of many set-backs and heart aches'.[111] However, rather than being cheerful and inspiring, the chapel had become

St Mark's Church, Elizabeth Street, Port Elizabeth

---

111 'St Marks's Mission House, Port Elizabeth', *The Newsletter (Official Journal of the Diocese of Grahamstown)*, March 1951, p. 34.

'very drab and uninspiring' and by 1951 a very great deal needed to be done to restore it. Aside from decorations and new lamps to help beautify the sanctuary, St Mark's was now to benefit from a large altarpiece. Sister Margaret had been working on 'The Blessed Sacrament' since 1947 and, with dimensions of about eight and a half feet wide by eight feet tall set across three panels, her picture was to be another large undertaking. She had noted the exact requirements on preliminary visits and completed the panels during 1953. They were to be installed on the east wall, above the altar, making good a space that was otherwise 'singularly bare', as it had 'only the slenderest of crosses above the altar' to adorn it.[112]

Altar and nave of St Mark's, Port Elizabeth, in 1947, before the art installation, which Sister Margaret's work was thoughtfully proportioned to enhance

With the chapel redecorated and other renovations done, Sister Margaret's work was placed above the altar in September 1953, to commemorate the church's centenary year.[113]

> Done in sections, it is not part of a formal reredos, but has obviously been given proportions relating perfectly to the fine altar of dark, gleaming timber, picked up by the frame of the picture, which is 'broken' upwards at the centre, and surmounted by a small but very clear cross. No other work shows quite how well Sister Margaret could use the offered space. It is a handsome altar, satisfactorily complete in itself; but it has been dwarfed by the great bare space above it.

'The Blessed Sacrament', for St Mark's, Crawford Street, North End, Port Elizabeth

---

112 Butler, *The Prophetic Nun*, p. 102.
113 *Grahamstown Diocesan Newsletter*, September 1953 and January 1954.

Sister Margaret does not attempt to add to the height of the altar. The lift is given by a free floating eight-foot picture framed in the manner described. The theme is the Holy Eucharist: Christ stands on the vertical between the Cross at the top of the frame and the Cross on the altar. In His hand, He holds a wafer; to His left stands a dark-skinned St Mark, holding the chalice; on His right is the Virgin; at His feet are two small black cherubs. Christ's head is higher than those of His companions and this fact, coupled with their containment within a rainbow, has the effect of giving an upwards emphasis not only to the picture but to the entire altar – an effect enhanced by the manner in which the bottom of the picture is dark in tone, relating to the dark wood of the altar, while much of the rest of the sky outside the rainbow is light, toning in with the wall.[114]

The installation of her magnificent work at St Mark's brought to a close Sister Margaret's most prolific period as an artist contributing to the beauty of holiness across southern Africa.

---

114 'St Marks's Mission House, Port Elizabeth', *The Newsletter (Official Journal of the Diocese of Grahamstown)*, September 1953.

Chapter Ten

Fulfilment of the Work

✳✳✳

ALTHOUGH SISTER MARGARET was described as 'very frail' in the early 1940s, she still managed to find the stamina to undertake numerous commissions and make several long journeys.[1] However, her return from Mount Frere in the Transkei in March 1950 and her completion of the panels for St Mark's in Port Elizabeth marked the end of such demanding works. She reached the age of seventy-five in May 1954 and, from then on, would remain in Grahamstown.

In 1950 the community numbered seventy-four active Sisters, with the addition of two postulants, seven novices, and forty elderly Sisters living at St Peter's Home. Among the elderly was Mother Florence, whose death on 8 August that year at the age of ninety-four was not unexpected. She had spoken just before she died about being 'almost on the other side'[2] and longed to be 'collected by the Angels'.[3] The whole community knew the day before that the beloved Mother had suffered a kind of collapse before 'very peacefully and quietly passing to the Master she loved so well and served so faithfully'.[4] A requiem was held in the Sisters' Chapel the following day before a 'lovely, triumphant funeral service', where Sister Margaret's flowers spoke of love and gratitude.[5]

---

1 Elizabeth Denton, letter to Prof. F.G. Butler, 7 August 1995.
2 A Sister of the Community, *The Story of a Vocation*, p. 69.
3 A Sister of the Community, *The Story of a Vocation*, p. 70.
4 A Sister of the Community, *The Story of a Vocation*, p. 70.
5 A Sister of the Community, *The Story of a Vocation*, pp. 70–71.

Mother Florence CR on the steps of St Peter's Lodge

At St Peter's, everyone had always taken on housekeeping duties on top of their regular work, but the rota became more frequent with fewer active Sisters. Sister Margaret took charge of the kitchen at various times and used to supervise operations in her white apron.[6] As sacristan, many chapel arrangements fell to her, and she continued instructing novices on this role.

Another responsibility she could not bear to see broken was the community's chain of intercession, which rolled on in the chapel from 6 a.m. until Compline at 8 p.m. each day to make up for the loss of personal prayer in the increasingly secular world. The chain sought to acknowledge God and recognise 'man's absolute dependence upon Him in everyday life'.[7] Every available Sister contributed a quarter of an hour daily. 'Any lapse or forgetfulness caused her real unhappiness, so much so that she took the intercession herself if she thought someone had forgotten.'[8]

Prayer had become one of the main contributions in Sister Margaret's life. She was frequently before the Blessed Sacrament in the Crucifix Chapel, where she felt most closely united with Christ. Some of her poems had a 'very deep mystical devotion', and she sometimes had 'intellectual visions' that she wrote down but only shared with Mother Edith, to whom she remained very devoted.[9] In a letter to her godson Geoffrey, Sister Margaret likened prayer to snow on mountain tops, which 'seems so useless'.[10] Yet 'when it melted [it] came down into the valleys and made them fertile – and so the hidden life of prayer in Religious Houses was one of the ways which Our Lord used for the subsistence of the world'.[11]

---

6   Sister Dorianne, letter to Prof. F.G. Butler, 2 June 1995.
7   Fitzherbert Fox, *A Chain of Prayer across the Ages*, p. xix.
8   Sister Dorianne, letter to Prof. F.G. Butler, 2 June 1995; & CR Remembrance Book, Sister Margaret CR (1879–1964).
9   Mother Joanna Mary, 'Reflections on the Life of Sister Margaret CR'.
10 Isaiah 55:10.
11 Sister Margaret, letter to Geoffrey & Kathleen Watson, 20 October 1948, Watson

Although she was never part of the Training College staff, Sister Margaret talked about her painting to students and conducted watercolour and handicraft classes.¹² Through these talks, students who had the opportunity to get to know her were struck by 'her sweet gentle smile and wonderful spiritual quality', which left lasting impressions.¹³ She is remembered 'sitting under the oak tree near the stream by the entrance to the Chapel, painting, in her habit of course, in watercolours happily'.¹⁴ When no other duties required her attention, Sister Margaret was 'upstairs working on her art in her studio'.¹⁵

Sister Margaret Evelyn CR, who took charge of the embroidery room at St Peter's Home

Another form of art she helped with was making processional banners for use at church festivals. These painted canvas panels combined with embroidered borders involved Sister Margaret Evelyn, who oversaw the embroidery room. She had overlapped with Sister Margaret for many years, having made her first profession at the end of 1908 before being sent to St Monica's Home in Queenstown.¹⁶ She 'loved beauty and many of the Community's treasured vestments were her work. Work done on them was truly exquisite and beautiful.'¹⁷ Such was the reputation of the embroidery room's fine work that churches across the diocese came to the Sisters to have altar frontals and vestments made. Sisters Margaret Evelyn and Margaret combined to make banners for the Cathedral and several of the community's churches in Port Elizabeth and at least two for use by the Sisters in their chapel at St Peter's, including 'Resurrexit' and 'St Peter'.¹⁸ Sister Margaret would paint the faces onto the fabric for Sister Margaret Evelyn to embroider.

---

family papers.
12 Elizabeth Denton, letter to Prof F.G. Butler, 7 August 1995.
13 Elizabeth Denton, letter to Prof F.G. Butler, 7 August 1995.
14 Joan [no surname], letter to Prof. F.G. Butler, c.1997.
15 Sister Dorianne, letter to Prof. F.G. Butler, 2 June 1995.
16 CR Remembrance Book, Sister Margaret Evelyn CR (1871–1961).
17 CR Remembrance Book, Sister Margaret Evelyn CR (1871–1961).
18 CR Annual Report [for 1925], March 1926; & Sister Dorianne, letter to Prof. F.G. Butler, 19 July 1995.

The community's ecclesiastical banner 'Resurrexit' by Sisters Margaret and Margaret Evelyn, in 2022

To help ensure that work was not unrelenting, everyone had a rest period each day to 'cultivate prayer and thanksgiving', which was regulated as strictly as work.[19] In addition, each Sister spent a day every month on retreat.[20] Sisters could also expect regular holidays, which were regarded as further opportunities for 'spiritual as well as mental and bodily refreshment'.[21] Had Sister Margaret joined a community in England, her holidays would most likely have been spent with relatives each year.[22] Some Sisters received visits from family members who travelled to the Cape, but these were rare and unlikely ever to have occurred for Sister Margaret. Frederick, who alone had the means to travel to South Africa, died before his retirement in 1947. Dorothy, who struggled to keep her pottery business going, could not have afforded it.

For annual holidays, many Sisters received invitations from local friends, such as Sea View for Sister Margaret in January 1934, while others stayed at Addo and Bushman's at the Kowie. St Peter's Lodge was built as a guest house during 1932 adjacent to the main home to accommodate Sisters from branch houses seeking to stay in Grahamstown. The Lodge also provided accommodation for visitors and lay workers who came on retreats.[23] In 1940, the building was extended to double its size so as to offer more rooms during the war when travel to England was not ordinarily possible.[24] Over time, the community acquired two other rest homes. The most prominent of these was at Stones Hill, about two miles south of Grahamstown.

---

19 Mumm, *Stolen Daughters*, p. 70.
20 CR Rule Book (1933), p. 49.
21 CR Rule Book (1933), p. 56.
22 Mumm, *Stolen Daughters*, p. 69.
23 CR Annual Report [for 1932], March 1932.
24 Mother Edith, Occasional Letter to Supporters and Associates, 6 March 1940.

CHAPTER 10 | FULFILMENT OF THE WORK

St Peter's Lodge

St Peter's Home of Rest at Stones Hill was a gift to the community in 1905 from Mrs. Cornish, wife of the Visitor, Bishop Cornish. She had hoped that it might offer some relief to Mother Cecile, who was terminally ill by that year. With the help of supporters in England, she laboured to raise funds and entirely equip the home. The building had been completed with four bedrooms, each subdivided by a curtain to enable eight Sisters to stay at any one time. There was a community room with a 'handsome bay window' and a spacious verandah extending around two sides.[25]

> The site selected was a fine healthy one on the eminence of Stones Hill, commanding extensive and interesting views on at least three sides, and situated within comfortable driving distance from town.[26]

> A most beautiful spot and healthy, with a variety of scenery, and distant glimpses of the sea 30–40 miles away.[27]

> Nothing was forgotten, even teaspoons, dusters, towels, and sheets, all beautifully marked and ready for use. There were, as well, easy chairs in the sitting room and beautiful altar frontals for the Oratory. The grounds round the house ensure privacy, and the name given, 'the Home of Rest', describes it perfectly.[28]

---

25 CR, 'St Peter's Home of Rest – Stones Hill'.
26 CR Quarterly Letter, July 1905.
27 CR Annual Report [for 1906], January 1907, p. 59.
28 A Sister of the Community, *The Story of a Vocation*, p. 35.

St Peter's Home of Rest at Stones Hill

On the stoep at St Peter's Home of Rest

The building included a 'beautifully fitted' oratory, for which Sister Margaret painted three altar panels depicting the 'Walk to Emmaus' in 1933.[29] Mother Joanna Mary later wrote that these works were among her best and that the central figure of Christ 'inspired many'.[30] Sister Margaret greatly appreciated her week-long stays at Stones Hill to sustain the 'required vigour for the carrying through of the arduous and devoted task in which [she was] engaged'.[31] She shared her contentment in a letter to her nephew Geoffrey Watson and his wife Kathleen on 20 October 1948. 'It is a beautiful spot up here – right out of town and on the top of the hills – on a clear day one can see the sea far away, and ranges and ranges of hills. Today I have had a lazy day of reading and writing, and it's such a joy to get more time for prayers.'[32] Her letter provides a glimpse of her contentment with the religious life which she had chosen, to undertake the 'highest work of man, the worship of God'.[33]

---

29 A Sister of the Community, *The Story of a Vocation*, p. 35.
30 Mother Joanna Mary, 'Reflections on the Life of Sister Margaret CR'.
31 CR Annual Report [for 1905], January 1906, pp. 55–58.
32 Sister Margaret, letter to Geoffrey & Kathleen Watson, 20 October 1948.
33 CR Quarterly Letter, October 1926, p. 3.

CHAPTER 10 | FULFILMENT OF THE WORK

East Bank, Port Alfred

Realising that more rest provision was needed, the community acquired additional premises to provide holiday accommodation. In early 1939, 'Old' St Paul's was acquired at Port Alfred, an hour from Grahamstown by car at the mouth of the Kowie River. For many years, the building served as St Paul's Church until it was superseded by a larger church in 1938. 'Old' St Paul's was a 'good substantial building', surrounded by grass and shady trees with 'fine views over the river, lagoon and coast'. The Sisters considered it ideal as the railway line connected Port Alfred directly with Grahamstown and 'Old' St Paul's was only about ten minutes' walk from the sea. The Sisters converted the property to serve as a rest home for themselves and provide foldaway dormitory accommodation with

Mother Edith CR at Salt Vlei, Port Alfred, in 1933

An outing to the beach at Port Alfred for Woodville children, 1940s

The Cottage, 'Old' St Paul's, at Port Alfred

plenty of activity space for large parties of Woodville orphanage children. Later, a small oratory and stoep were added, with more windows.³⁴ Neighbours were very friendly and welcoming, especially the rector, who did everything possible to help with the improvements.

> Many of those to whom the old church was very precious are glad to think that it has not had to go altogether to secular use. Strangely enough, our next-door neighbours are the Sisters of a Roman Convent long established there, and, courteously but with friendly interest, they look down on taking possession from their higher viewpoint, whilst we, from behind our shady sheltering hedge, smilingly congratulated ourselves that our obedience does not drive us to play tennis on January afternoons. So, we have been given another source of joy. Stones Hill will always have its charms and its own appeal, but the sea bears many meanings and suggests many thoughts.³⁵

Sister Margaret's first visit to 'Old' St Paul's was on 24 January 1944. She travelled down to the coast with Sister Katherine Maud to seek relief from the summer heat during a period of her life when she was described as 'very frail'.³⁶

Although she had last set foot in England twenty-four years previously, she kept in touch with her sister Dorothy and heard that Henry had died at Restronguet in Cornwall, aged seventy-two, on 4 February 1954. Her youngest

---

34 Mother Dorothea, general letter to Sisters, 18 August 1946
35 CR Annual Report [for 1938], March 1939, pp. 10 and 11.
36 Mother Edith, general letter to Sisters, 24 January 1944; & Beth Denton, letter to Prof. F.G. Butler, 7 August 1995.

Sisters' recreation in 1955

sister, Grace, also died that month on 28 February, aged seventy-three, at Hove in Sussex. Seemingly, all suffered from the family heart disease, with which she was also afflicted.[37]

Sister Margaret was asked to become godmother to two children, both daughters of Camilla Reppert, who had first come to the community after leaving school in 1928. Camilla had returned in April 1935 as a postulant and entered the noviciate in February 1935. She hoped to be able to teach domestic science in mission stations.[38] Although Sister Margaret did not have much to do with her in the community – 'just CR Rules', as Camilla explained – her gentle kindness left a lasting impression.

Through a dialogue that lasted almost thirty years, Sister Margaret's letters reveal her concern for Camilla as she made her way in the world after withdrawing from the community in 1936, and her continuing support for Camilla through marriage and the birth of her daughters. Although her letters were affectionate and conveyed some community news, they were largely devoid of opinion, being bound by the Rule of Intercourse with the Outer World.[39]

---

37 Dorothy Watson, letter to Stephen Watson, 24 April 1970, Watson family papers.
38 Cecily Camilla Bannister, letter to Prof. F.G. Butler, 7 September 1998.
39 CR Rule Book (1933), pp. 58–59.

Cecily Camilla Reppert on the occasion of her entry into the noviciate at St Peter's Home, Grahamstown, 2 February 1935

Sister Margaret CR standing proudly with her goddaughters Camilla Mary (left) and Merle (right) Bannister on the tennis court at St Peter's, Grahamstown, at Christmastide 1955

Sister Margaret wrote to Camilla on 19 January 1939, from St Joseph's House, Sophiatown, enclosing a little picture of Jesus she had just received on the twentieth anniversary of her profession, eleven days before. In 1945, she gave Camilla her much-treasured copy of *The Cloud of Witness*, presented to her by her uncle's family at Baldersby in July 1898. Giving away such personal items indicates a mind so contentedly settled in a higher space that it made parting with her few treasured possessions an obligation, as well as, no doubt, an act of immense satisfaction.

From the 1950s, correspondence widened to include letters to Camilla's children, her godchildren Camilla Mary and Merle. For Merle's confirmation in 1956, Sister Margaret again gave what she could: the mother-of-pearl crucifix she had received on her confirmation in her father's church at Stow-cum-Quy. There was an unusual exception in 1953 when Merle received another lifelong keepsake to commemorate the Queen's coronation, a pocket Bible, newly purchased from the Church Bookshop in the High Street of Grahamstown. On other occasions when she sought to give the girls small birthday presents, Sister Margaret's recourse was to ask Sister Elise, the Training College librarian, if she might look for suitable books. Sister Elise, a stalwart of the college, had taken over the fiction library on

CHAPTER 10 | FULFILMENT OF THE WORK

Sister Margaret's letter to her godson Geoffrey and wife Kathleen Watson, dated 20 October 1948, written on economy airmail paper with diluted ink, indicative of the austerity at St Peter's Home

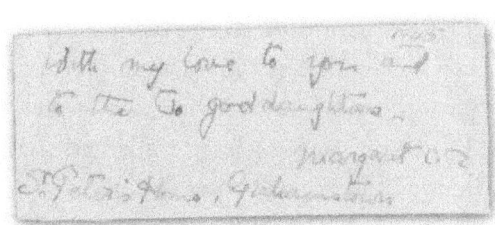

Painting of the 'Virgin Mary' surrounded by plants with the text 'Behold the handmaiden of the Lord', watercolour on paper, mounted on board, undated. This has a slip of paper stuck on the back reading, 'With my love to you and the goddaughters, Margaret, CR, St Peter's Home, Grahamstown'.

her retirement and ran it from her 'den'. She knew what was suitable for college girls, and when she doled out their books, they 'had to be good of their kind!' She would have found good reads for the girls.[40]

Amid the diversity of characters at St Peter's Home, Sister Heloise Lilian struck a different note. Rather than being brought up in England, as was the case for most at St Peter's, she was a 'true daughter of the Eastern Cape'.[41] Descended from General Jacob Cuyler, an American of Dutch origin, who commanded British forces in the frontier districts of the Eastern Cape, Sister Heloise Lilian had spent her childhood on a cattle farm at Uitenhage before studying at the Training College in the early 1930s. She asked if she might be admitted as a postulant when she returned for an Old Girls' reunion in 1938.[42] After her profession, Sister Heloise Lilian was able to dedicate her energies towards teaching and rose to become principal of the Good Shepherd School in Grahamstown and then at St Mark's School in Port Elizabeth.[43]

As an artist, Sister Heloise Lilian appreciated the magnificence and complexity of Sister Margaret's fresco in the apse of St Mary and All the Angels. She was anxious that as the years went by, Sister Margaret should write down the details of her work 'because she was concerned that no one would know how to restore it if she was no longer there'.[44] Late in her life, Sister Margaret followed Sister Heloise Lilian's advice and wrote a complete account. Her words were taken from her little exercise book and published 'just as she wrote it, in her own style, after her death' in 1964 as *Chapel of St Mary and All the Angels*.[45] A story handed down through the Watson family offers an antidote to the magnificence of Margaret's achievement, made by her sister Dorothy, as only a sibling could. When receiving her copy of the description of the work undertaken to complete the fresco at St Mary and All the Angels, Dorothy is said to have explained that Margaret was no good at painting limbs, hence the many flowing robes![46]

Sister Margaret's previous publications included *The Mind of Our Founders* (1948), which provided an account of the community's inception.[47] A third publication, *Mother Cecile, Foundress* (1961), published by the Church Bookshop

---

40 CR Remembrance Book, Sister Elise CR (1872–1960).
41 *Grocott's Mail*, 3 January 2003, '60 years since taking up her vocation – Sister Heloise celebrates'.
42 *Grocott's Mail*, 3 January 2003, '60 years since taking up her vocation – Sister Heloise celebrates'.
43 *Grocott's Mail*, 3 January 2003, '60 years since taking up her vocation – Sister Heloise celebrates'.
44 Elizabeth Denton, letter to Prof. F.G. Butler, 7 August 1995.
45 Sister Margaret, *Chapel of St Mary and All the Angels*.
46 Anecdote by great-nephew Richard Torrance.
47 Sister Margaret, *The Mind of Our Founders*.

CHAPTER 10 | FULFILMENT OF THE WORK

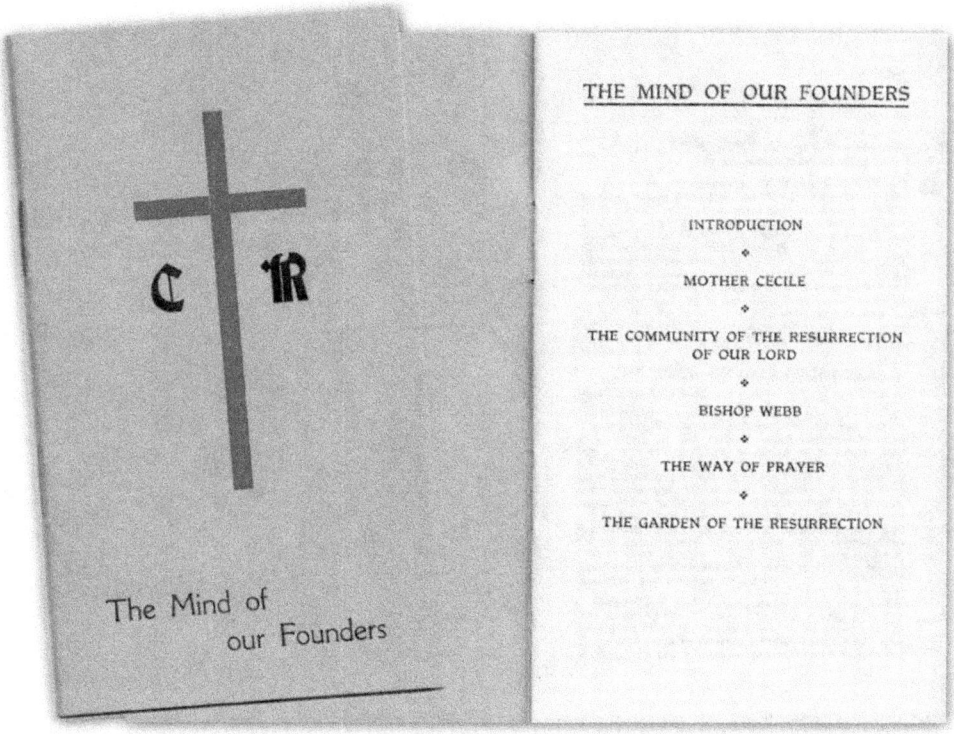

The Mind of Our Founders, c.1948

'Mother Cecile Foundress' Sister Margaret's final publication priced 1/- in the church bookshop, Grahamstown, c.1961

Cheerful Sisters in front of Winchester House

in Grahamstown, offered a sensitive and concise biography of the community's founder.[48]

Within the community, Sister Margaret played her part as a member of the Chapter and occasionally contributed to discussions. She also served on the liturgical subcommittee during the early 1950s, contributing her intricate knowledge of the feasts and customaries. Aside from helping with such ongoing occurrences at St Peter's Home, she found within her the energy to complete one final bold and colourful piece of art: a large canvas for the Cathedral.

As we have seen, when Sister Margaret arrived in Grahamstown in 1907, the city's principal landmark, the Cathedral of St Michael and St George, was still under construction. In 1912 the nave was completed, but the building still lacked the Lady Chapel which had been part of the architect Sir Gilbert Scott's original design. Despite Bishop Phelps's desire for this final piece to be built during his episcopate from 1915 to 1931, the Great War interrupted the project. An appeal launched in 1934 was again delayed by war, and 'it was not until peace returned that work on this piece of the puzzle could begin'.[49]

After James Morris Beaufort, a former Royal Air Force pilot and service chaplain, was installed as Dean in 1944, he was determined to see the Lady

---

48 Sister Margaret, *Mother Cecile, Foundress*.
49 Eve, 'New Features of Grahamstown Cathedral', p. A:3.

Chapel completed as a memorial to the fallen in both world wars. Under his direction, an architectural practice from Port Elizabeth was asked to put Sir Gilbert Scott's original plan into effect. As part of the Dean's vision for the chapel's dedication, the London artist Hugh Easton was commissioned to design the stained glass for three tall lancet windows to feature above the altar. He had a fine reputation for such memorial windows, having designed the notable Battle of Britain memorial window for the Royal Air Force Chapel at Westminster Abbey in 1947. Easton suggested that as the Lady Chapel was to be a war memorial dedicated to St Mary, the window should show 'Our Lord's mother tending her son after he had made the supreme sacrifice'.[50]

Building work commenced in 1950, and the roof was about to be put on by November of the following year.[51] Delays, however, prevented Dean Beaufort from ever seeing the work fulfilled as he died very suddenly in March 1952, less than a month before its consecration. 'He was a comparatively young man, and all thought that he had many years of work before him.'[52] The glass took longer and was not installed until 1954.[53] Beneath the lancet windows, a granite altar had been installed, backed by a lapis lazuli reredos to offset the 'severe style of the walls'. The reredos was also intended to form a 'pleasing focal point in an otherwise severely plain atmosphere'.[54] Unfortunately, this arrangement turned out to be unsatisfactory, as the blue tone chosen to signify the presence of the Virgin Mary was not well received by the Cathedral's congregation.

'Worship the King in the beauty of holiness', devotional card for Sister Jean May CR or Sister Mary Ursula CR on the occasion of their first professions, 7 September 1953

---

50 Eve, 'New Features of Grahamstown Cathedral', p. A:4.
51 Butler, *The Prophetic Nun*, p. 97.
52 'Bishop Etheridge's Memoirs'.
53 Butler, *The Prophetic Nun*, pp. 97 and 100.
54 *Grocott's Mail*, 25 April 1952.

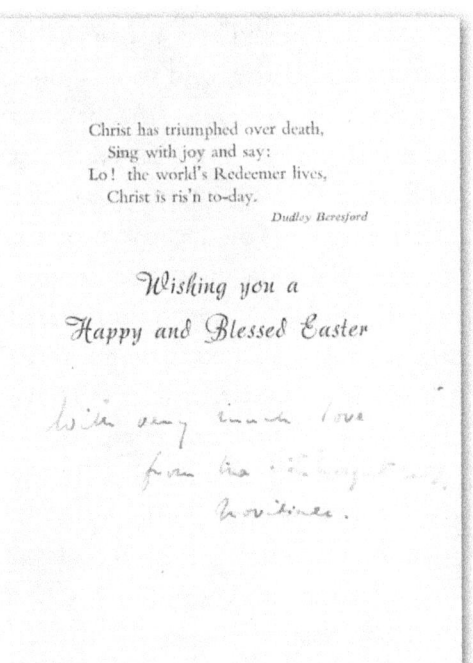

Easter greeting card for Mrs Camilla Bannister, c.1955

Sister Margaret CR, c.1955

Dean Beaufort had realised before his sudden death that something needed to be changed, and he agreed to a proposal by Archdeacon H.A.C. Hewitt that Sister Margaret might contribute a picture to stand in front of the reredos. Having served as Warden between 1938 and 1948, Archdeacon Hewitt knew her skills well. He suggested that the painting be sized to fill the space between the altar and windows, thereby hiding the lapis lazuli. Furthermore, the painting was to be a gift from his wife. The congregation approved, and Mother Dorothea gave her consent for the work to begin. Accordingly, Sister Margaret began working on a large and beautiful picture titled 'Madonna and Child' for this prominent position. Mary was to be composed sitting beside a stream surrounded by exotic and colourful local flowers with the Christ child in her arms. The canvas would be substantial, six feet wide by five feet tall, framed by architectural window mouldings with an additional top protrusion to tie into the elevated position of the central lancet window.

As with all her paintings, Sister Margaret took her time. However, after six years she was able to record that she had been so busy getting the picture finished that it left her no spare time. She movingly explained that 'I have put her [the Blessed Mary] in a garden enclosed with lots of flowers, and two angels, one on each side, to keep the way. There are some little angels over her head and I think she is listening to what they are singing, and pondering over all

The Cathedral Church of St Michael and St George, Grahamstown, showing the newly completed Lady Chapel, adjacent to the nave on the north side, with its three lancet windows

the wonderful things that would happen to her little child when he grew up – some of them very sad things which we think about in Holy Week and on Good Friday when he died for us. At the end, she stood by the Cross just loving, and so brave and quiet. We can stand there too on Good Friday and then on Easter morning we can rejoice that Jesus lives again.'[55]

Sister Margaret's joyous picture and yet sorrowful words suggest that she intended the work to be in place by Easter, 6 April 1958, before Dean John Hodson, who had succeeded Dean Beaufort, left for England at the start of May.[56] Many were delighted with the work, which filled the space with 'abundant joy and appreciation of colour'.[57] The painting served its purpose by adding a focal point to the austere chapel, and Mother Dorothea decided to use an image of the bright and joyful picture as the community's Christmas card.

Although the picture obscured the unloved lapis lazuli reredos, it started a new controversy. While, for some, the work was the 'most celebratory and

---

55 Sister Margaret, letter to Cecily Camilla Bannister, 17 March 1958.
56 CR Mother, general letter to Sisters, 8 September 1958.
57 Butler, *The Prophetic Nun*, p. 98.

'Madonna and Holy Child' by Sister Margaret, 1958, in position in the Lady Chapel of the Cathedral Church of St Michael and St George, Grahamstown, beneath the lancet windows by Hugh Easton, 1952

joyous of her pictures', for others it raised difficulties.[58] Criticism ranged from Mary's prominence on the canvas, rendering it too Catholic, to its being 'too flowery',[59] rendering it more decorative than devout. Others thought an overemphasis on the beauty of flowers was to the detriment of Mary. In summary, 'A number of people did not like it; it was not one of Sister's best.'[60] Another angle of concern was that the painting contrasted too much with Easton's sorrowful stained glass. Rather than echoing his theme of Mary as the Lady of Sorrows, the Mary in Sister Margaret's work was a 'joy-bringer, full of grace, the bearer of new life',[61] though those who thought this way perhaps did not appreciate that, as Sister Margaret had written, the joyous scene also foretold the mother's premonition about what lay ahead for her child.

Controversy over the picture did not abate and reached the point that a decision about its retention needed to be made. One view, made out of concern for Sister Margaret's feelings, was that it should be 'left in place for as long as the old nun who painted it lived. By that time, the Dean and Chapter would have got used to it and the criticism abated.'[62] However, Dean Hodson was not convinced. Some within the Cathedral hierarchy argued to him that it was 'too amateurish', others that it was 'too ornate'.[63]

Dean Hodson, therefore, arranged a temporary board to cover it as an interim measure.[64] Later, he revealed that he had never been happy about the painting,

---

58 Butler, *The Prophetic Nun*, p. 98.
59 Sister Dorianne, letter to Prof. F.G. Butler, 2 June 1995.
60 Sister Dorianne, letter to Prof. F.G. Butler, 27 February 1995.
61 Butler, *The Prophetic Nun*, p. 100.
62 Keith [former churchwarden], letter to Prof. F.G. Butler, 3 October 1997.
63 Joy Pain, letter to Prof. F.G. Butler, 25 October 1997; & Keith [former churchwarden], letter to Prof. F.G. Butler, 3 October 1997.
64 Keith [former churchwarden], letter to Prof. F.G. Butler, 3 October 1997.

CHAPTER 10 | FULFILMENT OF THE WORK

'Madonna and Holy Child' by Sister Margaret, 1958, for the Lady Chapel at the Cathedral Church of St Michael and St George, Grahamstown

but out of kindness he thought it better to leave it for the time being.[65] Finally, however, he announced in December 1960 that the recess behind the altar would be filled with a tapestry. With its fate sealed, the painting was repossessed by Archdeacon Hewitt. He moved it to the church of St Simon and St Jude in Peddie, a settlement about sixty miles east of Grahamstown, within his archdeaconry, where he regularly preached.[66] In the simple, rustic rural church, the picture was placed on the south wall by the font. By then, in the final years of her life, Sister Margaret may not have realised the full extent of the controversy her art had caused. Nonetheless, she may have been relieved to know that the future of her final significant painting was secure.

---

65 Butler, *The Prophetic Nun*, p. 100.
66 Prof. F.G. Butler, fax to Bishop Duncan Buchanan, 20 October 1997.

Chapter Eleven

Before the Throne

✳✳✳

WHILE THE SISTERS lived humbly at St Peter's Home and turned material shortcomings into virtues, they had difficulty applying the same equanimity towards political changes gathering pace from the late 1940s. These created new challenges for the country that Sister Margaret knew, loved and had served for most of her life.

Before the general election in 1948, a new word, 'apartheid', had begun to be used to characterise the racial policy of Afrikaner nationalists. No one quite knew what it meant, but everyone was clear that it did not mean racial mixing, equality, or political rights for black people.[1] For Sister Margaret's generation, brought up in a liberal tradition based on principles of justice and fairness and a belief in the virtues of a common society, apartheid caused great unease.

The Sisters' Rule required the 'avoidance of external cares', supposedly insulating them from such concerns.[2] However, being 'of the world' and having so lovingly built up institutions to serve all races of South African society, the Sisters at St Peter's could not help being concerned. Although it was their custom to keep out of politics, when Christian principles were at stake or matters were sufficiently concerning, they could vote in consultation with the Superior.[3] On 14 October 1945, Mother Dorothea included a reminder in

---

1   Worsnip, *Between the Two Fires*, p. 39.
2   Morton and Gasquet, *The Nun's Rule*.
3   CR, *Constitution, Rule and Customary* (1933), p. 76.

her general letter to all Sisters that at the 'election' on the 18th, presumably referring to a parliamentary by-election, a 'Progressive candidate' was standing in Grahamstown against the conservative United Party. 'The other evening the Warden gave us a useful talk on whether "Christian Principles" are involved in this election, and he believes that they are, so a number of Sisters will vote this time.'[4]

After the Afrikaner National Party won the elections in 1948, it proceeded to apply its programme of apartheid through legislation. The Group Areas Act of 1950, which sought to assign people by race to segregated urban areas, and the Bantu Education Act of 1953, which enforced racially segregated education, threatened several of the community's works. For Sister Margaret, who had been brought up by her parents in Cambridge to serve the Church, Nation and Crown, and, as her father implored her, to confront what was wrong so as to improve the circumstances of those less fortunate, the new political leadership in South Africa after 1948 would require profound readjustment on her part.

Although careful to refrain from expressing bewilderment, she wrote about the 'terrible world – troubles and distress' and the strength needed to counter it.[5] The Reverend Mother was more forthright in her letter to English supporters in July 1960, on the eve of a referendum to determine whether the Union of South Africa should become a Republic and possibly secede from the British Commonwealth and therefore dispense with the Queen as head of state.

> The month of May was a time of great strain in S. Africa as there were many rumours of what might happen when the Republic was inaugurated on the 31st. Meetings were banned and precautions taken to prevent violence. The Community entered on a Triduum of Prayer on 28th [May], asking for the forgiveness of GOD for the sins of racialism, falsehood and prejudice in the past and praying for a closer racial co-operation and more opportunities for the Africans and Coloured to express themselves in the future.[6]

Political changes and social unrest were not the only concerns for the community in the 1950s. The Warden appealed for help to counter the ever-present worry that the body of Sisters was shrinking and ageing. The community's decline would only accelerate in the forthcoming years owing to fewer active Sisters being available to cope with mission work and a greater number of them needing to shoulder the growing burden of caring for its elderly members. Attracting more women to replenish the Sisterhood was essential. The Warden wrote: 'This

---

4   Mother Dorothea, general letter to Sisters, 14 February 1945.
5   Sister Margaret, letter to Cecily Camilla Bannister, 3 November 1961.
6   Mother Joanna Mary, Occasional Letter to Associates & Friends, 1 August 1961, p. 6.

> **NOVENA. October 1945.**
>
> Let us acknowledge our utter helplessness – we can 'do no good thing without' God.
>
> Let us acknowledge that depending upon God we are supplied by His bountiful Grace with <u>all</u> the power and strength we need.
> "When our Saviour rose from the dead, He had taken on Himself and triumphed over every possible obstacle, in our past, in our future, in ourselves, or in our surroundings, which might interfere with our holiness."
> Boylan.
>
> Let us make an Act of Confidence in God's constant and loving desire to give us all we need to amend our lives.
>
> Let us offer an Act of Contrition for past failures, and let us acknowledge that they were caused principally by lack of the will to attain.
> "The first means, which, albeit seemingly the most ordinary, is in truth the hardest, is to will so to attain. But the will must be sincere, hearty, effectual and persevering; and such a will is no common thing."
> Grou.
>
> Let us pray that God will grant us a steadfast will and the grace of perseverance.
>
> Let us pray that:-
>
>   we may look to our Lord Jesus Christ in all things;
>
>   we may strive to imitate His Life on earth, uniting ourselves to Him day by day in heart and spirit;
>
>   we may observe our Rule to the best of our ability;
>
>   we may live in love and gentleness, humility and forbearance, with all our Sisters;
>
>   we may abide by our Vows, living in
>
>   POVERTY)   (as becometh a Sister
>   OBEDIENCE) (of the Community of
>   CHASTITY) (the Resurrection of our Lord.
>
> Let us pray especially that we may see and overcome the faults that often obscure the consecration of our lives – criticism, a grudging spirit, touchiness, impatience, making unnecessary difficulties, an unrecollected manner, a lack of serenity, of contentment, of thankfulness, of joyfulness.
>
> Let us offer a fervent thanksgiving for our vocation, for the happiness of Community Life, for the foundation of our own Community, for God's providential care of it, for our own place in it, and for the work it has been and is being allowed to do for the Church of God.
>
> Let us use the prayer 'For Religious Communities' from <u>Collects after Rule</u>.

Novena, October 1945

Community needs, and is most grateful for, your prayers: it needs also new members, new sparks of love, willing to dedicate themselves in Community to the service of God, their neighbours, and their country.'[7]

Although the overall number of Sisters in 1950 remained the same as in 1940 with a hundred and twenty women, postulants had declined from six to two, and active Sisters from eighty-five to seventy-one, while the number of elderly Sisters

---

7 CR Annual Report for 1960, January 1961, pp. 3–5.

had nearly doubled in ten years from twenty-four to forty.⁸ Accordingly, the community's branch house in London was required to play an even more essential role in attracting aspirants, helpers or anyone able to contribute.

Having been damaged by bombing in February 1944, the Lupton Street house was replaced by a considerably more substantial property at Oakleigh Park in North

The new noviciate built in 1949 beneath the Sisters' wing

London. This property, given to the community, was renamed St Peter's Bourne and was made ready for use in April 1948.⁹ With the resident Sisters at St Peter's Bourne supported by volunteers, it was hoped that the flow of women to Grahamstown could be restored to pre-war levels. Meanwhile, in Grahamstown, a new noviciate was built in 1949, tucked beneath the Sisters' wing, to provide more bedrooms and better facilities in anticipation of an upturn in new members.[10]

The community was to be disappointed. With many new opportunities opening for women in post-war English society, few were willing to commit to the uncompromising and irrevocable obedience of the religious life despite the attractions of travelling to and living in South Africa. In common with all other Anglican sisterhoods, the Grahamstown community began to realise that the religious vocation was no longer an attractive opportunity now that women were increasingly motivated by self-determination, remuneration and professionalism. Declining interest in the religious life was part of a broader crisis for the Anglican Church in post-war Great Britain, as it struggled to maintain relevance in an increasingly secularised society. Other communities found that their structured Anglo-Catholic traditions and institutionalised approach notably lacked appeal to young women in the liberated world.[11]

The community in Grahamstown now faced the same issues and reasons for decline as most prominent English orders for women had gone through. Their survival in the post-war years was beginning to look doubtful. Under these circumstances, every community needed to put its ability to survive before

---

8   CR Profession Register.
9   Mother Edith, Occasional Letter to Supporters and Associates, 9 March 1944; & CR 'English Branch House'.
10 CR Annual Report [for 1949], March 1950, p. 4.
11 Wilkinson, *The Community of the Resurrection*, pp. 340–346.

its work. 'However good any mission work may be, if its maintenance drains the vitality of the community as a religious Community, the exterior life must be sacrificed for interior values.'[12] Consequently, outlying establishments were relinquished to maintain the principal commitments in Grahamstown, Port Elizabeth, East London and Bulawayo. The Sisters had already withdrawn from the Grace Dieu Training College in 1951, and St Monica's Home in Queenstown closed in 1955.[13]

By 1960, the number of active Sisters had declined to sixty-seven, with thirty-one elderly Sisters to be cared for, including Sister Margaret, who celebrated her eightieth birthday that year. In January 1960, the Warden reported to English supporters that the community was 'stretched to the uttermost to maintain its works'.[14] More women were 'desperately needed', but few were forthcoming.[15]

Despite increasing frailty, the remaining Sisters at St Peter's Home strove to do all they could. The Warden wrote that though they were 'past their youth and middle-age too, and very often past their allotted span as well, they are by no means past their usefulness'.[16] Accordingly, at the age of eighty in May 1959, Sister Margaret was asked to take on the role of assistant novice mistress again, a position that she was more than familiar with from helping out a decade before.[17] She took charge of some of the novice classes to assist Sister Joanna Mary, the novice mistress since 1945. Unfortunately, they were not entirely successful, as, although she prepared very thoroughly and gave excellent notes, her approach was often above the novices' heads. One recorded that it was a beautiful class, 'but I don't really know what it was about, though she herself inspired us to love our Lord more'.[18] In 1959, there were six novices for her to guide, but not for long, as two soon left and three professed. The remaining novice was clothed in July but did not stay beyond December.

The decline in numbers and the new political obstacles were not the only reasons for the community's retrenchment. Increasingly, professionals were expected to provide public services. For Sister Margaret, who had written about Mother Cecile's optimism and witnessed the community's development over the following fifty years, the declining need for religious vocations to serve society might also have been disillusioning but for her strength of faith.[19]

---

12 Burne, *The Life and Letters of Father Andrew SDC*, pp. 58–59.
13 Mother Dorothea CR, Occasional Letter to Associates and Friends, 8 September 1956.
14 CR Annual Report for 1959, January 1960, pp. 2–4.
15 CR Annual Report for 1959, January 1960, pp. 2–4.
16 CR Annual Report for 1959, January 1960, pp. 2–4.
17 CR Remembrance Book, Sister Margaret CR (1879–1964); & Sister Dorianne, letter to Prof. F.G. Butler, 2 June 1995.
18 Mother Joanna Mary, 'Reflections on the Life of Sister Margaret CR'.
19 Sister Margaret, *The Mind of Our Founders*, p. 3.

At the end of 1958, Mother Dorothea's second term of office was drawing to a close. By then, she was aged seventy-two, had not been well, and perhaps believed that the community needed someone younger to face the challenges. Accordingly, on 2 January 1959, Sister Margaret voted for the last Superior she was to obey. Sister Joanna Mary was elected and installed by the Visitor eight days later.[20] Born and brought up in County Durham, where she had trained as a teacher, Mother Joanna Mary, unlike her Anglo-Catholic predecessors, had come to the community from a Pentecostal family.[21]

Mother Joanna Mary CR, following her installation as Superior on 16 January 1959

Regardless of the changes around her, Sister Margaret strove to care for the Sisters' Chapel for as long as possible, maintaining Mother Cecile's love for the place. She explained:

> Bishop Webb gave the Sisters definite Sacramental teaching: and it may be partly to him that Mother Cecile owed her deep love for the Blessed Sacrament. We can read this (for one thing) in her great love and care for the Chapel – nothing was too good for the Throne of the King; no pains were to be spared in beautifying the Altar and in the care of the Holy Vessels, vestments, linen, etc. Nothing was too small to be turned into an act of worship. If the Mother did the Altar flowers, nothing was lacking! One felt that she had loved to spend herself on anything that would add to the beauty of 'His Court on earth'. On one occasion she says with such joy 'The Bishop thought the Chapel perfect'. Indeed, the Chapel did grip one by its beauty.[22]

As Warden, Bishop Vyvyan had drawn on the religious writer Emma Herman's reflections on the 'law of the lily' to link its 'exquisite vestiture' with Mother Cecile's use of this flower to decorate the altar. Sister Margaret continued this custom. Just

---

20 Sister Margaret, letter to Cecily Camilla Bannister, 4 March 1959.
21 CR Remembrance Book, Mother Joanna Mary CR (1893–1978).
22 Sister Margaret, *The Mind of Our Founders*, p. 9.

The altar of the Sisters' Chapel, richly dressed by Sister Margaret with St Joseph's lilies

Bishop Archibald Cullen, with Mother Edith CR (sitting), Mother Dorothea CR (right), and Mother Joanna Mary CR (left). Photograph taken outside the Sisters' Chapel of the Resurrection on 29 June 1959, the day before his retirement, when he came to bid the community farewell after serving as Visitor for more than twenty-seven years.

as the lily's beauty stems from being 'deep-rooted in the earth in perfect adjustment to its environment' and its growth is determined by its 'complete responsiveness to sun and moisture and exact adaptation to the soil', so the 'spiritual beauty that is unconscious is as much under the reign of law as the lily's loveliness'. The lily symbolised the grounding and the sensitivity required for a religious life. Just as Mother Cecile's soul had been 'truly deep-rooted in the love of God, and her whole life gave out the fragrance which comes from that source', Sister Margaret sought to perpetuate the flower's decorative use on the altar, especially given its other associations of pureness and sorrow.[23]

---

23 Herman, *The Secret Garden of the Soul*, 'The Law of the Lily', pp. 61–69; & Vyvyan, 'A South African Jubilee' (1934).

Sister Margaret wrote that, whenever possible, she used pure white St Joseph's lilies cut from the Sisters' garden when they had not been 'held back by cold weather'.²⁴ To assist with this devoted duty, she had the use of a flower room from 1956, constructed at her request when the covered way connecting the chapel with St Peter's Home was widened.²⁵

However, in the final weeks of her life, her devotion to the beautification of the altar was challenged by a fresh opinion that sought to curtail this ritualism, as it was said to detract from the centrality and awe-inspiring symbolism of the Cross. Expense, time and simplicity were the reasons put forward at a Chapter meeting on 3 April 1964 to justify why there would be no more altar flowers, now that Sister Margaret could not carry on, except on special occasions.²⁶

The Reverend Bryan S.C. Knowles, Warden, in the company of his predecessor, the Venerable Henry A.C. Hewitt, on the occasion of the Archdeacon's retirement, on the steps of St Mary and All the Angels, 17 September 1960

One of the customs at St Peter's was for the elder Sisters to book interviews and walks with 'away' Sisters when they returned to Grahamstown. In this way, Sister Margaret got to know Sister Dorianne, who had come to the community from Highgate in 1940. She made her first profession in 1943, which placed the two women thirty years apart.²⁷ Sister Dorianne's experience contrasted with Sister Margaret's when her turn came to work away after taking her first vows. Mother Edith had told her: 'You always wanted missionary work, now you are being given your chance.' She was sent to serve alongside the CR Fathers at their great mission station of St Augustine's, Penhalonga. Sister Dorianne was to work here for the next twenty-two years.²⁸

---

24 Sister Margaret, letter to Cecily Camilla Bannister, 28 October 1963.
25 Mother Dorothea, Occasional Letter to Associates and Friends, 8 September 1956; & CR Chapter minutes, 23 April 1953.
26 CR Chapter minutes, 3 April 1964.
27 CR Profession Register, entry 239.
28 Sister Dorianne, letter to Prof. F.G. Butler, 3 July 1995.

Sister Dorianne received one of the devotional cards from Mother Edith in 1943, depicting 'Our Lord' suddenly appearing from a valley through trees. The image had left a deep impression. Accordingly, she wrote that she greatly valued her time with Sister Margaret.[29] 'These were valuable times for us. Sister Margaret always booked me whenever I returned, and I loved her. She was a lovely, gentle, holy person and it was a pleasure to be in her company.'[30]

In October 1963, Sister Margaret wrote that she 'cannot do so much nowadays'. Her correspondence had turned mainly to the health of other elderly Sisters, invalided in their final months.[31] She wrote lovingly about their deaths, always rejoicing that they had passed over to the 'other side'. Sister Jeanne had been 'longing to get to be with Our Lord', and, a week later, Sister Theresa 'looked so happy after death; it was such a sweet face'.[32] Perhaps mindful that her turn would soon come, she added that the All Saints festival was 'very especially dear this year'.[33]

> I do love All Saints hymns; there is one I am thinking of just now:
>
> > How long, O Holy Lord, how long
> > Must we and thee expectantly wait,
> > To hear the gladsome Bridal song,
> > To see thee in thy Royal State.
> > O light perpetual, Jesu blest,
> > Shine on them, Lord, and grant them rest.[34]

Sister Margaret also loved Christmas and wrote excitedly about the festivities in 1963. The custom for the celebrations included a performance of the Christmas story by children from the Woodville orphanage. On Christmas Eve, the carol service at St Mary's included a procession of children going to the crib. After this, Solemn Vespers was sung in the chapel, filling it 'with smoke as well as Alleluias!'[35] The chapel was again full at 11.30 p.m. for Midnight Mass conducted by the Bishop, in his capacity as Visitor, which included a wonderful plainsong chant leading up to 'O come let us adore Him, CHRIST the LORD'.[36] At dawn, on Christmas Day, Mass was sung at St Mary's at 7.30 a.m. with all the children present. Some Sisters would then visit Woodville and Bethlehem Homes for a

---

29 Sister Dorianne, letter to Prof. F.G. Butler, 3 July 1995.
30 Sister Dorianne, letter to Prof. F.G. Butler, 2 June 1995.
31 Sister Margaret, letter to Cecily Camilla Bannister, 28 October 1963.
32 Sister Margaret, letter to Cecily Camilla Bannister, 7 November 1963.
33 Sister Margaret, letter to Cecily Camilla Bannister, 7 November 1963.
34 Sister Margaret, letter to Cecily Camilla Bannister, 7 November 1963.
35 Mother Joanna Mary, Occasional Letter to Associates and Friends, 1 August 1961.
36 Mother Joanna Mary, Occasional Letter to Associates and Friends, 1 August 1961.

Christmas entertainment in the Chapel of St Mary and All the Angels performed under Sister Margaret's fresco, December 1960

nativity play and be with the children when they opened their presents. Workers and guests shared the Sisters' Christmas dinner, and although the weather could be scorching, there was turkey and plum pudding. In the afternoon, all assembled for a tea party on the Training College lawn to which the Bishop, clergy and many associates came. The big jacaranda trees provided shade for what was always a 'very friendly gathering'. 'Then follow Devotions before the Blessed Sacrament, the Second Vespers of Christmas, Compline and Lauds of St Stephen. So ends a wonderful day!'[37] Two years later, she wrote:

> We had a lovely Christmas. The Bishop came to sing Midnight Mass for us and it did seem a specially lovely one – the chapel was full, as all the Sisters go if they can – even the 90-year-olds. At midnight there is something so wonderful in the stillness all around, as there would have been when the Lord was born. But time does not really matter, it is the gift of the Presence of the Holy Child within us that we look for. Be born with us, abide with us, O Christ Emmanuel.[38]

Sister Margaret started the new year by joining the Sisters' retreat in early January, following the usual pattern. Then, on 22 January 1964, she celebrated the golden jubilee of her profession. By 30 March, however, a change had come about, as she had not been very well.[39] Mother Joanna Mary wrote that although Sister

---

37 Mother Joanna Mary, Occasional Letter to Associates and Friends, 1 August 1961.
38 Sister Margaret, letter to Cecily Camilla Bannister, 28 December 1963.
39 Sister Margaret, letter to Cecily Camilla Bannister, 30 March 1964.

Margaret 'had a weak heart, it had been a long time before she could be persuaded to come down to Peace from her room to avoid the stairs. When she did come, she was nearly at the end.'[40] Even then, she resisted, writing that the move made doing everything she should have liked more difficult.[41]

The House of Peace, the infirmary at St Peter's Home, had initially been built with five bedrooms in 1919 but was expanded to cope with the rising need. Another Sister described the arrangements:

> I found myself in a delightfully cool, airy room; a small table by the bedside has on it the books most likely to be needed, and behind it is a window from which one sees the chapel. The opposite end of the room is mainly a large French window leading onto the red-brick stoep, into which the sun at the moment is pouring a wealth of light and warmth. Beyond the stoep there is a pretty peep into the garden, with its old apple and plum trees.
>
> Then, as the daylight fades, one finds that one is indeed under the very shadow, or rather shall I say light, of the chapel, as its lights are reflected into the room and the soft cadence of the Sisters' voices as they chant Vespers is wafted in. Later on the murmur of Compline and Lauds' Psalms lull one to sleep till wakened again at daybreak by the chapel bell, when one can once more join in spirit in the morning offices and the daily Eucharist.
>
> I think it must be this feeling of close proximity to the Sisters in their times of prayer that prevents the days from seeming long or tedious, and imparts a strong sense of peace and quiet.[42]

On 29 March, Easter Day, the Warden conducted a special Mass for the Sisters in Peace at 6.30 a.m. before singing the principal Mass in the Sisters' Chapel. Sister Margaret wrote about her joy that morning: 'Such a happy service; the Altar was put up outside Mother Edith's door, and anyone helpless was wheeled or helped close by so that we all could hear and see. I thought how fortunate we were to have Our Lord's Risen Presence brought to us like that, early on Easter morning.'[43]

On 31 May, her eighty-fifth birthday, she again received Mass, 'her almost daily joy'. Camilla Bannister had sent flowers which looked 'so beautiful' the following morning when the Warden brought the Blessed Sacrament once more to her room.[44] For reading in her final weeks, she enjoyed a fresh account of

---

40 Mother Joanna Mary, 'Reflections on the Life of Sister Margaret CR'.
41 Sister Margaret, letter to Cecily Camilla Bannister, 30 March 1964.
42 CR Annual Report [for 1919], March 1920.
43 Sister Margaret, letter to Cecily Camilla Bannister, 30 March 1964.
44 Sister Margaret, letter to Cecily Camilla Bannister, 10 April 1964.

The Sisters' Chapel of the Resurrection looking 'east' and 'west', from transparency images of 1964

Mother Cecile's life by Margaret Cropper, recently published in her book *Shining Lights* (1963).[45] The author describes how other passengers had laughed at the young Cecile Isherwood on board the RMS *Trojan* for being dressed as the

---

45 Cropper, *Shining Lights*, pp. 135–165.

'Bishop's widow' when she sailed for the Cape Colony in October 1883. Yet she had overcome the ridicule, achieved so much, and inspired many others.[46] Mother Cecile's decisions were difficult, as was her journey into the community.

Sister Margaret reflected that as the years went on, she grew to live more continuously in a sacred space through the knowledge that came from the utter giving of self and the laying down of her life for others. She had followed One who was always with her and who had blessed her and kept her. She also wrote that she still had much to learn after six decades of a religious life. Yet, with the benefit of being able to look back on her entire life, she found to her great pleasure that in this closing stage 'spiritual things open out their treasures more and more'.[47] Sister Margaret's reflections for Trinity III also help to reveal the completeness of her dedication:

Humanity

O Lord, I thank Thee for thine almighty hand, which overshadows me in all the small occurrences Thou wilt place before me today. I rejoice in all the wonders of the happenings Thou wilt grant me, I thank Thee for all the sorrows and trials which will help to mould me in Thy purpose. O increase my faith, that I may learn to see Thy glory in all I meet, in all that may befall.

Amendment

O God, mend me, I would be broken for Thee but do though mend me, perfect me, stabilise me and strengthen me, so that I do not wallow in my sins, but look constantly up to Thee, who alone canst strengthen and perfect me.

Joy

Lord, in my own strength I can do nothing. All striving and anxiety is a block which prevents Thy strength and joy from reaching me. For Thou wilt never abandon me, Thy love cannot let me go. Thou wilt seek me in all the dark places which Thy son has made, and Thou wilt bring me home with joy. O Lord, that Thou shouldest want me!

How wonderful that even I, spoilt and hideous with sin, should be part of Thy heavenly creation; that the angels should rejoice for me to share Thy glory. O let me give Thee this joy each morning – help me come to Thee in trustful simplicity that Thou canst show me my day in the clear.

---

46 Cropper, *Shining Lights*, pp. 135–165.
47 Sister Margaret, letter to Cecily Camilla Bannister, 10 April 1964.

CHAPTER 11 | BEFORE THE THRONE

'O Lord, let me not go!', in Sister Margaret's hand

Also staying in Peace for her final stage was Sister Leila Mary, who had entered the community in 1949. She was only two years younger than Sister Margaret; she had been raised in a similar Victorian household, and they had much in common. Her family forbade her to leave England, so she entered the noviciate of the Community of St John Baptist in Clewer. She was only free to come to Grahamstown in her sixties after her parents had died. Younger Sisters much appreciated her clear and forthright guidance. Although failing, like Sister Margaret, she retained her sharp mind and helped Sisters in Peace who could no longer read, setting a wonderful example to the handful of elderly residents to the very end.[48]

Sisters learnt to submit willingly to sickness and suffering. They were to regard illness as a 'special

'My life is His within thy life', prayer card for Mrs Camilla Bannister

---

48 CR Remembrance Book, Sister Leila Mary CR (1881–1964).

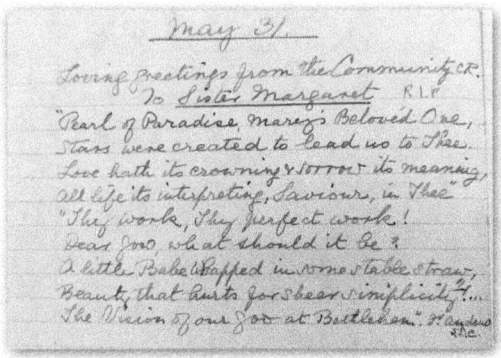

Extract from a copy of the Book of Birthdays of the Community of the Resurrection, compiled by Sister Charlotte Emily CR between 1909 and 1936, copied in 1957 by Sister Mary Christian CR

opportunity to fulfil their Vows and to look upon it as a means by which they may more perfectly take up the cross and follow Christ'.[49] Nursed by the Sister Infirmarian, Sister Mary Ursula, and inspired by Sister Leila Mary, Sister Margaret had already prepared for her death by tearing up letters and giving away her remaining personal things.[50] Her turn came almost a month after her eighty-fifth birthday, on Monday, 29 June 1964, St Peter's Day, a day of celebration which she loved so much. She knew she was near death and was anxious about the chain of intercessions, which she hoped would never be dropped.[51]

> She had been ailing for some time, had become weaker and was unable to get up on the previous Wednesday. The Doctor did not think seriously of her condition and on Saturday afternoon she chatted to me like her normal self, but early Sunday morning she had a coronary thrombosis and was in great pain until she was given an injection which relieved it. But after that, she gradually got worse all day, very weak and breathless, and she knew she would soon go. She said 'Be sure to write to Dot [her sister Dorothy]'.[52]

Sister Mary Ursula was with her when she died.[53] She was able to recount that just before passing away, Sister Margaret quoted two verses of a hymn she loved, the last one being:

Mother of CHRIST, Mother of CHRIST,
I toss on a stormy sea;
O lift thy Child as a beacon of light
To the port where I fain would be;
And, Mother of CHRIST, Mother of CHRIST,
This do I ask of thee –

---

49 CR, *Constitution, Rule and Customary* (1933), 'The Rule of Sickness', p. 62.
50 CR Remembrance Book, Sister Mary Ursula CR (1906–1995); and Sister Margaret, letter to Cecily Camilla Bannister, 3 November 1961.
51 Mother Joanna Mary, 'Reflections on the Life of Sister Margaret CR'.
52 Mother Joanna Mary, letter to Miss [Dorothy] Watson, 30 June 1964, Watson family papers.
53 Sister Dorianne, letter to Prof. F.G. Butler, 2 June 1995.

When the voyage is o'er,
O stand on the shore,
and show Him at last to me.⁵⁴

Mother Joanna Mary recalled that on her last night, Sister Margaret was so ill that she rested in a room close by so as to be ready to say the commendatory prayers. 'She said she would send for me when she knew the end was near. About midnight, the Sister Infirmarian called me. Sister Margaret was propped up in bed beside the open window and gasping for breath, but she tried to join in the prayers and was fully conscious when I finished. She said "Amen" and quickly gave up the ghost! I felt that the angels had come to fetch her and that a Saint had gone from us. She passed away at 9.30 a.m. on the 29th, St Peter's Day.'⁵⁵

The Oberammergau crucifix, Chapel of the Resurrection, from a transparency image of 1964

Her body was taken to the Chapel of the Resurrection at 5.15 p.m., where Sisters sang 'Safe in the arms of Jesus' before the Warden officiated at a service of Vespers. Then, at 7.15 p.m., a Solemn Requiem was held, followed by absolution and some hymns. Sisters kept watch until 10.30 the following morning when the funeral service commenced.⁵⁶ Finally, Sister Margaret was laid to rest in the Sisters' plot at the Old Settlers' Cemetery on the eastern edge of Grahamstown to the sound of 'The strife is o'er, the battle done'.⁵⁷ Mother Joanna Mary recalled: 'The sun was shining and all very peaceful and lovely.'⁵⁸ Sister Margaret's remains were buried just before the Celtic cross that marks the Sisters' plot.

Mother Joanna Mary wrote to Margaret's sister Dorothy in England that evening to describe the sad day. Unfortunately, the telegram sent to Sister Felicity,

---

54 CR Remembrance Book, Sister Margaret CR (1879–1964).
55 Mother Joanna Mary CR, 'Reflections on the Life of Sister Margaret CR'.
56 Mother Joanna Mary, letter to Miss [Dorothy] Watson, 30 June 1964; & Register of Services for the Chapel of the Resurrection, 29 & 30 June 1964.
57 *English Hymnal*, number 625.
58 Mother Joanna Mary, letter to Miss [Dorothy] Watson, 30 June 1964.

Sister Margaret's grave (foreground right, and inset) beneath the Celtic cross that marks the Sisters' plot in the Old Settlers' Cemetery, Grahamstown, in 2018

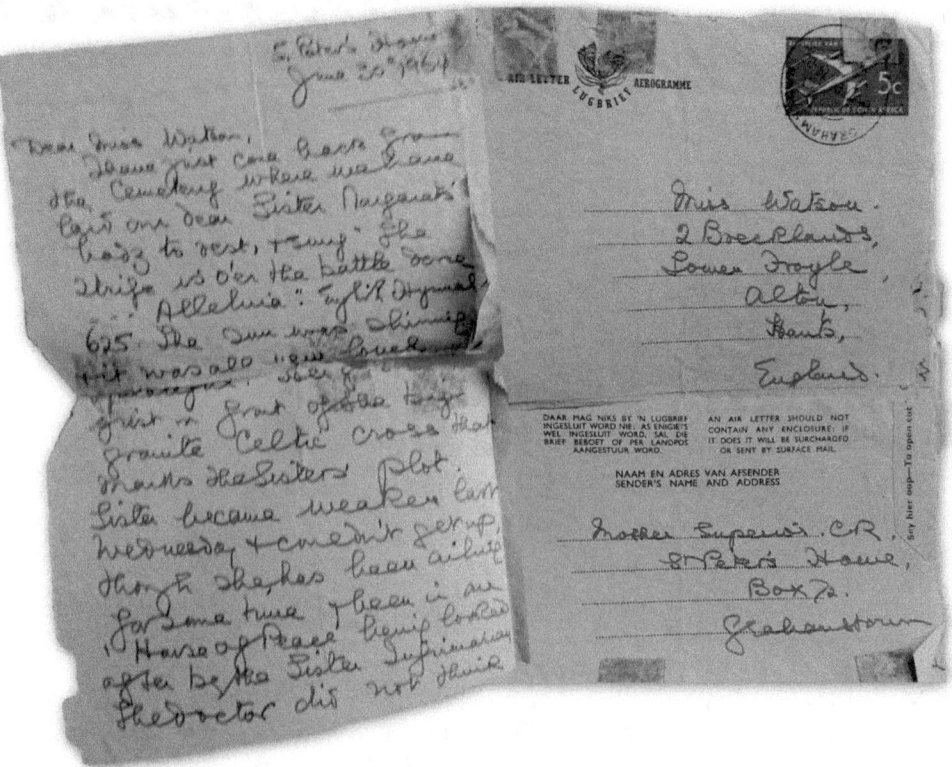

Mother Joanna Mary's aerogramme letter to Dorothy Watson, 30 June 1964

> COMMUNITY OF THE RESURRECTION OF OUR LORD
>
> HIL 5535
>
> S. PETER'S BOURNE,
> 40, OAKLEIGH PARK SOUTH,
> LONDON, N.20.
>
> 10th July, 1964.
>
> Dear Miss Watson,
>
> By some error – on whose part we know not – the cable telling us of Sister Margaret's death, has not been delivered, and so we heard only yesterday evening of her passing. I know our Mother Superior has already written to you, but I should like to add our quota of the sympathy for you. For our beloved Sister we can only rejoice that she has passed into the nearer Presence of the Lord she loved so much. She was such a splendid example and encouragement to us all, and our loss, in this world, is great, but we know how much she will be doing for us all in that other mysterious world.
> I heard from her in May, for my birthday, a letter of much loving prayer, and, when I go over to Africa in the autumn, for a short visit, she will be one of the many whom I shall miss very much.
>
> With kind regards,
> Yours sincerely,
> (Sister Superior)

Sister Felicity's condolence letter from the London branch house, 10 July 1964

> **THE COMMUNITY OF THE RESURRECTION OF OUR LORD.**
>
> "Christ died for us; Christ rose for us;
> Christ dwells in us; Christ reigns in peace."
>
> **Thanksgiving.**
>
> For the inspiration and joy of our dedication.
>
> For the prayers and lives of our aged and infirm Sisters, and for the example of Sister Eleanor, Sister Margaret, Sister Irene and Sister Leila Mary. R.I.P.
>
> For the prayers, gifts and help given us by so many Priest Associates, Oblates, Associates and Friends.
>
> For the work carried on at St. Peter's Bourne through the years.
>
> For the good relations between Church and Government in Zambia.
>
> For the call to new work at St. James' Mission, Rhodesia.
>
> For the love of many students of today and many yesterdays for the Training College.

Extract from the CR Annual Report for 1964

the Sister Superior at St Peter's Bourne in London, to alert Dorothy had failed to arrive owing to some error. Dorothy was therefore unaware of Margaret's death until she opened the blue aerogramme letter dropped through her letterbox the following week. For Dorothy, this was the eighth occasion of receiving such

Prayerbook page markers, given by the first Sister Margaret CR to Mother Florence, who later passed them to Sister Margaret CR, who left them to Sister Evelyn CR

news about her brothers and sisters. She carefully typed out the message to send to her remaining brother, John, and her nephew Geoffrey. Sister Anita, who had assisted with the painting at Christ the King in Sophiatown before she entered the noviciate in Grahamstown, also wrote to her. She travelled to Kent to meet Dorothy from the community's London branch house, St Peter's Bourne, in April 1961.

Two weeks after Sister Margaret's death, on the morning of 11 July 1964, her brother and sister, John and Dorothy, held a requiem at the Barn Church at Kew Gardens, the Church of St Philip and All Saints, just around the corner from where he lived. This service was to be her family's simple farewell. John also sent £10 to the community as a memorial gift. Given that there were to be no more altar flowers after Sister Margaret's demise, except on special occasions, there was a need for pedestals to hold flower bowls. 'Very good ones were obtained' with the gift, wrote Mother Joanna Mary in gratitude. 'I am sure this is what Sister Margaret would like as that will certainly beautify the chapel', as she had striven to do for so many years.[59] With another gift sent in her memory, 'we shall try to get some better bowls than those we have at present'.[60]

On Margaret's death, her large, vibrant family from Cambridge, of which she had been the first-born in 1879, was reduced to two. John, the youngest, died four years later, on 28 August 1968, at the age of seventy. Lastly, Dorothy, the family's beloved 'Dot', whom Margaret spoke about at her ending, died on 18 April 1971 where she lived in Cranbrook, Kent, aged eighty-three.

---

59 Mother Joanna Mary, letter to Mr [John] Watson 21 July 1964.
60 Mother Joanna Mary, letter to Mr [John] Watson, 21 July 1964.

Chapter 11 | Before the Throne

(Watson)

In Memoriam SISTER MARGARET C.R. 1914 - 1964.

Sister Margaret passed to her rest in the early hours of St. Peter's Day - a day she loved, as it is the Patronal Festival of our Home and the birthday of the elder of her priest brothers. Last January she had kept the Golden Jubilee of her Profession.

Sister Margaret was essentially a mystic and an artist and she has left behind her some very lovely and inspiring frescoes as well as many beautiful paintings. Her work always emanated from her prayer and before she painted Our LORD or Our Lady she spent hours in contemplation - then the result of her vision was translated into form and colour. She painted in obedience to authority but also in dependence on her inner vision, and when the fresco was complete she detached herself completely from it. It was her offering to Our LORD and did not belong to her at all. But she strove for perfection in every detail and would go on and on trying to improve the picture until under obedience she had to leave it! The fresco of Our Lady and the Holy Child in St. Mary's Chapel is probably her greatest work and has brought inspiration to generations of students at the Training College.

At the request of Father Raynes, C.R. Sister painted frescoes in the Church of CHRIST the King, Sophiatown, and there the central Figure is, of course, the Ascended and Glorified LORD. In between her hours of work on a high scaffolding, she made many studies of the African boys and girls, and introduced these into the panels of Our Lady and St. Francis of Assisi that surround the central Figure. Her frescoes can be seen also in churches in Port Elizabeth, in Zululand, Mount Frere and elsewhere. One of her most striking paintings is the "Walk to Emmaus" in three sections, set into the Altar of the Chapel at Stoneshill, with the Risen LORD breaking bread in the centre.

Sister Margaret's life was a hidden one, lowly and self-effacing and few could guess the depth of her contemplative prayer and intercession for others. For years she was responsible for the "Chain of Prayer" in the Sisters' Chapel daily, in which each Sister takes a share, and if anyone fell out Sister Margaret was always there to take her place as she could not bear the 'chain' to be broken. As she lay dying she was concerned in case her time for intercession should not be covered.

Only a few years ago she compiled "The Mind of Our Founders" which is treasured in the Community.

Hers was a life of love - love for the Community and a great desire for its perfection; love for souls, especially for those in difficulty or going through great trials. She had a real motherly love for the younger Sisters and for many years acted as Assistant to the Novice Mistress, giving a wonderful example of devotion to Our LORD, to Our Lady and to the Saints, both in her classes and in her own life. Although she cared for so many she kept her gaiety to the end and her face lit up with joy when speaking of the things of the Spirit, which she did only with great humility and diffidence. There was an inner radiance.

Sister had a very retentive memory, especially for poetry, and just before she passed away she quoted two verses of a hymn she loved - the last one being -
    Mother of CHRIST, Mother of CHRIST,
   I toss on a stormy sea;
   O lift thy Child as a beacon light
    To the port where I fain would be;
   And, Mother of CHRIST, Mother of CHRIST,
    This do I ask of thee -
   When the voyage is o'er, O stand on the shore,
    And show Him at last to me.

May she rest in peace.

Obituary record of Sister Margaret CR, which was included in the CR Annual Report for 1964

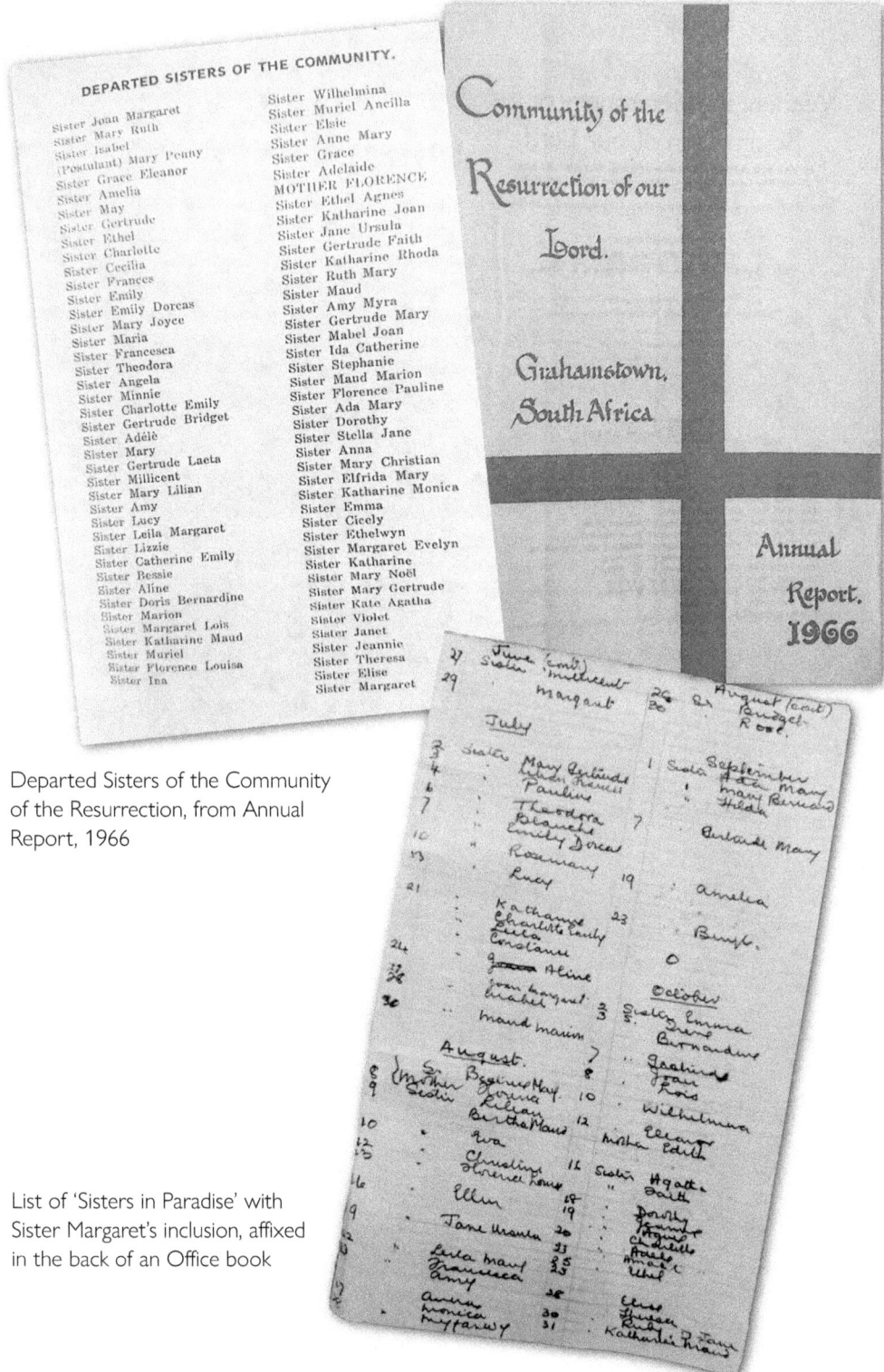

Departed Sisters of the Community of the Resurrection, from Annual Report, 1966

List of 'Sisters in Paradise' with Sister Margaret's inclusion, affixed in the back of an Office book

Illustration credits

All images of the Grahamstown Sisterhood and its activities are from the Archive of the Community of the Resurrection of Our Lord (CR). Other credits as follows:

Page xii: From Ethel Watson's album, courtesy of Paul Watson

Chapter 1
Pages 4, 5, 8, 12 (bottom), 13, 14, 18, 19: From Ethel Watson's album, courtesy of Paul Watson

Chapter 2
Pages 29, 31: From Ethel Watson's album, courtesy of Paul Watson

Chapter 3
Page 45: Church Education in South Africa: Works under the Care of the Sisters of the Community of the Resurrection, Diocese of Grahamstown (c.1907)
Page 48 (bottom): Sister Margaret Collection, Rhodes University
Page 55: From Ethel Watson's album, courtesy of Paul Watson
Page 58: CR Remembrance Book, Mother Edith CR (1868–1966)
Pages 63, 65: From Ethel Watson's album, courtesy of Paul Watson

Chapter 4
Page 69: CR Remembrance Book, Sister Gertrude CR (1860–1918)

Chapter 5
Page 93: Sister Margaret Collection, Rhodes University

Chapter 6
Pages 99, 101 (left): Archive of St Cuthbert's Mission, Tsolo, Historical Papers, Wits University, Johannesburg
Page 102: Harris and Ingpen, Mailships of the Union-Castle Line, p. 68
Page 104 (bottom): Richard Torrance

Chapter 7
Page 127 (bottom): *Port Elizabeth Herald*, 25 December 1951
Page 134: CR Remembrance Book, Sister Pauline CR (1883–1954)
Page 138: Paul Watson

Chapter 8
Pages 147, 148: Archive of the Community of St Mary the Virgin (CSMV), Wantage
Page 149: The Principal and Chapter of Pusey House, Archive of the Society of St Margaret, East Grinstead, Johannesburg Branch House 154
Page 150: Historical Papers, Wits University

Page 151: Archive of the Community of St Mary the Virgin (CSMV), Wantage
Page 153: CR Remembrance Book, Sister Anita CR (1898–1979)
Page 154: Archive of the Community of St Mary the Virgin (CSMV), Wantage
Page 155: From Ethel Watson's family scrapbook, courtesy of Paul Watson
Page 159: N. Mosley, The Life of Raymond Raynes

Chapter 9

Page 164 (middle): Amazwi South African Museum of Literature
Page 171: Lee, Charles Johnson of Zululand, p. 126

Chapter 10

Page 191: CR Remembrance Book, Sister Margaret Evelyn CR (1871–1961)
Page 197: Photograph by Sister Esme CR, courtesy of Miss Rosemary Boundy
Page 198 (bottom): Mrs Merle Metcalf
Page 199 (top): Paul Watson
Page 199 (bottom): Sister Margaret Collection, Rhodes University
Page 204 (top): Mrs Merle Metcalf
Page 205: The Cathedral Church of St Michael & St George, Grahamstown, South Africa (1958)
Pages 206, 207: Sister Margaret Collection, Rhodes University

Chapter 11

Pages 211, 214 (top), 217: From Sister Esme CR's album, courtesy of Miss Rosemary Boundy
Page 221: Mrs Merle Metcalf
Pages 224 (bottom), 225 (top): Paul Watson

Bibliography

Archives and Manuscripts

Amazwi South African Museum of Literature, Grahamstown (Makhanda)
F.G. Butler Papers: assorted correspondence relating to his book *The Prophetic Nun*

Berkshire Records Office, Reading, UK
Wantage Parish Register
Archive of the Community of Saint John Baptist, Clewer: Annuals, 1885–1906

Community of the Resurrection of Our Lord (CR), Cory Library, Grahamstown (Makhanda)
CR Annual Reports
CR Chapter minutes
CR, *The Constitution and Rule, Book II: The Rule* (1897)
CR, *The Constitution and Rule, Book II: The Rule* (1914)
CR, *The Constitution, Rule and Customary* (1933)
CR Logbook
CR Mother's general letters to Sisters
CR Occasional Letters to Supporters and Associates
CR Office Book, c.1930
CR Profession Register
CR Quarterly Letters
CR Reference Form for Aspirants
CR Register of Novices
CR Remembrance Book
CR Rule Book (1933)
'English Branch House' (TS)
Mother Edith, Logbook
Mother Joanna Mary, 'Reflections on the Life of Sister Margaret CR'
'Notes on the Chapel of St Mary and All the Angels'
'Novena for the Community of the Resurrection of Our Lord on the Occasion of Its Jubilee, April 13th–21st, 1934'
'A Record concerning the Chapel of the Resurrection at St Peter's Home, Grahamstown'
Register of Services for the Chapel of the Resurrection
'St Mark's School, Port Elizabeth (1887) – 1892 – 1970'
'St Peter's Home of Rest – Stones Hill'
St Peter's House, Visitors' Book

Sister Edith, 'Notes on Retreat Address by Father Noel, SSJE' (January 1914)
Sister Margaret, letters to Cecily Camilla Bannister and Merle Metcalf
Sister Margaret, 'Meditations on the Life of the Blessed Lord'
Sister Margery's Reminiscences
Sister Ruth, work record (MS)
Sister Valerie, long retreat timetable

Community of St Mary the Virgin (CSMV), Wantage, Archive
'The Apartheid Years'
'The Community of St Mary the Virgin in Southern Africa, 1948–1994'
'Ekutuleni Mission'

Historical Papers Research Archive, William Cullen Library, University of the Witwatersrand, Johannesburg
Community of the Resurrection, Sophiatown Minute Book, 1934–1942
Diocese of St John: E.H. Etheridge, 'Bishop Etheridge's Memoirs'
Grace Broughton, 'Early Days at S. Agnes' School, Rosettenville' (August 1963)
'Grace Dieu Diocesan Training College, 1906–1969'

Lambeth Palace Library, London
Archive of Randall Davidson, Archbishop of Canterbury, 1903–1928: letter from Mother Florence CR to the Most Reverend Randall Davidson, 8 October 1908

Queenstown Historical Society Archive, Eastern Cape
'St Monica's Home, Queenstown' (c.1955)

St Andrew's Church, Chilton, Eastern Cape
Vestry meeting minutes

St John's College, Cambridge, Archive
Minute book of the Ladies' Committee for St John's Missionary Parish of Lady Margaret, Walworth

UK National Archives, Kew, London
Board of Trade, Outward Passenger Lists
Parish of East Horsley, Surrey, Register of Marriages

Watson Family papers (in the possession of Paul Watson)
Dorothy Watson's childhood reflections

Dorothy Watson's childhood account (late 1960s)
Richard Torrance, 'Notes on the Family of (Rev.) Frederick Watson and Margaret Lockhart Adam'
Richard Torrance, 'John Douglas Watson'
Ethel Watson's diary, 1943
Dorothy Watson, letter to Basil Watson, 22 April 1912
Dorothy Watson, letter to Stephen Watson, 24 April 1970
Sister Margaret, letter to Geoffrey & Kathleen Watson, 20 October 1948
Mother Joanna Mary, letter to Miss [Dorothy] Watson, 30 June 1964

Printed works

Advisory Council on Religious Communities, *A Directory of the Religious Life for the Use of Those Concerned with the Administration of the Religious Life in the Church of England* (London: SPCK, 1943).

Advisory Council on Religious Communities, *Guide to the Religious Communities of the Anglican Communion* (London: A.R. Mowbray and Co., 1955).

Akyeampong, E.K. & Gates, H.L., Jr (eds.), *Dictionary of African Christian Biography* (Carey, NC: Oxford University Press, 2011).

Allchin, A.M., *The Silent Rebellion: Anglican Religious Communities, 1845–1900* (London: SCM Press, 1958).

Anson, P.F., *Call of the Cloister: Religious Communities and Kindred Bodies in the Anglican Communion* (London: SPCK, 1955).

Ashley, A., *Peace-Making in South Africa: The Life and Work of Dorothy Maud* (Bognor Regis: New Horizon, 1980).

Ball, R., 'The Noble Nuns Who Bridged Apartheid Divide', *Eastern Province Herald*, 5 July 2000.

Barham, W.D.C., *Forty Years a Potter: Dorothy Watson and the Bridge Pottery, 1921–1961* (Biddenden: You-by-You Books, 2020).

Brand, A., 'Sister Margaret's Fabulous Fresco', *Port Elizabeth Evening Post*, 17 June 1987.

Burne, K.E., *The Life and Letters of Father Andrew SDC* (London: A.R. Mowbray and Co., 1948).

Butler, F.G., 'The Nun's Pic's Tale', *Mail & Guardian*, 21 May 1998.

Butler, F.G., *The Prophetic Nun* (Johannesburg: Random House, 2000).

Caldecott, A., *English Colonization and Empire* (London: John Murray, 1891).

Caldecott, A., 'Frederick Watson', obituary in F. Watson and C.B. Drake (eds.), *Inspiration* (London: SPCK, 1906).

Carey, H.M., *God's Empire: Religion and Colonialism in the British World, c.1801–1908* (Cambridge: Cambridge University Press, 2011).

The Cathedral Church of St Michael and St George, Grahamstown, South Africa (Grahamstown: Cathedral Church of St Michael and St George, 1958).

Church Education in South Africa: Works under the Charge of the Sisters of the Community of the Resurrection of Our Lord (Grahamstown: CR, c.1907).

'Church of England: St Augustine's Mission', Rhodesian Study Circle, www.rhodesianstudycircle.org.uk.

Collier, J., *Frontier Post: The Story of Grahamstown* (Grahamstown: University Publishers and Booksellers, 1961).

Community of the Resurrection: Educational Work of the Sisters (Grahamstown: CR, c.1907).

Courtenay, J.W., *South Africa: The Railways of Cape Colony* (London: Jas. W. Courtenay, 1907).

Cropper, M., *Shining Lights: Six Anglican Saints of the 19th Century* (London: Darton, Longman and Todd, 1963).

Davies, H., *Great South African Christians* (Cape Town: Oxford University Press, 1951).

Day, P., *Life in Quy from the Beginning of Time to the Year 2000* (Cambridge, 2005).

Deacon, A. & Hill, M., 'The Problem of "Surplus Women"', in M. Hill (ed.), *The Nineteenth Century: Secular and Religious Alternatives; A Sociological Yearbook of Religion*, vol. 5, pp. 87–100 (London: SMC Press, 1972).

'Death of Dr Watson, Vicar of St Edward's Cambridge', *Independent Press* (Cambridge), 5 January 1906.

Doerner, M., *The Materials of the Artist and Their Use in Painting with Notes on the Techniques of the Old Masters*, translated by Eugen Neuhaus (New York: Harcourt, Brace and Company, 1934).

Dunn, L., *Ships of the Union-Castle Line* (London: Adlard Coles in association with George G. Harrap and John De Graff, 1954).

Elliott-Binns, L.E., *Religion in the Victorian Era* (London: Lutterworth Press, 1936).

Eve, J., 'New Features of Grahamstown Cathedral: A Guide to Post-1924 Developments', appendix to C. Gould, *Grahamstown Cathedral* (Grahamstown: Cory Library, Rhodes University, 2011).

Ferry, K., *The Old Convent, East Grinstead: John Mason Neale, George Edmund Street and the Society of St Margaret* (East Grinstead: The Old Convent Estate Residents, 2021).

Fitzherbert Fox, S., *A Chain of Prayer across the Ages: Forty Centuries of Prayer, 2000 BC – AD 1912* (London: John Murray, 1941).

From St Peter's Eaton Square to St Peter's Bulawayo: Jubilee Magazine of St Peter's Diocesan School (Bulawayo: St Peter's Diocesan School, 1971).

The Founders of Clewer: A Short Account of the Rev. T.T. Carter and Harriet Monsell to Celebrate the Centenary of the Community of St John Baptist in 1952 (London: A.R. Mowbray and Co., 1952).

Fulfilled in Joy: The Order of the Holy Paraclete and Its Foundress, Mother Margaret (Whitby: Order of the Holy Paraclete, 1964).

Gaitskell, D., '"Christian Compounds for Girls": Church Hostels for African Women in Johannesburg, 1907–1970', *Journal of Southern African Studies*, vol. 6, no. 1, Special Issue on Urban Social History (October 1979), pp. 44–69.

Gaitskell, D., 'Female Faith and the Politics of the Personal: Five Mission Encounters in Twentieth-Century South Africa', *Feminist Review*, no. 65, Summer 2000, pp. 68–91.

Gaitskell, D., 'Race, Gender and Imperialism: A Century of Black Girls' Education in South Africa', African Studies Institute Seminar series, University of Witwatersrand, August 1988.

Goedhals, M., 'Nuns, Guns and Nursing: An Anglican Sisterhood and Imperial Wars in South Africa, 1879–1902', *Studia Historiae Ecclesiasticae*, vol. XXXIV, no. 1, 2008, pp. 335–357.

Goodhew, D., *Respect and Resistance: A History of Sophiatown* (Westport, CT, and London: Praeger, 2004).

Gould, C., *Grahamstown Cathedral: A Guide and Short History* (Grahamstown: Grahamstown Diocesan Registry, 1924).

Grain, A.E., *Mission Unaccomplished: An Account of the Railway Missions in South Africa 1890–1980* (privately published, Lingfield, c.1987).

Granville Davis, P. (ed.), *Church of Saint Edward, King and Martyr Cambridge* (Cambridge: Black Bear Press, [1990]).

Hamilton Baynes, A., *Handbook of English Church Expansion: South Africa* (London and Oxford: A.R. Mowbray, 1908).

Harris, C.J. & Ingpen, B.D., *Mailships of the Union-Castle Line* (Cape Town: Fernwood Press, 1994).

Herman, E., *The Secret Garden of the Soul and Other Devotional Studies* (London: James Clarke and Company, 1924).

Hermitage Day, E., *Robert Gray: First Bishop of Cape Town* (London: SPCK, 1930).

Hinchliff, P., *The Anglican Church in South Africa* (London: Darton, Longman and Todd, 1963).

Hopper, E.C., *Some Account of the Parish of Starston, Norfolk* (Norwich: Agas H. Goose and Co., 1888).

Kelly, E., *Faithful to the Vision: A History of the Grahamstown Teachers' Training College, 1895–1975* (Grahamstown: NISC, 2018).

Knox, C., 'Guy Butler Rediscovers the Nun Who Painted like an Angel', *Grocott's Mail*, 5 June 1998.

Lee, A.W., *Charles Johnson of Zululand* (London: SPCK, 1930).

Le Tutla, M., *Bulawayo's Forgotten School: St Peter's Diocesan School, 1911–1977* (Bulawayo: Bulawayo1872.com, 2009).

Lewis, C. & Edwards, G.E., *Historical Records of the Church of the Province of South Africa* (London: SPCK, 1935).

Lowther Clarke, W.K., *A History of the SPCK* (London: SPCK, 1959).

Macmillan, A., *City of Grahamstown Illustrated* (Grahamstown, 1902).

Magee, W.C., *Anglican Sisterhoods: Their Inestimable Value in Rescue Work among Fallen Women; A Speech of the Right Reverend, the Bishop of Peterborough, Presented to the Council of the Church Penitentiary Society, 15th April 1886* (Torquay: The Directory Office, 1886).

Maughan, S.S., 'Imperial Christianity? Bishop Montgomery and the Foreign Missions of the Church of England, 1895–1915', in A. Porter (ed.), *The Imperial Horizons of British Protestant Missions, 1880–1914* (Grand Rapids: W.B. Eerdmans Publishing, 2004).

Maughan, S.S., *Mighty England Do Good: Culture, Faith, Empire, and World in Foreign Missions of the Church of England, 1850–1915* (Grand Rapids: W.B. Eerdmans Publishing, 2014).

McCleland, D., *Port Elizabeth of Yore* (Port Elizabeth, 2018).

A Member of the Community of the Sisters of the Church, *The Religious Life* (London: Church Extension Society, 1921).

Mitchell, W.H. & Sawyer, L.A., *The Cape Run: The Story of the Union Castle Service to South Africa and of the Ships Employed* (Lavenham: Terence Dalton, 1984).

Morton, J. & Gasquet, F.A., *The Nun's Rule: Being the Ancren Riwle Modernised by James Morton* (London: Chatto and Windus, 1924).

Mosley, N., *The Life of Raymond Raynes* (London: Faith Press, 1961).

'Mr E. Reginald Frampton, Obituary', *The Studio: An Illustrated Magazine of Fine and Applied Art*, vol. 86, no. 369, 1923.

Mumm, S., *Stolen Daughters, Virgin Mothers: Anglican Sisterhoods in Victorian Britain* (London: Lancaster University Press, 1999).

Naylor, A., *The Frampton Mural at St Peter's Church, Birstall: … His Life and Other Works of Art* (Gomersal: Alan Naylor, 1996).

Ollard, S.L., *A Short History of the Oxford Movement* (London: A.R. Mowbray and Co., 1915).

O'Meara, E. & Greaves, D.C., *Grahamstown Reflected* (Grahamstown: Albany Museum, 1995).

Page, B.T., *The Harvest of Good Hope: An Account of the Expansion of the Church of the Province of South Africa* (London: SPCK, 1947).

The Parish Church of St James the Great, Baldersby [guidebook] (2017).

Phelps, F.R., *Some Letters and Counsels of Francis Robinson Phelps, Archbishop of Cape Town, 1931–1938* (London: Bradley Press, [1938]).

Queenstown, Cape Province, South Africa (Queenstown Municipality and the South African Railway and Harbours Publicity Department, 1924).

Quint, F., 'The Way Out: Closure of and Departure from Anglican Religious Communities', *Ecclesiastical Law Journal*, vol. 18, no. 3, 2016, pp. 331–335.

Rickerby & Shekede, 'Church of St Michael the Archangel, Rushall: Walsall Report on Treatment of the Frampton Wall Painting' (unpublished, 2015).

Robins, M., *Mother Cecile of Grahamstown, South Africa: A Record of a Great Educational Work* (London: Wells Gardener, Darton and Co., 1911).

'Rorke's Drift – St Augustine's Mission', South African National Society, newsletter, April 2018, www.sanationalsociety.co.za.

St Gabriel's Home for Children, Bulawayo (Bulawayo: Board of Trustees, 1946)

Saint Giles' Church: A History and Guide (Cambridge: Parish of the Ascension, n.d.).

St John's College, University of Cambridge, *The Lady Margaret Mission in Walworth, 1888–1909* (Cambridge: St John's College, 1909).

St Mary's Diocesan School for Girls, Pretoria, 'History of the School', St Mary's DSG website

'The Sanctuary: The Story of St Monica's Home', *Church Weekly*, 12 December 1935.

Sedding, E.D., *Godfrey Callaway, Missionary in Kaffraria, 1892–1942: His Life and Writings* (London: SPCK, 1945).

'A Short History of the CPSA Congregation and Church in Thaba Tshwane (Voortrekkerhoogte, Roberts Heights)' (pamphlet, n.d.).

Sister Catherine Louise SSM, *The Planting of the Lord: The History of the Society of St Margaret in England, Scotland and the USA, 1855–1995* (East Grinstead: Society of St Margaret, c.1995).

Sister Gabriel, *Doing the Impossible: A Short Historical Sketch of St Margaret's Convent, East Grinstead, 1855–1980* (East Grinstead: Community of St Margaret, 1984)

Sister Janet CSMV, *Mother Maribel of Wantage* (London: SPCK, 1971).

Sister Kate CR, *Ventures for God: Mother Cecile* (London: SPCK, 1922).

Sister Margaret CR, 'Memories of the Past', *The Newsletter (Official Journal of the Diocese of Grahamstown)*, vol. XIX, May 1953, no. 4, p. 39; June 1953, no. 5, pp. 51–52; July 1953, no. 6, pp. 65–67; August 1953, no. 7, pp. 77–78.

Sister Margaret CR, 'The Apse', *Grahamstown Training College Magazine*, June 1929.

Sister Margaret CR, *The Mind of Our Founders* (Grahamstown: Community of the Resurrection of Our Lord, c.1948).

Sister Margaret CR, *Mother Cecile, Foundress* (Grahamstown: Community of the Resurrection of Our Lord, c.1961).

Sister Margaret CR, *Chapel of St Mary and All the Angels, Grahamstown Training College* (Grahamstown: Community of the Resurrection of Our Lord, c.1964).

A Sister of the Community [of the Resurrection of Our Lord], *Mother Cecile in South Africa, 1883–1906* (London: SPCK, 1930).

A Sister of the Community [of the Resurrection of Our Lord], *The Story of a Vocation: A Brief Memoir of Mother Florence, Second Superior of the Community of the Resurrection of Our Lord, Grahamstown, South Africa and the Works Undertaken by the Community during Her Superiorship* (Grahamstown: Church Bookshop, c.1952).

The Sisters of the Church: A Summary of Their Life, Work and Rule (London: The Community of the Sisters of the Church, 1894).

Sister Theresia Mary SPB, *Father Patrick Maekane MBK* [English translation], (Morija: Church of the Province of South Africa, 1987).

Sparrow Simpson, W.J., *The History of the Anglo-Catholic Revival from 1845* (London: George Allen and Unwin, 1932).

Steer, E.C.A., *The House of the Good Shepherd, East London: Twenty-One Years' Work, 1917–1938* (East London: Committee of the House of the Good Shepherd, [1938]).

Symonds, R., *Far above Rubies: The Women Uncommemorated by the Church of England* (Leominster: Fowler Wright Books, 1993).

Thomson, D.H., *A Short History of Grahamstown* (Grahamstown, 1952).

A Valiant Victorian: The Life and Times of Mother Emily Ayckbowm, 1836-1900, of the Community of the Sisters of the Church (London: A.R. Mowbray and Co., 1964).

Vallance, A., 'The Paintings of Reginald Frampton ROI', *The Studio: An Illustrated Magazine of Fine and Applied Art*, no. 66, 1919.

Venn, J. & Venn, J.A., *Alumni Cantabrigienses*, vol. VI (Cambridge: Cambridge University Press, 1954).

Vyvyan, W.L., 'A South African Jubilee: Work of Mother Cecile's Community', *Church Times*, 13 April 1934, p. 449.

Watson, F., *Defenders of the Faith* (London: SPCK, 1878).

Watson, F., *Inspiration* (London: SPCK, 1906).

Watson, F., *Sacramental Grace: A Lecture Delivered in Great St Mary's Church, Cambridge on Sunday, November 1st, 1885* (Cambridge: W.P. Spalding, 1885).

Watson, F., *The Seven Words from the Cross: A Course of Meditations* (London: Skeffington and Son, 1907).

Watts, P., *Late Victorian Quy, 1856–1897*, Parts One & Two (Cambridge, 2000).

Webb, A.B., *The Kingdom of Christ upon Earth and Other Sermons* (London: Skeffington and Son, 1909).

Webb, A.B., *Life of Service before the Throne: Notes of Meditations Given at Grahamstown, in the Chapel of the Community of the Resurrection of Our Lord, Whitsuntide to Advent with Certain Holy Days in Between* (London: Skeffington and Son, 1897).

Webb, A.B., *Sisterhood Life and Woman's Work, in Mission-Field of the Church* (London: Skeffington and Son, 1883).

Webb, A.B., *Women's Work for Foreign Missions of the Church of England* (London: J.T. Hayes, 1877).

Welham, S., *Hope Blossoms in Sophiatown: St Joseph's Home for Coloured Children; The Story* (Johannesburg: Anglican Diocese of Johannesburg, 2015).

Winter, A., CR, *Till Darkness Fell* (Mirfield: Community of the Resurrection, 1962).

Wilkinson, A., *The Community of the Resurrection: A Centenary History* (London: SMC Press, 1992).

Winterbach, H., 'The Community of the Resurrection's Involvement in African Schooling on the Witwatersrand from 1903 to 1956', research project submitted to the Faculty of Education, University of the Witwatersrand, Johannesburg, 1994.

Woodville Orphanage and Industrial School under the Care of the Community of the Resurrection, St Peter's Home, Grahamstown (Grahamstown: CR, c.1917).

Worsnip, M.E., *Between the Two Fires: The Anglican Church and Apartheid, 1948–1957* (Pietermaritzburg: University of Natal Press, 1991).

Periodicals

Church Weekly

Crockford's Clerical Directory (London: various publishers)

The Eagle (Cambridge: St John's College)

Grace Dieu Bulletin

Inverness Cathedral Magazine

The Mission Field

The Newsletter (Official Journal of the Diocese of Grahamstown)

St John's Chronicle

The Watchman: Gazette of the Diocese of Johannesburg

Who Was Who, vol. IV, 1941–1950 (London: Adam and Charles Black, 1951)

Index

Page numbers in *italics* refer to illustrations.

A

Adam, George Read 2–3
Adam, Margaret Euphemia 3
Adam, Margaret Lockhart *see* Watson, Margaret Lockhart (mother)
Algoa Bay 34, 35, 62, 67, 102, 135, 177
Alice, Princess 91
Allen, Donald 166
altars 99, *101*, 111, 127–128, 132–135, *133*, 169–170, *170*, 191, 213–215, *214*, 226
Anglican Church 2, 22–24, 26–28, 50, 170–171, 211
Anglo-Boer War 17, 40, 144
Anglo-Catholicism 2, 24, 51, 211
Anglo-Zulu War of 1879 170–171
Anita, Sister 153–154, *153*, 226
annual reports 88, *119*, *225*, *227*, *228*
apartheid 208–209
Arundel Castle, RMS 102, *102*
Athlone, Earl of 109

B

Baker, Herbert 81, 96, 146
banners 191, *192*
Bannister, Camilla Mary 198, *198*
Bannister, Camilla (née Reppert) 112, 197–198, *198*, *199*, *204*, 218, *221*
Bannister, Merle 198, *198*
Bantu Education Act of 1953 209
Barber, Mary Elizabeth 47
basket to transfer passengers *34*
Basutoland (now Lesotho) 174–175
Beatrice, Sister 163, 183–184
Beaufort, James Morris 202–204
Beaufort, Lady Margaret 8
Beresford, Rollie 166
Bernardine, Sister 169
Bessie, Sister 79–80, 82, 88
birthdays *222*

Blake, Mrs   172, 177–178
Boer War *see* Anglo-Boer War
Bognor, Sussex   65, *66*
Bongolo Reservoir   91, *92*, 94
Botanical Gardens   *48*, 95, *120*
brass crosses   71, *71*
Bridge Pottery   103, 136, 156, 178, 192
British Royal Family *see* Royal Family
Brook Green, London   64, *64*
Bulawayo, Southern Rhodesia   68–69, 111, 117, 125, *168*, 169–170, *170*, 212
Burvill, Father   175
Butterfield, William   13
Buxton, Lord   97

C
Caldecott, Alfred   15, 19, 62
'callings'   70
Cambridge
    Chesterton Road   4, *6*
    Hills Road   *11*
    Salisbury Villas   13, *14*, 15
Canterbury House   47, *61*, 115
Cape Town   31, *33*
Carter, T.T.   51
carvings *see* woodcarvings
Cathcart Road, Queenstown   *80*
Catherine, Sister   127
Cecile, Mother
    death of   40–42, 193
    photographs of   *26*, 106, *106*
    as Superior   26–28, 36–37, 40, 44, 50–51, 73, 120, 122, 213–214, 219–220
Chapel of St Mary and All the Angels   200
    see also St Mary and All the Angels, Chapel of
Chapel of the Resurrection   27, 77, 95–97, *96*, *97*, *121*, 123, 127–128, 132–134, *133*, 213–215, *214*, *219*, 223, *223*
Chapter, role of the   120–122
Charlotte Emily, Sister   *222*
Charlotte, Sister   67
Chesterton Road, Cambridge   4, *6*
children's homes   44, 117, 148, 169, 216

Chilton Farm   166–167
Chinese community   27, 117, 125, 163
Christmas   *125*, 216–217, *217*
Christ the King, Garrison Church of   165
Christ the King, parish of, Sophiatown   145–157, *148*, *151*, *154*, *155*, *158*
Church of England   1–2
City of Saints   21
Clayton, Geoffrey   153
Clewer House of Mercy   81
Clewer Sisters *see* Community of St John Baptist, Clewer
clothing *see* garments
Cloud of Witness, The   14–15, *16*, 71, 198
Cobden, Margaret   75
Colenso, John William   26–27
'coloured' community   27, 148, 186
Community of St John Baptist, Clewer   24, 51, 81, 221
Community of St Margaret   148–149, *149*, *150*
Community of St Mary the Virgin (Wantage Sisters)   24, 158–159, 165, 174
Community of St Michael and All Angels   22–25, 83, *83*
Community of the Resurrection, Mirfield   50, 144–145, 158
Community of the Resurrection of Our Lord (CR), Grahamstown
   annual reports   88, *119*, *225*, *227*, *228*
   Book of Birthdays   *222*
   Constitution and Rule   53, *53*, 57, *90*, 122
   CR Fathers   117, 144–145, 147–151, 153, 158, 215
   founding of   26–27
   jubilee of   131–132, *132*, *133*
   logbook listing Sisters present   *141*
Community of the Sisters of the Church   137–138
Cornish, Charles   53, 81, 193
correspondence *see* letters
Cowley Fathers   98
CR *see* Community of the Resurrection of Our Lord (CR), Grahamstown
Cromwell Road, London   63, *64*
Cropper, Margaret   219–220
crosses   71, *71*, 76, *90*, 122
crucifixes   72
   see also Oberammergau crucifix
Cullen, Archibald Howard   123, 162, 173, *214*

Cuyler, Jacob 200

D
Dakers, George Scott 166
Davidson, Randall, Archbishop of Canterbury 28, 41, 52
deaths 216, *228*
Debating Society 43
deference, rules of 72
Dell, Lavinia 167, 169
devotional cards *vi*, *128*, 163–165, *163*, *164*, *203*, 216
Doerner, Max 147
Dora, Sister 109, 138
Dorianne, Sister *103*, 215–216
Dorothea, Mother 173–174, *173*, 177–178, 181–184, 204–205, 208–209, 213, *214*
Dover Castle, SS 61, *62*
Dunbar Castle, MV 138–140, *139*
Durham Castle, SS 65, *66*
Durrell, Mary (later Watson) 62

E
Easton, Hugh 203
Eden Grove 27, 47, 95
Edinburgh Castle, RMS 104, *105*
Edith, Mother
    background of 57, 68, 122
    in Bulawayo 68–69, 125–126
    health of 151–152, 173
    as novice mistress 57–58, *58*
    photographs of *58*, *122*, *141*, *195*, *214*
    as Superior 122, 125–128, 130–132, 138, 142–143, 147, 157, 162–167, 172–174, 190, 215
Edith Perpetua, Sister 177
education 11, 120, 144, 209
Edward Storey Foundation 3
EHU *see* English Helpers Union
Ekutuleni Mission House, Place of Peace 145, *148*, 149, 158
election of 1948 208–209
Elise, Sister 198–200
Ellen, Sister 112
Ellison, Douglas 52

embroidery   191, *192*
England's Lane, London   136
English Colonialism and the Empire   15
English Helpers Union (EHU)   28, 104, 138
Ethel Maria, Sister   163
Etheridge, Edward   184
Eva, Sister   163
Evelyn, Sister   *226*
Everton Farm   91–94, *92*, *93*, *94*

F
Felicity, Sister   223, *225*
fire at boarding house   47
First World War *see* World War I
Fleming, Frank   146, 148
Florence, Mother
   background of   50–52
   death of   189
   page markers of   *226*
   photographs of   *89*, *122*, *142*, *190*
   as Superior   40, 50–53, 60, 69–71, 76–78, 80–81, 87–88, 91, 93–94, 96, 99–101, 105, 107, 116, 120, 129, 136, 169
flower arrangements   132, 142, 189, 213–215, *214*, 226
Frampton, E. Reginald   63–65, *64*, 100–101, 108, 147
Frere, Sir Bartle   183
fresco painting   63–65, 100–101, 147–156, *154*, *155*, *158*, 200, *217*
Frith, William E.C.   88, *88*, 99, 123
funding   27–28, 81, 88, 91

G
garments   55, 71, 76
Garrison Church of Christ the King   165
Gell, Mrs Littleton   15
George V, King   135
George VI, King   182–183
Gertrude, Sister   69, *75*
Gibbens family   166–167
Gilbert Scott, Sir George   22
Good Shepherd School   27, 117, 200

Gqeberha *see* Port Elizabeth

Grace Dieu Diocesan Training College   129–130, *129*, *131*, 132, 134, 212

Grahamstown (now Makhanda)   *viii*, 20–22, *23*, *24*, 33–34, *36*, *37*, 38–39, *38*, *45*, *110*, *118*, 140, *144*

Grahamstown Training College   42, 47, 117, 120, *121*, *161*, 191, 198–200

Great War *see* World War I

greeting card   *204*

Group Areas Act of 1950   209

H

habits *see* garments

'Hangklip from Nonesi's Nek, The' (oil painting)   93–94, *93*, *94*

Hart, Donald   91, *92*, 93–94

Hart, Letitia   91

Hart, Shirley   91, 93

Hart, Win   91

Hazelwood family   184–185

Heloise Lilian, Sister   200

Hely-Hutchinson, Governor and Lady   61

Herbert Baker, Kendall & Morris   81, 96, 146

Herman, Emma   213

Hewitt, Henry A.C.   204, 207, *215*

Hext, Edward   81, *82*

High Church   2, 6, 160

Highlands Farm   47

Hill, Arthur   *133*, 143

Hill, Charles   167

Hill, Gertrude *see* Gertrude, Sister

Hills Road, Cambridge   *11*

Hoddinott, V.A.   179, 181

Hodson, John   205–207

holidays   11–13, *12*, 129, 192, 195–196

Holmes, Edith *see* Edith, Mother

Holmes, Gertrude   174

Holmes, Mrs   126

Hours of Prayer   76

House of Peace   218–222

House of the Good Shepherd   175

Howson's Poort, picnic at   59–60

Hudson, Marjorie 'Anita' *see* Anita, Sister

Hunstanton, Norfolk   11–13, *12*, *29*
hymns   216, 222–223

I

Incomati, MV   158–159
indigenous people   160–161
Innes, Sister   112–113
Inspiration   19
Isherwood, Annie Cecile Ramsbottom   25–26, 131
Ivy, Sister   126

J

Jean May, Sister   *203*
Jeanne, Sister   216
Joanna Mary, Mother   194, 212–213, *213*, *214*, 217–218, 223, *224*, 226
Johnson, Charles   171–172, 179, 181, 183

K

Kate, Sister   90
Katherine Maud, Sister   196
Keynes, Maynard   9
King's College   9, *10*
Kitchener, Lord   165
Knowles, Bryan S.C.   *215*
Komani *see* Queenstown
KwaZulu-Natal *see* Zululand

L

Lady Margaret parish   8
laundry   *45*, 82, 88, 91, 100
lay workers at St Peter's Home   116
Leila Margaret, Sister   75, 89
Leila Mary, Sister   221–222
Lesotho *see* Basutoland
letters   72–73, 198, *199*, *224*, *225*
light, bright, in chapel   99–101, *101*
Llangibby Castle, MV   135, *136*
London
    Brook Green   64, *64*

    Cromwell Road   63, *64*
    England's Lane   136
    Lupton Street   *137*, 137–138, 140, 211
    Sumner Place   102
Lunn, Dora   103
Lupton Street, London   *137*, 137–138, 140, 211

M

Madeira   30–31, 102
'Madonna and Child' (painting)   204–207, *206*, *207*
Maekane, Patrick   174–175
Makhanda *see* Grahamstown
Mancoba, Ernest   132–135, *133*
maps   *viii*, *36*, *118*, *119*
Margaret Evelyn, Sister   191, *191*
Margaret, Sister (left community in 1905)   69–70, *226*
Margaret, Sister (1879-1964)
    as artist   17, 47–49, 63–65, 91–94, 98–101, 104–116, 120, 123–128, 130, 132–135, 143, 147–157, 160–170, 172–188, 200, 202–207
    as assistant novice mistress   212
    birthdays   153, 212, 218–219
    death of   222–226, *224*, *225*, *227*, *228*
    education of   7, 11, 17
    family of   1–7, *5*, *8*, *12*, 13, 17–19, *63*, *65*, 101, 156–157, 166, 178, 192, 196–197, 200, 225–226
    godchildren of   13, 62, *63*, 197–198, *198*
    health of   91–94, 117, 189, 196–197, 216, 217–222
    holidays in England   58, 61–65, *65*, 101–103, *103*, 135–140
    holidays in South Africa   47, 91–94, 129, 195–196
    journey to St Peter's Home   20, 29–37, *31*
    letters   198, *199*
    name 'in religion'   69–70
    as novice   68–75, *75*
    as postulant   49, 54–59, *55*, 65–67
    profession   *x*, 75–76, 88–90
    publications of   26, 123, *124*, 200–202
    retreats   89–90, 166
    at St Monica's Home of Refuge   78, 82–87, 90–91
    at St Peter's Home   41–42, 44, 47, 65–67, 104–115, 122–128, 130, *141*, 152, 174, 189–191, 202, *204*, 213–215, 220

    at St Peter's Home of Rest   194
    studio of   126–127, *161*, 191
    youth of   *xii*, 1, 3–20, *5*, *8*, *12*, *17*, *18*, *19*, *29*
Margery, Sister   73
Martha, Sister   177
Mary Christian, Sister   *222*
Mary Ursula, Sister   *203*, 222–223
Masite, Basutoland   174–175
Materials of the Artist and Their Use in Painting, The   147
Maud, Dorothy   145, 147, 149, 153, 156–158
Maud, John   147
'Meditations on the Life of the Blessed Lord' (booklet)   123, *124*
Mercury and Guardian   139
Merriman, Nathaniel   25
Millicent, Sister   75, 89
Mind of Our Founders, The   26, 200, *201*
Mirfield Fathers *see* Community of the Resurrection, Mirfield
Mitchell, Winifred   140
Mokhatio we Bahlanka ba Kreste   174
Moore & Son   71
Morning Post   21–22
'Mother Behold Thy Son, Son Behold Thy Mother' (painting)   167–169, *167*
Mother Cecile, Foundress   200–202, *201*
Mother Cecile Memorial Hall   60–61, *61*
Mothers' Union   5–6, 15
Muriel Ancilla, Sister   152

N

National Party   209
'Night at Highland's' (watercolour)   47, *48*
Noel, Frederick   98–100, *99*, *101*, 104, 107, 111, 113, 166
novenas   131, *132*, 210
novice mistress, role of   49, 53, 57, 68, 72, 74–75, 90
noviciate building   211, *211*
noviciate, Sister Margaret's time in   68–75, *75*

O

Oberammergau crucifix   127–128, *128*, *133*, 223
oil paint   *92*
Old Settlers' Cemetery   223, *224*

'Old' St Paul's   195–196, *196*
Our Lady and the English Martyrs, Roman Catholic Church of   11
Oxford Movement   1, 24

P

page markers   *226*
Paget, Edward Francis   170
paintbox and materials   *92*
Pauline, Sister   134–135, *134*
personal items   71, 222
Phelps, Francis Robinson   52–53, 70–72, *70*, 90, 97–98, 105, 107, 122–123, 202
picnic expedition   58–60, *59*
Pierson, George   13
Pierson, Susan   13
Pinnock, Burt   107
poems   190
political changes   208–209
Port Alfred   195, *195*, *196*
Port Elizabeth (now Gqeberha)   27, 33, *34*, *35*, 117, 162–163
postulants   49, 54–59, *54*, *55*
pottery *see* Bridge Pottery
prayer   *76*, 190, 222
prayer cards   *221*
Price, Helen   140
Princess Dock, Southampton   30, *30*, 65

Q

Queen Alexandra Home for Infants   117
Queenstown (now Komani)   78–81, *80*, *83*, 85–86
Queen, The   28
Quy *see* Stow-cum-Quy

R

railways   33–34, *36*
Raynes, Raymond   145–148, 150–153, 157–158, *159*
religious communities   24, 26–28, 98, 137, 211–212
Reppert, Camilla *see* Bannister, Camilla (née Reppert)
rest homes   116–117, 192–196, *197*
retreats   98–99, 123–124, 143, 166
Rhodesian Church Magazine   111

Rhodes University College   21, 96, *144*
rings   *90*
Rosemary, Sister   163, *164*
Royal Family   182–183
Rule for Intercourse with the Outer World   102, 197
Rule of Life   *53*, 54–55
Rules for Workers and Visitors at St Peter's Home   *46*
Runge, Carl   143–145
Russell, Ethelwyn   178

S
sacristan duties for Sisters' Chapel   123
Salisbury, Southern Rhodesia   117, 125, 135
Salisbury Villas, Cambridge   13, *14*, 15
Saxon, RMS   30, *30*, *31*, *32*, *33*
Schauder, Adolph   162
Schauder Township (Schauderville)   162, *176*
schism between bishop and dean, Grahamstown   22, 26–27
schools *see* education
Scott, Sir Gilbert   22, 202–203
Sea View   129, 192
Second World War *see* World War II
Seven Words from the Cross, The   19
Shining Lights   219–220
silence   55–56
silver crosses   76, *90*
Sisters' Chapel of the Resurrection *see* Chapel of the Resurrection
Sisters' Rule   208–209
Slater, Father   2–3
Society for the Propagation of the Gospel (SPG)   5–6, 145
Sophiatown   145, *146*, *148*, 157–158
South African Emigration Expansion Committee   15
South African War *see* Anglo-Boer War
Southampton, Princess Dock   30, *30*, 65
Southern Rhodesia
    Bulawayo   68–69, 111, 117, 125, *168*, 169–170, *170*, 212
    Salisbury   117, 125, 135
SPG *see* Society for the Propagation of the Gospel
St Agnes's Home   151–152, 179

stained glass panels   165, 203
St Andrew's Church   127, 166–167, *166*, *167*
Starston, village   1, 3, *4*
St Augustine's Mission, Zululand   171–174, *171*, 177–183, *180*, *181*, *182*
St Augustine's, Penhalonga   117, 215
St Barnabas, church of   174–175
St Cyprian's School   *148*, 151
St Edward King and Martyr, church of   9, *10*, 19
St Francis Xavier Mission   117, 125, 163
St Gabriel's Home   75, 117, *168*, 169–170
St George's Church   184–186, *184*, *185*, *186*
St Giles's Church   2–3
St Gregory, parish of   163
St Helena   135, *137*
St James the Great, church of   13, *15*
St James the Less, church of   127, *127*, 167
St John's College, University of Cambridge   1, 3, 17
St John's Gospel   132–134
St John the Baptist, Anglican Church of   *11*
St Joseph's Home   148–149, *149*, 157
St Joseph's lilies   213–215, *214*
St Luke's, Baragwanath   165–166
St Mark's Mission   163, 177, 182, 186–188, *186*, *187*, 200
St Mary and All Saints, Chapel of   135
St Mary and All the Angels, Chapel of   98, *98*, *100*, 104–115, *108*, *112*, *114*, *115*, *133*, 143, *161*, 200, *217*
St Mary the Virgin, parish of, Aldworth   103, *104*
St Mary the Virgin, parish of, Stow-cum-Quy   3–7, *5*, *7*, *8*
St Mary with All Souls, church of, Kilburn   2
St Michael and All Angels, church of   83, *83*, 162, 174–177, *176*
St Michael and St George, Cathedral Church of   22, *24*, *25*, *144*, 202–207, *206*
St Monica's Home of Refuge   74–75, 78–88, *84*, *85*, *86*, *87*, *89*, 90–91, 126, 183, 212
Stow-cum-Quy   3–7, *5*, *7*, *8*
St Peter's Bourne   211, 225, 226
St Peter's Diocesan School for Girls   75, 111, 117, 125, 170, *170*
St Peter's, Eaton Square   25
St Peter's Home
   Christmas   *125*, 216–217, *217*
   description of   36–39
   growth and decline of   27–29, 49–51, 72, 116–117, 131, 143, 160, 189, 209–213

holiday accommodation   195–196
　　　lay workers at   116
　　　logbook   *141*
　　　map   *118*
　　　photographs of   *41*, *117*, *120*, *121*, *141*, *144*, *161*
　　　refectory at   124, *125*
　　　roles at   52–55
　　　routine at   42–44, 55–56, 82–87, 192–193
　　　rules   *46*, *54*
St Peter's Home of Rest   124–125, 193–194, *194*
St Peter's Lodge   *161*, *190*, 192, *193*
St Peter's School   27, *45*, 47, 120, *120*, *161*
St Simon and St Jude, church of   207
studio of Sister Margaret   126–128, *161*, 191
Sumner Place, London   102
Sunday Express   155–156, *155*
Superior, role of   53, 57, 72, 75–76, 120–122, *122*

T
Tambo, Oliver   152
Theresa, Sister   163, *164*, 216
Thornley, Charles E.   113, *113*, 123
Tractarianism   1–2
Training College *see* Grahamstown Training College
trains *see* railways
Transkei   98, 182–184
Trojan, RMS   219–220

U
Union-Castle Line passenger information leaflet (1911)   *32*
Union of South Africa   67, 209
University of Cambridge   1, 3, *10*, 17, 144

V
veils   71, 76, 102
Victoria Falls   125–126
Victoria, Queen   79
Visitor, role of   52–53, 123
Vyvyan, Edith   123, *142*, 172–173, 178–179, 181

Vyvyan, Wilmot Lushington   123, *133*, 140–143, *142*, 145, 170, 172, 178, 213

W
Wales, Prince of   109–110, *110*
'Walk to Emmaus'   124–125, 194
Wantage Sisters (Community of St Mary the Virgin)   24, 158–159, 165, 174
Warden, role of   52–53, 55, 57, 72, 75, 88, 209
Watchman, The   156
watercolour paintings   *48*, 94, 166, 191, *199*
Watson, Arthur (brother)   3, *8*, 11–13, *12*, *18*, 62, 103, 138, 157
Watson, Basil Lockhart (brother)   7, *8*, *12*, 63, 87, 101, 136
Watson, Christopher (brother)   3, *8*, 11, *12*, 63, 87, 103, 157, 166
Watson, Dorothy (sister)
   Bridge Pottery   103, 136, 156, 178, 192
   childhood of   4, 6–7, 9, 13, 63
   death of   226
   death of Sister Margaret   222–226, *224*
   photographs of   *8*, *12*, *18*
   Sister Margaret and   57–58, 102, 136, 192, 196, 200
   World War I   88
   World War II   156
Watson, Ethel Mary (sister)   3, *8*, *12*, 17, 55, 63, 88, 102–103, 136, 156, 178
Watson, Frederick (brother)   3, *5*, *8*, 11, *12*, 58, 62–63, 103, 178, 192
Watson, Frederick (father)   1–11, *2*, *8*, *12*, 17–19, 49, 68
Watson, Geoffrey (nephew and godson)   101, 194, *199*, 226
Watson, Grace Hilda (sister)   7, *8*, *12*, *18*, 63, *63*, 88, 103, 156, 197
Watson, Henry (brother)   3, *5*, *8*, *12*, 17, 87, 103, 196
Watson, John Douglas (brother)   11, *12*, 13, *18*, 63, 87–88, 103, 156, 178, 226
Watson, Kathleen (wife of nephew)   194, *199*
Watson, Margaret *see* Margaret, Sister (1879-1964)
Watson, Margaret Elizabeth (niece)   138, *139*
Watson, Margaret Lockhart (mother)   1–3, *3*, *8*, *12*, 57–58, 102, 136, 156, 166
Watson, Mary Monica (niece and goddaughter)   62, *63*, 103, *104*
Watson, Mary (née Durrell) (sister-in-law)   63
Watson, Olive (sister-in-law)   *18*, 62, 138
Watson, Susannah (grandmother)   *8*
Webb, Allan Becher   22–27, 40, 42, 50, 95, 106, *122*, 131, 213
Webb, Merle   166
wedding dress   76
West, Margaret Isabel *see* Margaret, Sister

Wilkinson, George Howard 25
Willett, Millicent Helen *see* Millicent, Sister
Williams, Dean 22, 26–27
Winsor and Newton Company *92*, 93
women
    opportunities for 24, 65, 211
    role of 22–24
woodcarvings 132–135, *133*
Woodfield, Canon 129, *133*
Wood, Grace Eleanor 70
Woodville School and Orphanage 44, 117, *195*, 196, 216–217
World War I 86–88, 99, 148, 202–203
World War II 156, 158–160, 178, 192, 202–203, 211

Z

Zimbabwe *see* Southern Rhodesia
Zululand 170–173
    see also St Augustine's Mission, Zululand

www.ingramcontent.com/pod-product-compliance
Lightning Source LLC
Chambersburg PA
CBHW080409230426
43662CB00016B/2357